Multicultural Encounters

Multicultural Encounters

Sanjay Sharma

First published 2006 by
PALGRAVE MACMILLAN
Houndmills, Basingstoke, Hampshire RG21 6XS and
175 Fifth Avenue, New York, N.Y. 10010
Companies and representatives throughout the world

PALGRAVE MACMILLAN is the global academic imprint of the Palgrave Macmillan division of St. Martin's Press, LLC and of Palgrave Macmillan Ltd. Macmillan® is a registered trademark in the United States, United Kingdom and other countries. Palgrave is a registered trademark in the European Union and other countries.

ISBN 13: 978–1–4039–3556–4   hardback
ISBN 10: 1–4039–3556–4   hardback

This book is printed on paper suitable for recycling and made from fully managed and sustained forest sources.

A catalogue record for this book is available from the British Library.

Library of Congress Cataloging-in-Publication Data
Sharma, Sanjay, 1967–
     Multicultural encounters / Sanjay Sharma.
        p. cm.
     Includes bibliographical references and index.
     ISBN 1–4039–3556–4 (cloth)
        1. Multiculturalism. 2. Multicultural education. I. Title.

HM 1271.S46 2006
305.8–dc22   2006045714

SHA

10   9   8   7   6   5   4   3   2   1
15   14 13 12 11 10 09 08 07 06

Printed and bound in Great Britain by
Antony Rowe Ltd, Chippenham and Eastbourne

For my mother, Narinder V. P. Sharma

Contents

Preface

I don't know why, the black people continue with the problems of
hundreds of years ago, with huge chips on their shoulders. Having
attended the lectures and read the readings, it is still not apparent
to me, just what the underlying issues are, apart from being very
emotional and why they are continued – but I am not black.
(Student essay)

How do we judge the efficacy of a multicultural pedagogy? The epigraph above suggests that the anti-racist teaching goals of an *'Identity,*
Difference and Race' undergraduate module were far from realized. The
response, from a white male student, appears to embody a 'structure of
feeling' indifferent to appeasing a ('minority') lecturer. The student's
concluding comment 'I am not black', purports to indicate the in-
adequacy of his own identity for grasping the vestiges of racism. The
specific reasons for his antipathy are undoubtedly over-determined by a
multitude of racialized affects and practices, operating both inside/
outside the teaching encounter. Nonetheless, as 'cultural workers'
(Giroux, 1992), isn't our aim to contend with this student's entrenched
racialized subjectivity? His troubling response exemplifies the pedagogic
challenges and resistances of confronting 'race' and difference.

Notably, the im/possible goal of transforming a student's subjectivity
has figured cultural identity as the problematic for pedagogy. The politics of *identity* has been inseparable from the practice of pedagogy for
multicultural and anti-racist education (Kincheloe and Steinberg,
1997).[1] Yet, how have existing conceptualizations of identity impacted
upon the praxis of critical multicultural pedagogies? How have they
materialized an anti-racist 'erotics' of teaching? (hooks, 2003). Identity
as originary, unified and predicated on a self-sustaining subject has
undergone sustained philosophical and cultural critique. The de-
centring of the sovereign subject has inured a critique of identity from
which there appears to be no return. When Stuart Hall (1996) asked
'who needs identity?' his response continues to mark a terrain pre-
occupying those of us concerned with relations of culture, power
and knowledge. Hall invokes the Derridian notion of 'thinking at the
limit' – putting a concept 'under erasure'. Thus, *identity* cannot be
simply superseded with something better, because '... without which

certain key questions cannot be thought at all' (p. 2). For Hall, the seemingly irreducible concept of identity arises in relation to the set of *problems* it has emerged from: '... its centrality to the question of agency and politics' (p. 2).

The persistence of identity is also echoed by Lawrence Grossberg (1996). He cautiously notes how the influence of post-colonial and critical race theory has led to 'narrowly' equating cultural studies with theories of the politics of identity and difference, while paradoxically the discipline itself has expanded its theoretical and spatial borders beyond these issues. Still though, for cultural studies, '... discussions of multiculturalism too quickly assume a necessary relation between identity and culture' (p. 88). In questioning identity as the cardinal site of all political struggles, Grossberg turns to a reflection on the politics of black documentary practice by David Bailey and Hall, which is worth reproducing:

> It is perfectly possible that what is politically progressive and opens up new discursive opportunities in the 1970s and 1980s can become a form of closure – and have repressive value – by the time it is installed as the dominant genre ... It will run out of steam; [...] people will use it not because it opens up anything but because they are being spoken by it, and that point, you need another shift. (Bailey and Hall, cited in Grossberg, 1996, pp. 87–8)

Bailey and Hall point to more than only the contextual, shifting nature of the political and pedagogical struggles over racialized representations. They intimate how regimes of power-knowledge may appropriate and neutralize the grounds upon which struggles over identity and representation are played out. It follows that identity needs to be relocated away from reductive, binaristic oppression/resistance models of power. This move requires rethinking *agency*.

Multicultural Encounters seeks to activate a shift from identity to agency for innovating a pedagogy of cultural difference. It questions why identity continues to be at the heart of multicultural and anti-racist educational approaches. Significant developments in multicultural pedagogy have taken place since the 1970s in the USA, Canada, Australia and UK for example. These have been in response to a (belated) recognition of the diversity of the nation in order to refashion a cultural citizenship. The ideologies of multiculturalism, and its educational conceptualization, implementation and practices of pedagogy have widely varied in different national contexts. Much of these developments though have been governed by an encroaching neo-liberal educational agenda, and a '... normative politics of cultural difference in the form of practical concerns for teachers and administrators.' (Grant and Sachs, 1995, pp. 89–90)

In opposition to this de-politicization of pedagogy, the emergence of a 'critical multiculturalism' (Sleeter and McLaren, 1995) and its dialogue with other inter-disciplinary fields of cultural, media and postcolonial studies is to be welcomed. The trajectory of identity remains the common ground of these fields of study in relation to their multicultural pedagogies, yet none have adequately examined their own praxis of representing difference. This book remains preoccupied with questions of identity, though in order to explore a *pedagogic agency* for living with difference. It grapples with the problem of teaching difference in the age of multicultural globalization by asking: What constitutes a 'multicultural' curriculum and pedagogy? How is the difference of 'others' *conceived*, *represented* and *encountered* in the supposedly radical pedagogies of cultural and media studies? The challenge is to develop an educational practice that eludes reifying cultural identity, by engaging the racialized 'other' outside a pedagogic encounter of idealization or domination. It necessitates questioning the *logic of identity and representation* as the only grounds for a critical multicultural pedagogy.

Teaching difference

The *problem* of teaching difference should however, not just be considered in terms of its solution(s). 'We are led to believe that problems are given ready-made, and they disappear in the responses or the solution' (Deleuze, 1994, p. 158). Gilles Deleuze insists problems do not seek to uncover a solution and nor do solutions define or exhaustively capture the problem. Problems open up new ways of thinking differently; they can be 'inventive' and constitutive. Cultural identity as the *normative* site of agency for multicultural pedagogy is only one solution (adequate or otherwise) of many. Problematizing teaching difference thus can move away from thinking that encountering the 'other' or the mere inclusion of 'other cultures' engenders a multicultural curriculum and practice.

To encounter the 'other' begs a consideration of how Western regimes of knowledge and representation have incited and perpetuated states of domination. In tackling the specific problem of teaching difference, I draw upon the critique of the foundational subject as ultimate ground of knowledge and action, whose universality has suppressed otherness (Falzon, 1998). The philosophical thinkers Gilles Deleuze and Félix Guattari, (and more obliquely, Emanuel Levinas) have been influential for developing my project. Admittedly, the book is parasitic upon selective elements of their work and the reader should not expect a treatise on these thinkers. The engagement is more tactical in order to mutate their ideas for my own ends. We need to recall that concepts for Deleuze and Guattari (1994) are invented to address specific *problems* – it is how we *'put to use'* (Schrift, 1995) such concepts that determine their efficacy.

Deleuze and Guattari (1984; 1987), inspire what I would crudely label as *'alter*-representational' conceptualizations of identity and difference. Their work far from possesses ready-made solutions to the problem of realizing a multicultural pedagogy, but it offers another means of working through questions of identity, representation and power for becoming otherwise – activating an alternative pedagogic agency. To construct their work as simply post-representational (as has become commonplace) fails to acknowledge the continuing force of identity and representation (Kawash, 1998). Increasingly fashionable Deleuzo-Guattarian[2] concepts such as 'rhizomes', 'multiplicities', 'becoming', 'lines of flight' exhaustingly abound and proliferate in recent cultural critique. McKenzie Wark warns that the work of Deleuze especially '... lends itself to the trap of purely formal elaboration of the kind desired by the Anglo-American market particularly' (Wark, 2004, fn. 7).

I also turn to the grounds of the 'ethical' as way of thinking through questions of encountering otherness for an alterity pedagogy. This turn should come as little surprise, as the '... decentring of the subject has brought about a recentring of the ethical' (Garber *et al.*, 2000, p. ix). A Levinasian inspired ethics (especially influenced by Derrida's re-reading through considerations of justice) has found favour in the humanities (Biesta and Egéa-Kuehne, 2001; Zylinska, 2005). It is an ethics without foundations, devoid of moral prescription, rules or codes of conduct. Yet it offers a unique account of *living with difference* that resists charges of cultural relativism aimed at so-called anti-foundational 'postmodern' thought. Levinas (1981) begins from a position of a 'responsibility' towards the other, who cannot be reduced to 'the same'. The primacy of the self is overturned in his account – there is always a response and obligation to the other *before* anything else (Nealon, 1998). The 'other' calls into question the same, rather than the other way around. A Levinasian perspective appears to offer a 'non-conceptualization' of the other as *singular*, 'recognizing' its irreducible alterity outside of domination. Mirroring a fervent celebration of Deleuze in cultural critique, a (re)turn to the ethical has generated a 'Levinas effect' (Johnson, 2000). And the (increasingly banal) exultation of difference, acknowledgement of otherness and incessant liberal invocations of respecting the other are not far behind. The 'Levinas effect' isn't necessarily based on a mis-reading of Levinas, but has more to do with the turn to the ethical being appropriated as a turn to the 'other' as a lauded site of multicultural difference. The valorization of cultural difference (shifting identities, fragmented subjectivities and hybridities), in the age of global multicultural capitalism continues to haunt cultural studies. Judith Butler also worries that 'the return to ethics has constituted an escape from politics' (2000, p. 15). My fleeting, equivocal encounter with Levinas, is driven by the concern that by denying politics there is no ethics for the 'other'. Undoubtedly, it will be found wanting by those bent on pursuing the ethical as a sacred multicultural stomping ground of the 'other'.

This book is not only concerned with making a theoretical intervention. The onerous task of *realizing* a practice of a pedagogy for alterity is also pursued. Hall's (1983) claim that there is 'no general pedagogy' remains apposite, because a universal alterity pedagogy does not exist. Pedagogy needs to be conceptualized as a *site-specific* activity which *responds* to the conditions of its practice. Moreover, there is no general 'other' and its alterity refers to a specific social agent (Chapter 1). Consequentially, while a conceptual understanding of an ethical agency is presented, an alterity pedagogy is also outlined by offering a particular example of critical multicultural practice.

It is a pedagogy which is developed from already existing practices of cultural, media and film studies. While Deleuze urges us 'to experiment' (often exalted as an avant-garde activity by imperious Deleuzians), my efforts are far more modest, and firmly located within *existing* educational institutional settings. Moreover, I draw on texts of popular media culture which resonate with the everyday experiences of students. In the fields of cultural and media studies, the use of texts from popular culture for teaching about the relations of power and representation has become a significant activity (Buckingham and Sefton-Green, 1994; Giroux, 1994). Clearly, the use of 'minority' texts and cultural productions in teaching has endeavoured to examine complex issues of identity and difference. Writers such as Kobena Mercer (1994), Paul Willeman (1994) and Laura Marks (2000) have highlighted that the cultural politics of minority film creatively interrogate questions of otherness. Nevertheless, the use of manifestly *popular* minority film for a critical pedagogic practice has not been adequately scrutinized, especially in relation to a critical engagement with the ethics of difference. In this study, the work of British-South Asian British film-makers has been utilized, and more specifically, films such as *East is East* (1999) and *Bend It Like Beckham* (2002) have been deployed for thinking through the *practice* of an alterity pedagogy.

The use of these types of popular texts is a fraught undertaking, however. While there appears to be a contemporary political recognition of multiculture, this has also been accompanied by an increasing commodification and fetishization of ethnic difference in neo-liberal democracies (Root, 1995; Chow, 1998). The reification of otherness makes a pedagogy for alterity a risky activity. To use 'ethnically marked' texts in teaching runs the danger that it inadvertently leads to further objectifications of otherness. But it is specifically this problem of teaching difference that I seek to addresses: how we can ethically encounter the representation of already racialized minorities in a pedagogic situation? The 'other' has been subject to contemporary forms of racialization in the spheres of public and popular culture. The challenge for an alterity pedagogy is encountering the 'other' outside of reductive categories of racialized knowledge and experience. It would be a relationship to the 'other' which resists reifying its identity, and instead enters into a productive ethical 'alliance'. In other words, it is a pursuit of the *im/possibility* of engaging with otherness which compels an alterity pedagogy.

The structure of this book

Multicultural Encounters addresses the question of alterity and pedagogy in two related parts. Firstly, from an interrogation of the politics of identity and difference, and secondly, by attempting to develop a site-specific pedagogic practice for alterity.

Part I identifies three different 'multicultural educational standpoints' and their articulation of particular pedagogic practices that engage with cultural difference. These standpoints have been labelled as *'identity'*, *'border difference'* and *'the other'*, respectively. In the Introductory chapter, both liberal multicultural and anti-racist pedagogies are discussed in terms of the first standpoint of 'identity'. It involves developing an understanding of the contested idea of multiculturalism, especially in relation to the (essentialist) discourses of identity, culture and nationhood. This educational standpoint is considered lacking for an ethical pedagogy because it can reproduce many of the difficulties and closures associated with practices of identity politics more generally.

Chapter 2 goes on to interrogate educational standpoints of 'border difference' and 'the other'. The second standpoint of difference advances an anti-essentialist critique of identity politics, and offers an inter-subjective account of identity formation (as an effect of difference). Its 'critical multiculturalism' recognizes the need to rethink identity and culture in terms of hegemony and power, and this standpoint's pedagogy advances a contemporary understanding of 'border identities' as 'cultural hybridity'. While a pedagogy of border difference appears to be attractive, it is liable to objectify supposedly transgressive hybridities. As in the case of the first educational standpoint, it actually remains grounded on and limited by a logic of identity. Conceptually, the standpoint of border difference is bound by a dialectic of self/other identity relations predicated upon a negation or 'lack'. That is, its inter-subjective notion of identity is unable to account for more than one identity-difference at a time (Nealon, 1998).

The third standpoint of the 'the other' offers an alternative non-dialectical account of identity formation. There is a recognition of the relational nature of identity formation, though the *agency* of a subject is not conceptualized as a failure in the plenitude of identity as a lack (the self requiring the other in order to be 'complete'), but in terms of the possibility of difference (alterity) in the production of identity. It is this constant process of the making and remaking of identity which allows subjectivity to be articulated otherwise. This performative understanding of identity draws on Grossberg's (1993; 1994) move to dis-articulate cultural identity from a subjective agency that is not secured by a negation of otherness. Agency rather than identity is the practice of this pedagogy. A student's agency is conceived in terms of mobilizing their 'affective investments' to an alternative set of places that may not be framed by existing cultural hegemonies. This argument is developed further via Jeffrey Nealon's work of *Alterity Politics* (1998). Nealon, drawing on Levinas, stresses the ethical relation to otherness in terms of a site-specific performative subjectivity which is always responding to alterity. It is through the productive movement of 'becoming-other' that students have the possibility to ethically encounter alterity outside of a relation of appropriation or domination. In particular, this notion of an ethical performative subjectivity allows the possibility of pedagogically engaging white students from an anti-racist position that does not condemn whiteness.

In Chapter 3, the limitations of existing multicultural/anti-racist pedagogies founded upon rationalist assumptions and realist notions of
curriculum knowledge are highlighted. The second educational standpoint of border difference supersedes such realist practices of 'ideological demystification' and focuses instead on the complex processes of
meaning-production (signification) in the classroom. While this standpoint's pedagogy offers a compelling mode of critical textual analysis
for students, it is unable to engender an ethical encounter with alterity.
There is a need to move beyond only asking about the meaning and
ideological interpretation in the critical reading of a text. Instead, we
can ask the celebrated Deleuzo-Guattarian question of 'what does a text
do?' It involves considering how a text works as an assemblage in terms
of its affective capacities, and how it may be pedagogically utilized for
mobilizing (deterritorializing) students to other sites of ethical investment – productive places to move towards. In particular, popular media
texts are significant because students are already invested in these texts,
and the challenge would be to move them to other ethical ways of
'knowing' and encountering otherness. Such an 'open-ended' pedagogy
aims to advance a reading praxis that encourages students to make
'rhizomatic' connections and linkages, operating outside of existing
hegemonic frameworks of racialized knowledge.

This reading praxis is developed in *Part II* of the book from the third
educational standpoint of a politics of the other. Chapter 4 is concerned with the need to grasp and 'read' the contemporary *crisis of
race* in order to realize a critical multicultural praxis. Contemporary
multiculturalism is driven by a global capitalism able to penetrate
extant borders by increasingly commodifying and subsuming ethnic/
racial differences and hybridities, while advancing a (cultural) racism
of 'differential inclusion'. Conceiving these operations of a neo-liberal
multiculturalism is presented through a framework developed by
Michael Hardt and Antonio Negri (2000) in *Empire*. I argue that the
universality of whiteness as an integrating force and assimilative
power over other racialized differences is in crisis. The deconstruction
of whiteness in crisis is a necessary point of departure for rethinking a
critical multiculturalism and pedagogy.

Chapter 4 goes on to explore the problem of *reading* the crisis of race
(whiteness) itself. I examine three sets of films, *Menace II Society* (1993),
La Haine (1995) and *The Matrix* trilogy as a way of opening up an
understanding towards how these popular texts are *symptomatic* of this
crisis, rather than merely reflecting the contradictions of neo-liberal
multiculturalism. This approach lays the groundwork for subsequent

chapters by maintaining that reading a *racialized* text only in terms of its ideological meanings and signifying practices reduces the pedagogic encounter to one of competing or contestable interpretations. The 'materialist' contention (Montag, 2003) of *why* such interpretations arise and *what* this obfuscates in our understanding of the hegemony of neo-liberal multiculturalism, are otherwise foreclosed.

The realization of an alterity pedagogy is pursued in Chapter 5 by exploring the cultural productions of Black (South Asian) film-makers. These cultural productions have been characterized as directly engaging the contested politics of difference and otherness (Hall, 1988; Mercer, 1994; Marks, 2000). While it is not claimed that these texts autonomously perform a radical pedagogy of alterity, they nevertheless can be tactically deployed as offering performative sites for encountering alterity. Moreover, much of the analysis of Black film has focussed on critical 'avant-garde' work rather than the more *popular* narrative based films, such as *Bend It Like Beckham* or *East is East.* These types of films offer the possibility for opening up questions of cultural difference through demotic aesthetics and languages that readily resonate with students. However, the difficulty is that such films offer a recognizable set of representations of 'Asian culture' and 'identity': it is what ethnically marks these as 'Asian' in the first place. Their popular status means these texts are politically ambiguous due to their ambivalent utilization of extant racialized stereotypes. Nevertheless, they can also be conceived pedagogically as 'minor' texts (cf. Deleuze and Guattari, 1986). Arguably, they have the potential to deterritorialize the 'norm' because they are not simply determined by hegemonic culture, but offer a different exercise of affective power that deviates from the norm. It enables the consideration of the expressive cultural politics of these *'minor-popular'* films in terms of their potential to disrupt normative racialized representations of otherness or the exclusionary practices of multicultural national formation.

In Chapter 6, the claims made about the 'minor-popular' status of the films *Bend It Like Beckham* and *East is East* are elaborated through a close 'reading' of their expressive and affective cultural politics, (rather than only in terms of an ideologically driven interpretative reading). The (anti-)methodology for reading these films is based on creating the conditions of possibility for an ethical encounter between these texts and students in a teaching situation. This approach does not prescribe a specific 'method' of reading, but attempts to understand these films in relation to how they could be *put to use* for realizing an alterity pedagogy. While these texts inhabit the contradictory racialized terrain of the popular, it is maintained that in a site-specific pedagogic encounter they can institute the possibility of mobilizing students to non-appropriative sites of an ethical agency. Although this movement of deterritorialization can never be guaranteed to engender ethical relations with the 'other' – it makes a pedagogy for alterity a risky enterprise. A specific example from my own teaching practice is presented in the deployment of *East is East* as an instance of what an alterity pedagogy may look like in practice. It is a modest attempt at exploring how such an 'imperfect' pedagogic praxis may work in a concrete teaching situation.

Acknowledgements

This book has been a long time in the making. Without the encouragement and support of my family and close friends it would have never seen the light of day. Nirmal Puwar, my intellectual and emotional soul-mate, enabled me to keep going, especially during those times when things seemed insurmountable. My brother (and occasional collaborator), Ashwani Sharma, has been a constant source of inspiration.

I would like to thank Nikos Papastergiadis and Gajendra Verma for their patient support and advice on a very early version of this book. I would also like to thank my former colleagues and students in the Department of Cultural Studies, University of East London for their assistance during the project. Les Back has been invaluable for his continuing encouragement. The friends who have helped me along the way, I remain indebted to.

Short segments of Chapters 2 and 5 respectively, have been published as 'The problem with multiculturalism', in I. Law *et al.* (eds) (2004) *Institutional Racism in Higher Education*, Stoke on Trent: Trentham Press, and 'The sounds of Alterity', in M. Bull & L. Back (eds) (2003) *The Auditory Culture Reader*, Oxford: Berg. A section of Chapter 4 appeared as 'White Paranoia: Orientalism in the age of Empire', *Fashion Theory*, 7(4), pp. 301–18 (written with Ashwani Sharma). I am grateful to the publishers for permitting the reprinting of the above material.

Part I
Educating Identity

1

Introduction: What's Wrong with Multiculturalism?

> There is a growing awareness that other cultures, non-European, non-Western cultures must be met by means other than conquest or domination ... This awareness will have to translate into a type of intellectual work different from that of the modernist intellectual who typically spoke with the confidence of standing at the cutting edge of time and of being able to speak for others. (Huyssens, 1986, p. 220)

> Central to a pedagogy of and for difference is the questioning of the grounds on which identity is constituted within specific historical, cultural, and political contexts and redefined as these contexts (demand) change. To question identity is not to erase or to negate identity, although the latter, as a condition of the refusal of identity, can be a consequence of what might be deemed at the time as political necessity. In fact, such refusals are imperative to the disavowal of forms of subjectivity that oppress others and invade their efforts to forge lives of dignity and meaning. Thus, identificatory positions have a powerful ethical dimension, which extends to points of avowal as well as disavowal. (Kelly, 1997, p. 119)

How do we approach the challenge of teaching difference? Is it possible to ethically encounter the cultural differences of so-called 'others' outside of a relationship of appropriation and domination as Andreas Huyssens urges? And what could this new intellectual and educational work that no longer 'speaks for others' look like in practice? For post-imperial nations the discourse of multiculturalism has been at the heart of the development of educational approaches attempting to engage with 'others'. However, the imbrication of 'identity' and 'culture' has governed and delimited debates of multiculturalism. As Ursula Kelly points out, the un-doing of identity is a critical challenge for a radical pedagogy in creating the conditions of possibility for the production of alternative forms of ethical subjectivity that offer a non-appropriative relationship to otherness.

Pedagogy is inextricably tied to identity and knowledge through which students learn to see themselves and others in the world (Kincheloe and Steinberg, 1997). In relation to questions of multiculturalism, this understanding of pedagogy makes the politics of identity production pivotal for instituting practices that confront racialized regimes of power-knowledge. This opening chapter maps three 'educational standpoints' and their articulation of pedagogic practices that engage the multicultural. These educational standpoints are identified as: (i) 'identity'; (ii) 'border difference'; and (iii) 'the other'.

The first standpoint of 'identity' characterizes the conventional educational approaches of both liberal multicultural and anti-racist education. While this standpoint appears to supersede Enlightenment thought by recognizing difference in the constitution of particular identities, it nevertheless advances a fixed and immutable (essentialist) notion of an autonomous unified subject. Its pedagogy rests largely on Enlightenment occidental rationality and reason. The second standpoint of 'border difference' is present in the work of influential theorists of critical multiculturalism and critical pedagogy, such as Henry Giroux (1992; 1994; 2000), Peter McLaren (1995; 1997), Christine Sleeter (1996), Stephen May (1994; 1999a) and Ali Rattansi (1992; 1999). This standpoint embraces a 'postmodern' critique of the universal rational subject and Enlightenment reason. It advances an anti-essentialist and inter-subjective understanding of identity formation, which recognizes that racial, gendered and sexual social differences are formed through historical and political struggles of power. It also questions rationalist forms of pedagogy and the belief of Enlightenment reason as liberating a unified subject.

These first two educational standpoints of 'identity' (as liberal diversity or anti-racist) and 'border difference' (as critical multiculturalism), are seemingly predicated on distinct notions of subjectivity for establishing their educational goals and strategies. Yet they both figure *identity* as their problematic. I argue that both standpoints (i) and (ii) actually exhibit forms of 'identity politics', which respectively account for 'difference' in particular essentialist and anti-essentialist ways. The trouble is that both standpoints are liable to reproduce many of the political closures found in the social practices of 'identity politics'. The term 'identity politics' has a wide number of meanings and uses, and it is conceived here as a deployment of identity in some form or manner in grounding a pedagogical practice and agency. This includes identity as something fixed and immutable (*essential*), and conversely, a social constructionist anti-essentialist account which recognizes the inter-subjective formation of identity (*specificity*) as an effect of difference. In the first part of the chapter, I maintain that both these forms of identity productions are actually modalities of 'identity politics' predicated on a logic of identity and representation unable to pedagogically encounter alterity – 'the other as other' (Nealon, 1998). It is the third educational standpoint of 'the other' itself which addresses the ethical agency of the subject (as a *singular* individuation), and displaces identity as the site of pedagogic agency. This latter standpoint offers the possibility of engaging with the ethical challenge of alterity.

However, it is important to stress that for these three standpoints and their concomitant deployments of 'identity' – essential, specific and singular – the intention is not to claim that each successive standpoint is simply politically and pedagogically superior to the former. In practice, educationalists may enact more than one form of production of subjectivity without apparent contradiction. It requires examining the standpoints and questioning their ethico-political efficacy in relation to given pedagogical situations. In fact, the pedagogic value of all three of these educational standpoints is not a question that can be always decided in advance – at stake too is the *praxis* of pedagogy. Praxis can be conceived as open-ended rather than possessing a teleological goal. Postmodern critiques of the Enlightenment have challenged the legitimacy of emancipatory politico-educational discourses (Lyotard, 1984; Peters, 1996). The ideals of modernist forms of education to interpellate students to predetermined 'liberatory' subject-positions has been called into question, (though the impact on multicultural and anti-racist pedagogies is questionable). An open-ended praxis is concerned with connecting 'theory' with a transformative practice. 'This entails a reflexivity where we learn to attend to the politics of what we do and do not do at a practical level' (Lather, 1991, p. 21). By scrutinizing these standpoints we can begin to develop an informed understanding of the conceptual and political grounds on which their pedagogies operate – something which has been lacking even in radical multicultural educational accounts of difference.

The problem with identity politics

The first educational standpoint of identity, including both liberal multicultural and anti-racist educational approaches, has promoted varied progressive forms of teaching and learning about difference. Nonetheless, its explicit imbrication of culture and identity engenders this standpoint's pedagogic limits. Both multicultural and anti-racist approaches assume a deterministic relationship between culture and identity leading to limiting the ethico-pedagogic possibilities of students engaging with other differences, as well as their own.

Central to the project of liberal-pluralist multicultural education has been the advocacy of a group-based cultural (ethnic) identity (Verma, 1989). Its logic of recognizing cultural diversity seemingly legitimizes a type of 'communitarian' multicultural educational strategy that encourages the preservation of particular ethnic identities (based on claims of cultural authenticity). The discourse of liberal multicultural education has forwarded a communitarian goal of education as affirming and maintaining cultural identities, yet in the last instance this is subsumed under a liberal universalist claim. The opposition to liberal multiculturalism from anti-racist educational perspectives have largely focussed on rejecting the significance of ethnicity for education. In fact, the anti-racist position championing the category of the 'Black community' in Britain for example, as a collective 'racial' group identity exhibited a radical potential for contesting the white 'transparent norm' of liberal multicultural education (Rattansi, 1992).

Nevertheless, both liberal and anti-racist pedagogic approaches advocate some form of a communitarian group-based cultural/ethnic identity. Their mode of identity production assumes that a particular identity expresses a true natural essence and cultural disposition, 'which can be traced to some authentic common origin or structure of experience' (Grossberg, 1994, p. 12). James Donald and Ali Rattansi (1992) have contended that 'culture' in relation to identity formation can no longer be understood and explained as shared descent, language and custom as present in many multicultural accounts, nor that of shared socio-economic position or colonial history as found in many anti-racist approaches. While multicultural and anti-racist education expound different political ideologies for social transformation, they nevertheless occupy the same ground in their articulation of identity. In their pedagogy, there is an 'underlying similarity between multiculturalist attempts to combat racial prejudice by the provision of "positive images" and the anti-racist injunction to present black histories primarily as narratives of resistance and struggle against racism' (Rattansi, 1992, p. 33). Arguably, such a conceptualization of identity formation and the pedagogies it generates may a have critical pur- chase, particularly in politico-educational conditions in which racially marginalized groups continue to have little means or access to forms of (self-) representation. However, the issue is not to simply advance a cri- tique of the limits of the educational standpoint of identity, but rather to analyse the *investment* of its mode of identity politics (cf. Brown, 1995).

The emergence of forms of identity politics in the West is dependent on national context, though it can be historically understood as the tension between universal and particularistic claims of political rep- resentation in post-Enlightenment liberalism. Identity politics is con- ceived as 'political practices and mobilizations that are based on cultural and social identities' which attempt to resist and struggle against self-negation (Clarke, 1991, p. 37). It has become common to identify contemporary marginalized social groupings based on a part- icular articulation of identity such as 'women', 'black', 'gay' or 'Islamic' as exhibiting an identity politics. Moreover, identity politics based on ethnic affiliation have become especially prominent in late modernity (McCarthy, 1998).

The reasoning of identity politics intends that 'identity necessarily determines a particular kind of politics' (Fuss, 1990, p. 99). This has been most readily expressed in British anti-racist education which advanced a 'politicized Black' racial self-identity. Comparatively, we find that within the discourse of liberal multicultural education there has been an essential relation assumed between cultural diversity and identity – a relation which sublimates ethnicity. Liberal multicultural and anti-racist pedagogic practices do not necessarily promote an iden- tity politics in the classroom as some type of political activity, but their (unintentional) production of a 'politicized' ethnic or racial identity is of concern here. Moreover, as Wendy Brown points out, politicized identity is discursively produced across a number of sites, '... as both a production and contestation of the political terms of liberalism, dis- ciplinary-bureaucratic regimes, certain forces of global capitalism, and the demographic flows of postcoloniality' (1995, p. 54).

It is not the case of wilfully rejecting this form of identity politics for critical pedagogy, though its mode of operation still warrants an unpacking. While identity politics appears to make legitimate demands for recognition and equality, its demands are nevertheless governed by existing regimes of power and domination. Brown maintains that identity politics seek to challenge social inequalities by invariably resorting to claiming political rights based on moral and juridical grounds within late-modern democracy. The question of the relations of domination which engender rights-based discourses remain foreclosed, giving rise to a troubling paradox for identity politics:

> What kind of political recognition can identity-based claims seek – and what kind can they be counted on to want – that will not resubordinate a subject itself historically subjugated through identity, through categories such as race or gender that emerged and circulated as terms of power to enact subordination? (p. 55)

Brown's provocation captures the problematic governing all forms of identity politics: they are ensnared by the very regimes of power they wish to challenge and transcend. Her intervention points towards the necessity of thinking 'beyond' identity as the ground for a political and pedagogic agency.

An interrogation of identity politics reveals that its practices reduce the complex discursive formation of identity to simplistic (observable) social attributes. Rather than exploring the 'effects of discursive and institutional power' (p. 66) in the production of identity-differences, specific social differences are valorized resulting in identities becoming normatively defined and regulated. For example, the state may choose only to legally recognize or provide assistance to particular social groupings representing themselves in terms of their claim to an ethnicity (cf. Sivanandan, 1990). Similarly, neo-liberal multiculturalism may only educationally legitimize certain 'ethnic' ways of life. In this respect, we can further consider the problem of the educational standpoint of identity by examining the charges of 'essentialism' made against it (Rattansi, 1992; May, 1999a). Identity politics is accused of advancing social and cultural differences into particularist self-constituting identities, which are self-interested and unable to take account of other identity-differences (Bourne, 1987). An essentialist understanding of identity formation ignores the intersubjective social construction of all identities; rather it maintains that identities are already trans-historically posited and irreducible to other differences. The educational standpoint of identity found in multicultural and anti-racist education has been disputed and challenged not only because of the conflation of culture with (a politicized) identity, but the essentialized categories that this form of identity production is premised upon.

The critique of essentialism has not only been directed against liberal multicultural education and its affiliate notion of ethnicity. In Britain for example, Rattansi (1992) has highlighted that while an anti-racist form of identity politics has denoted an often successful political alliances against racism, the term 'Black' has also operated as 'profoundly a cultural category, an attempted representation of particular experiences and a particular construction of unity around those experiences' (p. 40). And this cultural essentialism of 'Black' has tended to marginalize questions of class, ethnic, and gender differences for the sake of the 'the black struggle'.[1] The central tenets of anti-racist education, the comprehension and dismantling of racism and the forging of political alliances particularly within the 'Black community' (Brandt, 1986; Troyna, 1987) while important, have been rendered problematic by an anti-essentialist critique against identity politics.

We need to be cautious of embracing an anti-essentialist critique, and too readily dismissing an educational standpoint advancing forms of supposedly essential identity politics. Notably, the impressive analysis and critique against essentialism made by Diana Fuss (1990) in her classroom example, *specifically* rejects the deployment of essentialism by 'minority' students. In a critical response, bell hooks raises the question that directing an anti-essentialist critique solely against students from marginalized groups ignores and misrecognizes 'the subtle and overt ways essentialism is expressed from a location of privilege' (1994, p. 82). The issue for hooks is not simply erasing so-called essentialist standpoints in the classroom, but to interrogate the situations and configurations of power they are deployed in, and by whom.[2] Therefore, while the stance against an essentialist identity politics is compelling, we need to take account of how this form of identity production operates in specific pedagogic situations.[3]

Moreover, the anti-essentialist critique does not capture, perhaps, a more serious risk of identity politics. A number of theorists such as Cameron McCarthy (1998), Nealon (1998) and Brown (1995) have highlighted the 'failure' of identity politics because it is considered as inherently reactionary – structured by the logic of *'ressentiment'*. This Nietzschean term is elaborated by Brown:

> it delimits a specific site of blame for suffering by constituting sovereign subjects and events as responsible for the 'injury' of social subordination. It fixes the identities of the injured and the injuring as social positions, and codifies as well the meanings of their actions against all possibilities of indeterminacy, ambiguity, and struggle for resignification or repositioning. (p. 27)

Brown is careful to distance herself from neo-conservative attacks on minority rights, or to disingenuously oppose anti-discriminatory laws. However, the point she and other theorists raise is that 'social injury' – expressed most powerfully in the developments of highly specified identity-based rights – should not be the *constitutive* grounds for claiming an identity for marginalized groups. It should be noted that an educational standpoint of identity would not necessarily produce a reactionary in-ward looking stance amongst its students, (one reason being that multicultural and anti-racist pedagogies are often unsuccessful!). However, students would be subject to the hazards of an educational strategy based on identity and the essentializing closures it may engender.

To argue that identity claims are pedagogically limiting also requires acknowledging their imbrication with discourses of multiculturalism (see Chapter 3). Notably, this has led to rethinking *critical* multiculturalism for the educational standpoint of border difference, which overcomes the supposed dichotomy of liberal and anti-racist ideologies present in the educational standpoint of identity. The second part of this chapter pursues an interrogation of two significant contemporary discourses of educational multiculturalism, namely 'neo-liberal' and 'critical' (McLaren, 1995). While critical multiculturalism imparts a cogent critique against neo-liberalism, it has not come to terms with the problem of alterity. For its standpoint of border difference, the nation becomes the fault-line that exposes the antagonism of the multicultural, and the impossibility of the representation of alterity. And it is from this challenge of alterity that third educational standpoint of the 'other' is outlined in the final part of the chapter.

Multicultural contestations

> [M]ulticulturalism has served variously as code for assimilationism and cultural separatism; campus marxism and ethnic nationalism; transnational corporate marketing strategies and minority competition for state resources; radical democracy and cosmetic adjustments to the liberal-democratic status quo. Multiculturalism in its various guises clearly signals a crisis in the definition of 'nation'... [It] assumes a different complexion depending on whether the term is regarded as alien or integral to discourses of national identity, and whether it is interpreted as naming that have been called 'top-down' (state-sponsored) or 'bottom-up' (minority-led, oppositional) strategies for reinventing the nation. (Bennett, 1998, pp. 1–2)

David Bennett attempts to capture the ambivalences of multiculturalism. Multiculturalism is figured as a contested terrain of multiple
meanings within differing social and national contexts, and expressive
of a variegated set of political 'projects'. The ambivalent status of
multiculturalism has meant a lack of agreement as to its meanings and
effects (Gordon and Newfield, 1996). To state that multiculturalism is a
contested site has become almost customary, as its manifold meanings
allude to a range of issues and social exclusions: 'race', socio-economic
class, gender, sexuality and disability (Kincheloe and Steinberg, 1997).

Bennett highlights the need to locate its emergence and deployments
within a particular national context. He outlines (rather too schemat-
ically) that multiculturalism in Britain has been largely 'state-managed'
('top-down') in comparison to the USA, where it has been ostensibly
driven by identity-based 'minority demands' ('bottom-up'). Although,
the political forces behind multiculturalism do not necessarily determine
its potential for progressive social transformations. For example, the
contested nature of multicultural demands within a hegemonic national
formation, in which both state-managed and minority multicultural pre-
scriptions may coincide as well as collide (Anthias and Yuval-Davis,
1992). However, the production of national unity by the staging of a
common national culture which attempts to transcend racial antagonisms and other cultural differences has been reproduced in the discourse
of neo-liberal multicultural education. As Maria Koundoura (1998, p. 70)
writes: 'Such is the history ... from which multiculturalism as an educational policy – with its agenda of representing and teaching cultural
difference – arises.'

'Cultural diversity' has been the dominant motif in the representation
and teaching of difference in contemporary liberal-pluralist multiculturalism, for both schooling and university education. From neo-marxist anti-
racist perspectives, this educational approach has been admonished for
reifying culture and ethnic group identity at the expense of examining
power relations in society (May, 1999b). While ostensibly a convincing
critique, the anti-racist approach according to Rattansi (1992; 1999)
mistakenly entailed a rejection of 'ethnicity' (culture), rather than examining the cultural politics of representation. The ideology of cultural
diversity has not only intended to manage (incommensurable) cultural/
racial differences within the nation. Homi Bhabha (1990) has suggested
that it also seeks to control and repress cultural difference:

> although there is always an entertainment and encouragement of
> cultural diversity, there is always a corresponding containment of it.

A transparent norm is constituted, a norm given by the host society or dominant culture, which says that 'these cultures are fine, but we must be able to locate them within our own grid' ... a containment of cultural difference. (p. 20)

Bhabha alerts us to the danger of notions pertaining to the construction of a unitary or *common* culture, whether in a crude conservative sense of the exclusive nation or the liberal sense of 'diversity within unity'. It is a transparent (white) norm which is erased in accounts of liberal or benevolent multiculturalism. As McLaren has asked: 'Who has the power to exercise meaning, to create the grid from which Otherness is defined, to create the identifications that invite closures on meanings?' (1995, p. 213).

The containment of cultural difference constructs culture epistemologically as an 'empirical object of knowledge', and compels it to be understood as a discrete category that can be *discovered, observed, evaluated* and *contextualized* – though always governed by a transparent norm. Liberal multiculturalism in reifying culture ignores the operations of power that *produce* culture as a knowable 'anthropological' object in the first place. For the project of multicultural education, the appreciation and knowledge of *other* cultures, or the encouragement of cultural diversity in curriculum practices can only manifest itself through an absolute or relative difference against an invisible Eurocentric frame of reference. At the heart of this compensatory multiculturalism there subsists an acknowledgement of 'otherness' only as a balkanized or domesticated other. The act of making (ethnic) otherness a knowable object of knowledge can be understood as making the other the 'same'. That is, the relationship or encounter with the 'other' is one of appropriation or domination (Chow, 1998; Nealon, 1998; Ahmed, 2000).

While Bhabha has provided a cogent critique of liberal multiculturalism and its ideology of cultural diversity, an educational multicultural *versus* anti-racist oppositional divide has led to an occlusion of more profound theoretical and pedagogical questions concerning the constitution of cultural identities, and the political significance of national formation. The limitations of this opposition have been addressed by identifying an anti-essentialist strategy in the attempt to rethink culture (Donald and Rattansi, 1992). It has signified a radical departure from conventional (and incorrectly assumed antagonistic) multicultural and anti-racist positions that have been divided over the issue of culture. The move beyond the multicultural/anti-racist opposition is an attempt to rethink multiculturalism more *critically*, although until recently this politically charged divide impeded such a development (May, 1999b). In particular, it has been the work of McLaren who has attempted to promote a critical rethinking for developing a contemporary understanding of multiculturalism.[4]

McLaren (1995) advances a concept of 'critical multiculturalism' which seeks to be distinct from other forms of multiculturalism identified as 'conservative', 'liberal' and 'left-liberal'. He acknowledges that these are 'ideal-typical labels' which serve as 'heuristic devices', and in reality each of the positions blend into one another. Nevertheless, in relation to 'race' and ethnicity, McLaren's aim is to formulate a 'theoretical grid that can help discern the multiple ways in which difference is both constructed and engaged' (p. 120). His codification of multiculturalism is significant because it readily brings questions of the theorization of cultural difference to the forefront in an interrogation of the discourse of educational multiculturalisms.[5] His elucidation of a 'critical multiculturalism' is motivated by what he identifies as the insights of post-structuralist thought, though he is keen to ground this in relation to 'material' struggles:

> The perspective of what I am calling critical multiculturalism understands representations of race, class, and gender as the result of larger social struggles over signs and meanings ... [It] stresses the central task of transforming the social, cultural, and institutional relations in which meanings are generated. (p. 126)

McLaren points out that the liberal (and conservative) stress on 'sameness', and the left-liberal emphasis on absolute 'difference' are a false binary opposition based on essentialist logic of identity. In contrast,

> critical multiculturalism interrogates the construction of difference and identity in relation to a radical politics. It is positioned against the neo-imperial romance with monoglot ethnicity grounded in a shared or 'common' experience of 'America' that is associated with conservative and liberal strands of multiculturalism. (p. 126)

By drawing upon Bhabha (see earlier), McLaren is vigilant against the regulation of difference through liberal and conservative notions of a common (national) culture. He stresses the 'terror of whiteness' as the invisible cultural norm against which 'others' are defined against. Unlike liberal-pluralist multiculturalism, McLaren's formulation is astutely aware of the social and political relations of power which produce cultural differences both between and amongst groups. From the perspective of a 'politics of difference' (cf. Hall, 1988; West, 1990), McLaren outlines a radical educational practice that promotes 'border identities' which are not tied to essentialist practices of identity formation (see Chapter 2). Nevertheless, McLaren's mapping of critical multiculturalism still demands further scrutiny in relation to the danger of reproducing untenable ideological divisions, and the urgent issue of deconstructing national formation. While the codifications of multiculturalism by McLaren are made on heuristic grounds, they still have a tendency to suffer from reproducing unusable 'critical/liberal' or 'left/right' ideological divisions. McLaren's schema is liable to operate from a politics of positing a (reductive) choice between 'reform' and 'revolution' (Rattansi, 1999). It is unsurprising that critical multiculturalism is promoted for its revolutionary potential of social transformation, but it also limits an understanding of the politics of representation and alterity for multiculturalism. This issue becomes more apparent by exploring the exposition of a 'discrepant multiculturalism' by Barnor Hesse (1999).

Hesse begins from a deconstructive impulse seeking to interrogate the politics of the *Western* status of multiculturalism in relation to representations of the modern nation and identity. We know that contemporary national discourses of multiculturalism signify cultural differences principally as 'race' and ethnicity, but also more broadly in terms of gender, class, sexuality, religion etc.

> What these contracting and expanding poles of the multicultural suggest is not only the incidence of diverse cultural responses to the experience of national entanglement, but the political irreducibility of racialisation in any formation of Western multiculturalism. It is the articulation of racialisation in Western multiculturalism that is its configural dimension. Without this neither the contractive nor expansive pole can be constituted. It is for this reason that multiculturalism in the West needs to be understood as discursively organised around the various discrepancies that circulate within the cultural afterlife of modern Europe's imperialisms. (Hesse, 1999, p. 207)

Hesse lays emphasis on Western multiculturalism being premised upon the 'political irreducibility of racialization' in its constitution. The operations of 'race' are integral to, and formative of, identity and nation. Moreover, the politics of multiculturalism is figured on the 'exposure of the discrepant', which involves the need to make explicit the inconsistencies and political antagonisms disavowed in Western national formations. What is at stake is not only grasping that the discourses of 'race' and ethnicity are articulated through gender, sexuality and class for instance, but that multiculturalism signifies a 'point of entanglement' which is repressed in the narration and formation of Western nations (see also Bhabha, 1994).

> What is disavowed in the official versions of the Western nation is its implication both in the hegemonic construction of 'Europe' as the universal/ideal and its acculturation through an antagonism with the subaltern construction of 'non-Europe' as the differential/ pathological. (Hesse, 1999, p. 215)

This mapping of multiculturalism concerns itself with the representation of the nation which is revealed by the

> contestation of different multicultural imaginaries ... Imaginaries are important ... as they express desires to overcome incompleteness or insufficiency in the construction of identities ... [T]he nation ... is affirmed through particular imaginaries which give meaning to the proliferation and interaction between its cultural differences. (pp. 216–17)

In Hesse's account, and somewhat in contrast to McLaren's, all forms of political imaginaries (conservative, liberal and left) are motivated by the task of transforming social, political and institutional relations – not just critical multiculturalism. A key distinction lies in the emphasis placed by Hesse on the codification of the nation in the identification of multicultural imaginaries. The nation cannot be fully accounted for by any particular representation of a multicultural imaginary. While the nation attempts to delimit cultural identity and difference, it is also politically contingent upon these multicultural imaginaries. Rather than a single point of 'origin', the nation is multiply inscribed, and founded upon a series of inclusions/exclusions (Bhabha, 1994). There is always an 'excess' to the nation, that what remains as excluded. Cultural differences are not simply congruent with the national space. Thus, there is a paradox of multiculturalism: 'the impossibility of full national representation' (Hesse, 1999, p. 206). Western forms of multiculturalism are unproblematically tied to the idea of a single unitary nation, how ever much the nation may purport to recognize cultural diversity. The emergence of liberal multicultural education has embodied a project of nation-building. Its idea of a multicultural democracy that has faith in the nation as an arbiter of identity-differences cannot be countenanced.

The quandary of identity and nationhood is not confined to conservative or liberal forms of multiculturalism; though the account of critical multiculturalism forwarded by McLaren is not oblivious to the problem of the representation of identity and multicultural democracy. McLaren (1997) has highlighted concerns with the aporia of a liberal multicultural democracy. While working from a 'revolutionary' transnational multicultural perspective, he begins to confront the question of national formation for critical multiculturalism. There is a possibility nonetheless, that a critical multiculturalism's standpoint leaves open the idea of affirming a multicultural nation which in the last instance assimilates cultural identity through the recognition and representation of difference. There is a need '... to offer a different articulation of the multicultural nation that would accommodate its multiple cultural histories without resolving them into a unitary narrative of nationhood' (Koundoura, 1998, p. 71).[6]

Alterity pedagogy

The problem of the nation and representation of difference is symptomatic of a more profound challenge of multiculturalism, which the educational standpoints of identity and border difference are unable to substantially address. As Cameron McCarthy writes, a '... fundamental issue ... posed by theories of identity formation, is the challenge of defining identity in ways other than through the strategy of negation of the other. This, I wish to suggest, is the fundamental challenge, of multiculturalism' (1998, p. 92). At stake here is the ethico-political issue of how students pedagogically engage difference without a relation of exclusion, negation or domination. I have claimed that only the third educational standpoint of the 'other' can address an ethics of alterity. This contention, of course, is in need of further elaboration. The final part of the chapter outlines the provocation of alterity for rethinking the project of multicultural pedagogy. It returns to the vexed question of 'identity' but moves beyond critiques of essentialism which have stifled the standpoints of identity and difference. Instead, a more fundamental question of subjectivity and agency is elaborated.

Hall (1996) has elaborated an influential notion of identity which continues to circulate in contemporary cultural theory:

I use 'identity' to refer to the meeting point, the point of suture, between on the one hand the discourses which attempt to 'interpellate' ... hail us into place as the social subjects of particular discourses, and on the hand, the processes which produce subjectivities, which construct us as subjects which can be 'spoken'. Identities are thus points of temporary belonging which discursive practices construct for us. (pp. 5–6)

Hall enables us to understand that pedagogy as an institutionalized discursive practice is involved in the process of 'articulating' subjects to positions made available for their adoption. This raises the problem that subjects are not necessarily always 'hailed' (interpellated) successfully, and more significantly, that these subject-positions are not identical to the subject. It means that subjects also 'invest' in these positions in the formation of identities. What is of most interest in this account however, is an implicit understanding of subject-formation based on identity being non-identical to itself. It highlights a dialectical understanding of self/other identity relations.[7] William Connolly offers one of the clearest accounts of how identity is dialectically conceptualized in many 'post-structuralist' accounts.

An identity is established in relation to a series of differences that have become socially recognized. These differences are essential to its being. If they did not coexist as differences, it would not exist in its distinctness and solidity ... Identity requires difference in order to be, and it converts differences into otherness in order to secure its own self-certainty. (Connolly, cited in Brown, 1995, p. 54, fn. 2)

Connolly stresses the dialectical inter-subjective and relational operations of identity formation. A particular identity-difference relies on the *negation* of another difference (otherness) to establish itself.

The challenge for an alterity pedagogy is the need to break out of this problematic of identity in order to think through an alternative mode of subjectivity – an ethical agency – which does not negate otherness in the process of its articulation. At the risk of grossly simplifying complex bodies of thought, the two educational standpoints of identity and difference are more or less founded on a Hegelian dialectic of self/other relations. Deleuze famously summarizes a key aspect of what underpins the Hegelian dialectic:

> The Hegelian dialectic is indeed a reflection of difference, but it inverts its image. For the affirmation of difference as such it substitutes the negation of that which differs; for the affirmation of the self it substitutes the negation of the other, and for the affirmation of affirmation, it substitutes the famous negation of negation. (Deleuze, 1983, p. 196)

Deleuze's challenge to the Hegelian dialectic is beyond the scope of this book. Instead of negation however, the alternative Deleuzian proposition of an affirmative, immanent difference – multiplicity – is of interest. Identity or rather 'individuation' as Peter Hallward states, from a Deleuzian perspective is derived from the *singular* which 'creates the substance of its own substantial existence or expression ... [it] is self-constituent, an on-going differentiation' (2001, pp. 2, 4). Hallward contrasts the *singular* with the *specific* which is an inter-subjective individuation, the contextual specificities of 'race', class and gender for example (as found in the educational standpoint of border difference). The concept of the singular raises the possibility of considering the other in terms of its own positivity, the 'other as other', because such a conceptualization works outside of dialectical self/other identity relations. The educational standpoint of the other is predicated on a non-dialectical ontology of difference which encounters the other on its own terms. The implication is that it makes possible to institute an 'ethical' engagement with difference for critical multiculturalism. It means attempting to develop a singularizing practice that creates the *conditions* for in which students acknowledge and affirm alterity. But what does an *ethical encounter* actually involve in the practice of an alterity pedagogy?

The ethical provocation posed by alterity may be grasped by first asking the seemingly innocent question: 'What or who is "the other"?' (Rajchman, 1995, p. xiii). The apparent separation of the 'what' from the 'who' marks the aporia of 'Otherness', and reveals its 'doubling' movement. The explication of Otherness has traditionally been understood as belonging to the realm of Western philosophical inquiry. Rey Chow highlights that Otherness in these accounts refers to the attempt to un-do the logocentric metaphysical tradition of European thought from within, which actually precedes the subversive challenge of post-structuralism in its 'theoretical dislocation of the sign' (Chow, 1998,

p. 5). In simple terms, 'logocentricism' refers to the grounding of truth and unity in language. The traditional Western philosophical project has 'privileged oneness and unity (the Same) at the expense of manyness and plurality (the Other). Accordingly, '[it] can be understood as the repeated effort to overcome plurality and establish unity by reducing the many to the one' (Taylor, cited in Scheurich, 1997, p. 85). Otherness – *autre*, understood as ontological difference – in post-structuralism has challenged the idea of unity vis-à-vis a critique of the transparency of language and the stability of the meaning of a sign. Chow argues that the emergence of the field of cultural studies (while indebted to post-structuralist theory) turns to otherness not only as a deconstructive mode of inquiry, but also to Europe's 'actual others' forged by a history of violent imperialism and colonial encounters. She makes the bold statement that cultural studies has forced post-structuralist theory 'to confront the significance of race – and with it the histories of racial exploitation – that is repressed in poststructuralism's claim to subversiveness and radicality' (Chow, 1998, p. 5).

One of the difficulties of undertaking a study which attempts to engage with what we can now refer to as the 'concrete other' (*autri*) is that it is entangled (and often conflated) with an 'ontological Other'. The reification of the concrete other (*autri*) slipping into an objectified *unknowable* object of western knowledge (*autre*), an abstract 'generalized Other' has plagued discourses of alterity (Hanssen, 2000). Moreover, it has been argued that merely inquiring 'Can we know the other?' is implicitly Eurocentric (cf. Kaplan, 1997). This question can conflate concrete others, with the ontological Other as a marker of the limit of Western knowledge. While the Western quest for knowledge (the process of making the Other the Same) has been structured by an imperialist epistemological violence (Spivak, 1988b), it does not follow that an encounter with the concrete other outside of domination is futile. Neither does this mean that the alterity of the concrete other can be wholly 'known' through existing hegemonic representational practices. Alterity cannot be captured through representation – made into to a knowable object of knowledge – else the other no longer remains other (Levinas, 1979). The 'other' being referred to in this book is a concrete social agent whose own irreducible differences (alterity) has been historically subordinated.[8] If multicultural education is to be a worthwhile project, it is compelled to engage alterity outside of a pedagogical relationship of appropriation, domination or exclusion.

How do we then conceive of such a non-appropriative relationship with the other? It necessitates an acknowledgement of the force of the

'ethical'. The ethical here does not refer to a universal prescriptive set
of principles or foundational rules to follow (Levinas, 1979; Foucault,
2000). Nor is it expressive of the banality of the liberal aphorism of '*we
must respect and tolerate others*' (which insidiously harbours a violence).
Rather, ethics is to be conceived as a grounded social and political
relation. Christopher Falzon offers such an understanding of ethics in
relation to concrete others:

> Ethics is not a matter of justifying or legitimating principles and
> forms of life. Normative principles, along with the social forms
> they inform, emerge out the play of dialogue. Dialogue itself, as
> I am presenting it, is not itself a normative notion, an ideal to be
> realised. On the contrary, it is an inescapable fact of life, of our
> historical existence. We are inevitably caught up in the ongoing
> play of dialogue, the movement of ordering and resistance to
> ordering. And it is in this context that ethics can be understood.
> Ethics becomes an instrument, a tool, a means of facilitating the
> movement of dialogue in which we are always involved. (Falzon,
> 1998, p. 60)[9]

Falzon's notion of 'social dialogue' contends that encounters with
others are historically forged and unavoidable because they are an
inescapable fact of human existence. Forms of ordering and domination emerge when social dialogue is arrested in the attempt to domesticate the other (which invariably fails). However, appropriation or
domination are not the only types of encounters that are possible. Any
encounter with the other (unequally) affects and alters both sides. It
inevitably involves judgement and the imposition of meaning-
categories, though for this 'is not a final understanding, but only the
beginning of an open-ended process' (p. 93). Hegemonic frameworks of
categorization and ways of knowing are not absolute, but historically
determined because they have emerged from encounters with others in
the first place. It means that on-going social dialogue allows the possibility of the transformation of these frameworks leading to 'new
forms' and 'ways of knowing'. To encounter, or be 'open to the other'
means promoting or accelerating social dialogue which the ethical
facilitates. It is a fraught and risky activity because it means being confronted with new ways of knowing and other 'ways of life'. In terms of
materializing the notion of social dialogue further, Mary Louise Pratt's
account of 'contact zones' goes towards grasping how encounters are
played out: 'social spaces where disparate cultures meet, clash, and

grapple with each other in often highly asymmetric relations of domination and subordination' (1992, p. 4).

An alterity pedagogy thus can be characterized as attempting to activate ethical encounters which resist the domination and exclusion of the other, though not by ignoring how such risky engagements are subject to illicit capture and appropriation. We shall find in the following chapter, this educational standpoint of an affirmative other emerges out of an intervention by Grossberg (1993; 1994). He has been one of the few cultural studies educationalists to recognize the need to develop a multicultural pedagogic practice which begins by acknowledging the singularity of the other.

2
Borders, Agency and Otherness

Over a decade ago, Stuart Hall (1988) inaugurated an influential critique against an essentializing identity politics advanced by both liberal multicultural and anti-racist discourses. The challenge of what he dubbed as the *'new ethnicities'* demanded rethinking identity in terms of the contested, uneven processes of globalization and transnational formations:

> A recreation, the reconstruction of imaginary knowable places in the face of the global postmodern which has, as it were, destroyed the identities of specific places ... So one understands the moment when people reach for these groundings ... is what I call ethnicity. (Hall, 1991a, pp. 35–6)

Hall's move to re-appropriate cultural identity outside its narrow multiculturalist conceptions and racialized nationalist discourses highlighted that the new ethnicities 'speak from a particular place, out of a particular history, out of a particular experience, a particular culture, without being contained by that position' (Hall, 1988, p. 29). Ethnicity reconfigured as a site of identification, 'belongingness' and positionality acknowledged that the groundings of identity are neither exhaustive nor *determinate* of our political and cultural identifications. New ethnicities captured 'the astonishing return to the political agenda of all those points of attachments which give the individual some sense of place and position in the world' (Hall, 1989, p. 33). This intervention by Hall sought to rework the imperious relationship between culture and identity, and spawned extensive discussions of a politics of *hybridity* amongst cultural theorists. Hybridity signalled the complex condition of globalizing cultures, but what tended to be passed over in

Hall's account is that more fundamentally, re-appropriating ethnicity also marked an attempt to displace cultural identity as the cardinal site of *agency* of the subject in the 'global postmodern'.

Identity continues to remain an inexorable force in our fractious global times, and Hall recognized that the 'persistence of the subject' (Williams, 2001) is not just a problem of theory. While the over-determined categories of identity and culture delimit discourses of multiculturalism, the question of the agency of the subject (student) in multicultural education has remained muted. How have critical multicultural pedagogies constructed the subject in their praxis? Where is the agency of the subject located? What is the pedagogic relationship to otherness (alterity) of the subject? The most difficult challenge for multicultural pedagogy is how to engage with a racialized subject-position articulated by *ressentiment* (Chapter 1).

Howard Winant (2004) identifies a 'new politics of whiteness' in *crisis* that is entangled with *ressentiment* when he writes:

> On the one hand, whites continue to inherit the legacy of white supremacy ... But on the other hand, they are subject to the moral and political challenges posed to that inheritance by the partial but real successes of the black movement (and affiliated movements). These movements advanced a countertradition to white supremacy ... they did not destroy the deep structures of white privilege, but they did make counterclaims on behalf of the racially excluded and subordinated. As a result, white identities have been displaced and refigured: They are now contradictory, as well as confused and anxiety-ridden, to an unprecedented extent. (p. 4)

A key problem for a multicultural praxis is how to advance an anti-racist perspective which avoids denouncing the racialized subject-position of a white student. To put it more starkly, the 'white angry man' (Nealon, 1998) is the exemplary subject of *ressentiment* in the age of neo-liberal multiculturalism.[1] We shall discover that this primal figure of *ressentiment* is in fact a critical limit point for any multicultural pedagogy.

In Chapter 1, potential closures of the educational standpoint of identity was examined. Agency for this standpoint is limited by an essentializing identity politics, governed by a determinate relationship between identity and culture. Moreover, I asserted that the second educational standpoint of the border, while advancing an anti-essentialist position, was also governed by a modality of identity

politics. That is to say, the entangled relation between cultural identity and agency persists for this standpoint. The first part of this
chapter interrogates the standpoint of the border by it being
premised upon a rendering of identity as an *effect* of 'difference'. It is
not merely a matter of recognizing or valorizing a particular identity-
difference – a racial, class or sexual identity – but of attending to the
more difficult issue of 'the *kind* of difference that is acknowledged
and engaged' (Mohanty, 1994, p. 146, my emphasis). This standpoint's pedagogic enterprise is realized through the trope of 'border
crossing' as generative of difference (Giroux, 1992). Border differences have been most readily conceived as expressive of cultural
hybridity – the site of a dialogic mode of inter-subjectivity (cf.
Bakhtin, 1981; Bhabha, 1994). Hybridity as a location of difference
operating in cultural studies and critical pedagogy approaches will be
considered against the ethical provocation of otherness. It transpires
that a dialectical, inter-subjective account of identity formation as
hybridity is still tied to a modality of 'identity politics', and thus is
unable to acknowledge, politically or ethically, more than one identity-difference at a time.

In contrast, the third educational standpoint of the 'other' evades
the problematic of identity as the negation of difference. Part two of
this chapter develops an alternative multicultural praxis of alterity that
disarticulates cultural identity from pedagogic agency. Influenced by
Deleuze and Guattari (1984; 1987), and the notable intervention by
Grossberg (1994; 1996), a non-dialectical notion subjectivity is
advanced allowing for *agency* being 'located' outside of identity, and
towards another set of possibilities. Agency is reconsidered in terms of
a student's 'affective investments' which may be productively mobilized otherwise. This rethinking of identity as pedagogic agency is
pursued further via Nealon's (1998) stress on activating a performative
subjectivity which is always responding to alterity. It offers a means
of conceiving a pedagogy that addresses the possibility of a non-
appropriative ethical agency and engagement with otherness.
Although, how it responds to the figure of the 'white angry man'
exposes the *im/possibility* of an alterity pedagogy.

Border pedagogy: hybridity and its discontents

There are a number of educationalists whom, while proposing a range
of critical multicultural pedagogies, share an opposition to essentialist
forms of ethnic/racial identities for the educational standpoint of the

border.[2] Inspired by the promise of 'new ethnicities', the turn towards deconstructive conceptualizations of 'culture' and identity production has invoked the key concept of 'hybridity' as difference. Over the last decade, this trope of difference has gained a critical educational purchase for a globalizing cultural/media studies, particularly in relation to describing the transformations of national cultures, and the formation of new 'border crossing' student subjectivities.[3]

It is worth examining the semblance and ontological groundings of this standpoint's deployment of hybridity. The interactions and exchanges between and across different cultural formations are primal to how identity and difference are forged for a border pedagogy. Central to this standpoint's praxis is the stress on cultural commutation across boundaries of difference. More generally, as Grossberg (1993) points out, the spatial figure of the 'border' has articulated accounts of inter-subjective identity formation in post-colonial cultural studies. While the standpoint of border pedagogy has much to offer a critical multiculturalism, it runs the risk of over-valorizing 'boundary crossing' as the *condition* of hybridity. Hence, it is necessary to closely examine the figures of the *border* and *hybridity* as generative of identity for their value and potential limits in realizing an alterity pedagogy. The anti-essentialist critique of cultural identity has engendered differing notions of hybridity, which often exist collaterally in many accounts (Young, 1995).[4] At least two modes of hybridity can be identified in terms of their installation of difference: (i) hybridity as a fusional or syncretic notion of identity and cultural formation; and (ii) hybridity as a radical form of cultural difference produced in the space of liminality.[5] As many accounts of identity slide between these distinctions and simultaneously draw on more than one production of 'difference', this schema is of course heuristic.

Donald and Rattansi (1992) were one of the first British educationalists to consider the implications of contemporary theoretical developments in cultural theory for the question of identity. Clearly influenced by the 'new ethnicities', these authors reassessed the question of culture in terms of cultural authority and individual agency, and opposed culture being reductively conceived as the expression of identity, either as a social collectivity or a community. They advanced an educational standpoint which urged for innovating pedagogic strategies based on acknowledging de-centred subjectivities and the discursive conditions of identity formation. Donald and Rattansi did not specify in any great detail how such educational approaches may be realized, or what they could look like in practice. Although, they referred to the pedagogy of celebrated Black British-based diasporic aesthetic practices of art, music and film,[6] and lay emphasis on the emergence of *hybrid* youth identities in urban spaces. Rattansi pointed towards the educational potential of acknowledging the

> creative explorations of the shifting contours of black and white British cultural identities ... [Students] are engaging in their own complex negotiations and renegotiations around language and music, for example borrowing elements from 'white', Afro-Caribbean and Asian forms and creating new syncretic versions. (Rattansi 1992, p. 41)

Rather cautiously, Rattansi (1999) also highlighted that hybrid youth identities and cultures are transitory and situational in their marginality, and cannot be readily conflated with 'new social movements' in offering a transformative politics for a radical multicultural practice. Hybridity as a mode of fusion or syncretism may offer counter-hegemonic formations of identity production, and the potential to disrupt exclusionary notions of national identity that rest on a culturalist neo-racism (Gilroy, 1987). The problem is that the condition of syncretic hybridity is not necessarily transgressive – it does not prefigure or guarantee a cultural or political identity would challenge or transform the present racial order (Shohat and Stam, 1994; Rattansi, 1999). For instance, multi-racial urban areas have been noted for their production of creative syncretic musical youth cultures and identities (Gilroy, 1987; Jones, 1988). Some of these areas are however, simultaneously the very centres which continue to produce virulent forms of inter-racial conflict (Back, 1996; Banerjea and Barn, 1996). Furthermore, specific ethnicized and gendered forms of hybridity have become re-assimilated as a crucial component of consumer identity in the expansion of global multicultural capitalist markets (Sharma *et al.*, 1996; Puwar, 2000). Hybridity may be re-appropriated as no more than a form of neo-Orientalism which continues to render the other knowable in the power-knowledge nexus of the Western gaze.[7]

Syncretic hybridity in the educational standpoint of the border renders difference as the friction of already constituted, unitary components of identity – national, racial or gender etc. – and these border differences are actually located 'beyond' identity (Fuss, 1990). The valorization of cultural diversity sublates the (post)modern hybrid, by first claiming and then rejecting a supposed anterior cultural purity for those identities marked as non-syncretic and essentialist (Diawara, 1991; Back, 1996; Pieterse, 2004). Hybridity seemingly relies on an a priori purity, and it exists almost exclusively in those ethnicized border spaces which are marked by unequal or asymmetric cultural exchange. The agency of the minority subject is reduced to its ability to engage in modes of cultural fusion. This type of hybridity may become an essential component of ethnic/racial difference for 'marginalized' or racialized 'minority' groups. As a consequence, multicultural *diversity* is in danger of being replaced unwittingly by a postmodern *hybridity* in an adulation of cultural difference and otherness. The upshot is that pedagogies predicated on this deployment of hybridity are significant for validating and focussing on new emerging forms of syncretic and diasporic youth culture. The danger is that such an understanding of hybrid identities reproduces the logic of an essentialist difference found in liberal multiculturalism, underlined by a determinate relationship existing between culture and identity.

Rattansi while questioning the limits of syncretic hybridity, alongside other critical educationalists, has continued to focus on 'border cultures' when suggesting that what 'can be learnt from the new spaces and cultures of *liminality* is how to live with cultural difference, rapid social change and the complexities of the local/global interface' (Rattansi, 1999, p. 106). It is the North American educationalists of critical pedagogy who have most readily embraced liminal hybridity in their projects of 'border pedagogy'.[8] In particular, the theorists Giroux (1992; 1994; 2000) and McLaren (1995; 1997) have utilized the hybridity discourses of cultural studies and post-colonial theory, even though these theorists do not possess a unitary educational project. Giroux's inaugural call for a 'border pedagogy' encourages students to transgress and redefine current borders forged in domination and opposition, so that educationalists create the pedagogic conditions for students to become 'border crossers'.[9] Similarly, a key thread in McLaren's work has prescribed the need to encourage the pedagogic production of 'border identities' which challenge ethnocentric forms of knowing, and identity formation and subjectivity that are discursively produced by oppressive structures of power. Border pedagogy transgresses both a liberal cultural pluralism and an essentializing (anti-racist) identity politics. This standpoint of difference confronts the ambivalent processes of identity and cultural formation while still attempting to acknowledge ideological and discursive operations of power, including the media, transnational capitalism and the nation-state.

Giroux (1992) coined the term 'border pedagogy' in an attempt to redefine radical educational theory and practice in order to attend to the shifting configurations of power and the complex discursive sites of identity formation. He identifies at least three key considerations which inform a border pedagogy.

> First, the category of the border signals a recognition of those episte-mological, political, cultural and social margins that structure the language of history, power and difference. That is, it signals a trans-gression in which existing borders forged in domination can be challenged and redefined. Second, it also speaks to the need to create pedagogical conditions in which students become border crossers in order to understand otherness on its own terms, and to further create borderlands in which diverse cultural resources allow for the fashioning of new identities within existing configurations of power. (Giroux, 1992, p. 28)

Thirdly, Giroux highlights the importance of recognizing the language of the political and the ethical. He casts the political in terms of '... how institutions, knowledge, and social relations are inscribed by power differently' (p. 28). The ethical is understood 'by examining how the shifting relations of knowing, acting and sub-jectivity are constructed in spaces and social relationships based on judgements that demand and frame "different modes of response to the other"' (pp. 28–9). Giroux's outline of a border pedagogy high-lights a number of key concerns for developing a multicultural ped-agogy, particularly for raising the question of the ethical relation to otherness.

Crossing borders

A central tenet of border pedagogy focuses on encouraging students to transgress and redefine current borders forged in domination, and create the pedagogic conditions for students to become border crossers, enabling them to refashion or rewrite their identities from another position. That is, 'to develop a relationship of non-identity with their own subject positions and the multiple cultural, political, and social-codes that constitute established boundaries of power, dependency and possibility' (Aronowitz and Giroux, 1991, pp. 199–200). The idea of students adopting a relationship of non-identity with their 'own self' implies that they would have to iden-tify with another subject position and develop an 'antagonism' to their own. Abdul JanMohammed (1994) explores this same issue by pointing out that non-identification requires a movement of both dis-identification and re-identification in order to form affiliations with other positions. He contends, drawing on Laclau, that this antagonism is based on a 'constitutive outside' which impedes the identity of the 'inside', but is still necessary for its constitution. He also suggests that antagonism cleaves identity from the 'inside': 'it manifests itself as a fundamental incompatibility between different subject positions that one occupies at a given point' (JanMohammed, 1994, p. 247). Antagonism is crucial for the defining of identities by creating borders, and also in the construction of hybrid identities, within the subject and between subjects and groups. Border pedagogy premised on the idea of students becoming 'border crossers' who examine the constitution of their own hybrid identities is a critical activity for a multicultural pedagogy that seeks student self-reflexivity in relation to everyday experiences, their access to privileges and conditions of identity formation. To conceive the refashioning of student identities through the process of 'non-identification' is however open to scrutiny for this standpoint. The insight that borders are produced through a set of irreducible antagonisms accounts for how conflictual political identifications emerge, and we shall discover invokes Bhabha's (1994) 'third space' of liminal hybridity.

The liminal condition of hybridity is also central to McLaren's (1995) development of border pedagogy, which advances a logic of identity as an effect of difference. McLaren recognizes the significance of the border processes in North America when he writes:

> In Los Angeles, for instance, it is possible that an inner-city neighborhood will contain Latino cultures, Asian cultures and Anglo cultures and students live interculturally as they cross the borderlines of linguistic, cultural and conceptual realities. (p. 140)

The conception of a border pedagogy and identity is informed by Hick's (1988) notion of 'border writing' as an 'anti-centring strategy', which itself is based on the heterogeneous and hybrid border cultures of Latin America. The desire to borderize identity is expressed especially in the work of Anzalduà (1987), Rosaldo (1993), and Saldívar (1997), as a counter to essentialist and hegemonic Western notions of culture and identity formation. These authors emphasize, though in quite different ways, the liminal and discordant practices of culture which disrupt the exclusionary politics of whiteness. McLaren elaborates his idea of 'border identity' via Anzalduà's description of a '*mestiza*' identity.

> The new mestiza copes by developing a tolerance for contradictions, a tolerance for ambiguity. She learns to be Indian in Mexican culture, to be Mexican from an Anglo point of view ... [S]he operates in a pluralistic mode – nothing is thrust out ... Not only does she sustain contradictions, she turns the ambivalence into something else. (Anzalduà, cited in McLaren 1995, p. 112)

Here, McLaren draws upon notions of liminal hybridity in relation to the trope of the border. We may note that Anzalduà's formulation of the border as a site of ambivalence and incommensurability closely echoes Bhabha's notion of the 'third space'. In fact, McLaren also insists that we need to develop pedagogic practices which advocate the process of identity formation to occur in the 'third space', because the intervention of otherness 'challenges the essentialism of origins and the discourse of authenticity' (McLaren, 1995, p. 109) that characterize the Western sovereign individual.

McLaren recognizes the political limits of a naive rendition of syncretic hybridity and difference, and emphasizes that we need to 'intervene in the power relations that organize difference [as] ... differences are produced according to the ideological production and reception of cultural signs' (pp. 132, 214). He urges us to understand differences in terms of a politics of signification in order for different cultural identities both within and across different social groupings to be grasped and located in political terms. The cultural signs that constitute identities and mark out boundaries 'are neither eternally pre-determined nor pan-historically undecideable: they are rather "decided" or rendered as "undecideable" in the moment of social conflicts' (Zavarzadeh and Morton, cited in McLaren 1995, p. 214).

McLaren's position mirrors Bhabha's 'third space' of liminal hybridity and identification, and directs us to resist thinking this site as free-floating, already replete with a permanent politically paralysing mode of undecidability and ambiguity. As Bhabhà (1990; 1994) has maintained, the ambivalent subjectivity and identification produced in the 'third space' is not constituted by an unfettered voluntarism or anarchic liberalism, but forged in difference and displacement. The third space imagines the construction of forms of solidarity or alliances which conceive 'political subjectivity as multi-dimensional, conflictual form of identification' (Bhabha, 1990, p. 221). McLaren stresses the importance of recognizing both the discursive and ideological processes of identity formation. The educational goal of 'crossing' borders and engendering political alliances amongst and across differing cultural identities occurs in a non-totalizing arena of negotiation and contestation, and cannot be based on some pre-conceived, finalist *common* identity, or pre-determined political location.

> Identities constructed in the act of solidarity will be provisional, and the alliances formed will be contingent on the strategies, negotiations, and translations that occur in the act of struggle for both a common ground of alliance-building (rather than a common culture) and a radical transformative politics. (McLaren, 1995, p. 109)

McLaren attempts to displace and *re-articulate* – though not erase – cultural identities in favour of the formation of political alliances which transcend the potential limits of cultural specificity and the premature ideological closure of essentialist subject-positions. Moreover, the insight that we cannot specify in advance, a pre-destined political location (or subject-position) and common identity for students to occupy liberates pedagogy from being not only teleological, but also politically dogmatic and naively manipulative (see Chapter 3).

Nonetheless, it is important to ask what constitutes this 'common ground of alliance-building' for a border pedagogy? And on what grounds does 'non-identification' discussed earlier by Giroux and JanMohammed operate on? At best this ground is to be negotiated, and 'alliances' would be temporary, contingent and situational (Hall, 1986). In principle, this would resist border differences from becoming ideologically marked as hegemonic identities. But the problem persists that a 'common ground' is founded upon a 'lack' as Nealon (1998) insists. That is, the agency of the border subject is governed by a 'lack'. Any alliance based on forging a common 'non-identification' through struggle is founded on a commonality of a 'we' that shares a collective lack: no one identity can claim a hierarchy of oppression or marginalization. The difficulty here is not only that this form of politics of representation (as a modality of an identity politics) is liable to collapse and splinter back into its self-interested singular group identities (Grossberg, 1992). There is also always the danger that the very real social exclusions of specific marginalized groups are conflated and homogenized to a common theme of expropriation or a more generalized lack (Nealon, 1998). To elaborate the critique of 'agency as lack' against a pedagogy of the border requires interrogating the key concept it is underwritten by: liminal hybridity (Bhabha, 1994).[10]

Liminality

Bhabha has observed that the problem of cultures most intensely emerge at their boundaries, at points of political conflict and crisis. It is at this boundary (or border site) that meanings and values are lost or misread in the contestation

> of everyday life, between classes, genders, races, nations. Yet the reality of the limit ... of culture is rarely theorised outside well-intentioned moralist polemics against prejudice and stereotype, or the blanket assertion of individual or personal racism – that describe the effect rather than the structure of the problem. The need to think the limit of culture as a problem of enunciation is disavowed. (Bhabha, 1994, p. 34)

This passage neatly captures Bhabha's consideration of cultural difference. His reading of culture counters the liberal multicultural myth that cultural diversity emerges through an accumulative process of synthesis and accretion of difference (Papastergiadis, 1997). Bhabha seeks to offer an alternative to the account that cultural differences are irrevocably connected to or ordered by the principle of identity – as still figured in practices of identity politics. The differences that mark current borders of identity – such as gender, 'race', sexuality, religion, nation – are not where Bhabha locates the problematic of cultural difference (Johnson and Michaelson, 1997). He contends that the articulation of cultures is possible because they are a 'signifying or symbol forming activity' lived out through forms of representation which can never be complete in themselves. He understands cultural difference as a 'process of translations' which implies that it

> can never be said to have a totalised prior moment of being or meaning – an essence ... [C]ultures are only constituted in relation to that otherness internal to their own symbol-forming activity which makes them de-centred structures – through that displace-

ment ... opens up the possibility of articulating different, even incommensurable cultural practices and priorities. (Bhabha, 1994, p. 211)

Bhabha points to the inherent process of the *hybridity* of culture, which is not dependent on accretive processes or a mutual cultural interaction of unmediated exchange based on 'the illusion of transferable forms and transparent knowledge' (Papastergiadis, 1997, p. 279). It is at the borders where these already de-centred cultural practices are contested, and cultural hybridity as a form of cultural difference 'gives rise to something different ... a new area of negotiation of meaning and representation' (Bhabha, 1994, p. 211). Bhabha labels this as a nascent 'third space' which he contends has the potential to open up possibilities for new structures of counter-authority and novel political initiatives that may not fit into our conventional (political and ethical) frames of reference or rules of interpretation.

The 'third space' of cultural hybridity is however, not simply a ground of identity or a border site in which differences are to be 'crossed over' (Johnson and Michaelson, 1997). Rather, it is a liminal space and *ambivalent* ground of a cultural authority that is hazardous to a unitary identity. Bhabha is concerned with the *conditions of emergence* and address of a culture, which is always marked by an 'undecidability' in the advent of its arrival (Bennett and Bhabha, 1998). This is not to say that judgements cannot be made or differences cannot be marked, rather it is to highlight that there are no anterior unambivalent grounds of cultural authority that determine which identity-differences are to matter or the form of representation. To put it more simply, the significance of the representation of our identities is governed by a set of contestable political-ideological operations.

Bhabha's anti-essentialist proposition that the articulation of a culture is in itself an incipiently hybrid process is compelling as a potent antidote to the culturalist discourse of the new racism, and any simple (anti-)essentialist notions of cultural and identity formation.[11] For a critical multicultural education, the study of 'other cultures' based on their content is no longer viable. The conditions in which a particular 'culture' and 'identity' emerge and the constant negotiations, dissonant exchanges, struggles and operations of power which mark those conditions and inscribe particular differences – the liminal site of the border – would inform pedagogical practices.

Bhabha's account of a politics of border difference can be understood as focussing on the differences *within* identity, whereby identity is no longer the ground for a political agency (see Fuss, 1990).[12] Nevertheless, it raises the question of where the *agency* (of the other) is located. Bhabha frames this issue in terms of exploring a 'minority' agency both in colonial and post-colonial national and metropolitan contexts. Drawing on Bakhtinian concepts of the 'dialogic' and the 'hybridity of language' – the ability of one discourse to unmask another – a unitary or hegemonic national culture is unable to secure its dominance because

> the hybrid strategy or discourse opens up a space of negotiation where power is unequal but its articulation may be equivocal. Such negotiation is neither assimilation nor collaboration. It makes poss- ible the emergence of an 'interstitial' agency that refuses the binary representation of social antagonism. (Bennett and Bhabha, 1998, p. 34)

Bhabha situates the agency of the minority in the 'in-betweeness' or the liminality of a third space. It is the 'thirdness' or 'supplementar- ity' of the discourse of the minority which is disruptive of any totaliz- ing and exclusivist production of nationhood. This analysis attempts to break the binarism which locates minority agency as merely auto- nomous or oppositional and outside of the power of dominant culture. The other is already present in the dominant (colonial and post-colonial) national discourse which is internally marked by cul- tural difference. The nation produced or rather 'performed' as a unitary whole is founded on an originary lack because it is always interrupted by an alterity – the subversive 'counter-authority' and 'ethical site' of resistance of the other. In Bhabha's account, the bina- rism and opposition between the dominant self and subordinant other is deconstructed and challenged. The ambivalence of the third space and the liminality of identification ensures that the demand for wholeness and an essential difference is breached (Papastergiadis, 1996). Furthermore, identity and agency (as resistance) are produced as an *effect* of difference – the impossibility of a supposed wholeness or plenitude.

The politics of 'lack'

Bhabha's far reaching contentions have been subject to a range of crit- icism,[13] though it is the problem of his 'politics of originary lack'

(Chow, 1998; Nealon, 1998) which is of concern as it as it opens up to a critique of the *pedagogic* limits of border difference (as still being governed by a modality of identity politics). Arguably, Bhabha's rendition of culture as unfinished process is based on the '... result of ontological "ambivalence" of signification in general' (Chow, 1998, p. xiv). The trouble with his position is that the crisis of signification in modernity is liable to be mapped too quickly as a process describing the structure of social relations. The formation of cultural hybridity can be universalized to the limit that it has little pedagogic purchase or radical potential. If the agency of the minority is only an effect of an ambivalence, it denies and fails to examine adequately the practices that produce specific subjects in particular social configurations and circuits of power[14] (cf. Spivak, 1988b; cf. Shohat and Stam, 1994). Furthermore, locating agency of the minority subject as an effect of the ambivalence of the third space is unable to cast the 'other' as a positive term. The other is effectively already present only as a deconstructive (ontological) 'negative other' (Chapter 1). Bhabha evidently draws on linguistic post-structuralist accounts of inter-subjective identity formation that are predicated on the dialectical principle of 'sameness' (Self) requiring 'difference' (Otherness) in order to structure itself (secure an identity). This dependence on the other has led to the recognition of alterity in radical multiculturalism: identities have to be in constant negotiation with other differences, and cannot be complete in themselves. But as Nealon observes,

> contemporary intersubjective or multiculturalist reinscription of identity politics remains unable to deal with the other *as* other, it continues to thematize difference among persons, groups, and discourses in terms of (the impossibility of their) sameness. (1998, p. 7)

Inter-subjective identity is therefore founded on a 'lack of wholeness' or a certain kind of 'failure'. The other is needed in order for the subject (self) to be complete, but this is not possible, therefore we individually and collectively share this 'lack' in some way and it is this groundlessness which structures all modalities of identity politics. It is worth bearing in mind that Bhabha's understanding of difference is concerned with the *emergence* of a particular cultural formation and the contested grounds of a performative political subjectivity, rather than identity simply as political agency. Nonetheless, Nealon maintains that in Bhabha's compelling account of cultural difference and agency, the subject is founded on an originary lack or failure, as it is still governed by a normative plenitude (even though it is recognized that this cannot be fulfilled).[15]

> [I]ntersubjective theories argue that we need each other for recogni-
> tion and happiness, such theories continue to harbour a regulatory
> ideal of complete subjective freedom, which is actually freedom
> from recognition, freedom from difference itself. (p. 7)

Thus, the paradox of 'freedom from difference' is caught in double-bind of dis/avowing the other – it has not led to an increased social respect and tolerance of 'others' (Brown, 1995). In fact, this paradox of needing the other can lead to *ressentiment* because '... we've been excluded from the privileges of an ideal or autonomous self' (Nealon, 1998, p. 7). Ironically, the subject-position of the 'white angry man' as Nealon suggests, is emblematic of the limits of modalities of identity politics. For this group, charges of 'reverse racism' and discrimination are made from a position which claims that privileges and power of the 'ideal' – the norm of white, middle-class masculinity – are being denied. While claims of discrimination and social exclusion made by the 'white angry man' are hardly politically or historically comparable or equivalent to claims made by other racialized or marginalized groups, the very structure and ground(lessness) of identity politics in the final analysis is inclined to flatten out these socially produced differences: 'the horizon of expropriation (which identity politics depends upon) reduces rather than heightens attention to the specificities of interpellation and identity production' (p. 8).

The figure of 'white angry man' is a limit point for the educational standpoint of the border as it leads to an unravelling of the praxis of its pedagogy. Although the question of this pedagogy's efficacy is more involved. A border educational practice would not necessarily attempt to forge any lasting classroom 'political alliances', or conflate specific political struggles with everyday classroom practices. While its pedagogy of difference is unable to reconcile specific identity-differences in a classroom situation, its practices may not pursue such a goal. Nevertheless, it has become apparent that the problematic of its modality of identity politics (agency), is still structured by a *demand of identity*. And the subject-position of the 'white angry male' is exemplary here for questioning the grounds of border pedagogies of difference. How would his claims of social exclusion be managed in a classroom situation? What kind of alliances or affiliations with marginalized and radicalized identities could we expect from him? What ethical relation to otherness could this subject-position express? The white angry man poses an intractable challenge for multicultural border pedagogies. The second part of this chapter works through an alternative ontology of identity and agency for coming to terms with the ethical im/possibility of his subject-position.

Alterity pedagogy

A handful of critical educationalists such as Kanpol and McLaren (1995) have recognized the limits of articulations of border difference which privilege 'social conflicts' rather than 'political antagonisms'. As they point out, it is Grossberg (1993; 1994) who directly confronts this issue for pedagogy in his attempt to dis-articulate political agency from cultural identity. He shares alongside other theorists of alterity that against the negation of the other found in the representational logic of identity, there needs to be a 'positive' account: a singularizing ontology of the other that 'exists in its own place, independently of any specific relation of difference' (Grossberg, 1993, p. 96). Before moving on to examine Grossberg's intervention for critical pedagogy, it is useful to outline some key concepts in the work of Deleuze and Guattari (1984; 1987) which he utilizes.

Deleuze and Guattari: a primer

It is hardly surprising that Grossberg turns to the theorists Deleuze and Guattari, as they have advanced an influential critique of 'lack' for rethinking subjectivity and agency. However, their ideas are not easy to grasp, which probably accounts for why the impact of their work on educational praxis remains relatively limited. A provocation of Deleuze and Guattari is that we need not worry too much about searching for the exact meaning of a concept, and rather think about how it works and what possibilities it may open up. There is no single entry point in the work of these theorists as their philosophically orientated writings proliferate concepts which circulate, multiply and unfold. A good place to start as any other is through their concept of 'desire' and its relation to 'lack' in the production of the social.[16] A Deleuzo-Guattarian deployment of 'desire' does not define it in terms of the realm of an unreal fantasy or as an individual lack (as found in psychoanalytical accounts). Desire is not figured as lacking an object or fixed to an individual, rather it is conceived as being intimately tied up with the *production* of the social (Deleuze and Guattari, 1984). Deleuze and Guattari consider 'reality' in a machinic sense, that is, reality is always being 'produced' (because the function of a machine is to produce things). Their alternative conception of reality collapses everything into 'machinic' terms, which includes the formation of social subjectivities. For Deleuze and Guattari the social emerges from multiple interconnecting machines, and '[d]esire is a machine and the object of desire is another machine connected to it' (Deleuze and Guattari, 1984, p. 26). The social field is therefore not only inseparable from 'desiring-machines', but is also produced by them.

Desiring-machines have been *socially* organized as producing a *'lack'* in liberal-capitalist societies, for example through the site of the family and the media. These sites of specific social desiring-machines connect together and produce individuated and disciplined social subjects (identities) whose possibilities to become otherwise are constrained. A critical task for these theorists – and in our case, the pedagogue – is then to 'insert' other desiring-machines which breakdown existing connections (social codifications) and create alternative connections, interactions and contagions for producing new ways of life. This understanding of desire in machinic terms (as constituted/constitutive) means that 'desire is always assembled' (1987, p. 531) in relation to how it links with other things – it is not a metaphysical condition or natural state of reality.

Deleuze and Guattari augment their understanding of desiring-machines through the complex concept of the 'assemblage'. The assemblage can be characterized in terms of two poles, the 'molecular' and the 'molar'. These poles are not in a binary opposition but are qualitatively different. The molecular acts as a virtual potential within the molar. The molecular is the site in which desire resists organization and instead, it breaks/flows, giving rise to 'a-signifying signs', 'affects' and 'singularities' which escape structural representation and meaning (1987). In contrast, the molar is through which desire is solidified, and desiring-machines are organized by hierarchies of social power. Meanings are stabilized and movements are arrested at the level of the molar, giving rise to social identities that are restricted by their lack of ability to transform. In this respect, all social identities exist on this plane, and therefore modalities of identity politics also operate on this level. (The molecular and molar should not be ascribed in positive or negative terms, rather their inter-relations account for the production of the social).

In a basic sense, assemblages are the machinic relations, connections and arrangements of things. To simplify, along one axis their operations are structured by the two-fold movement of the molecular and molar. On the one hand an assemblage has a molecular movement of 'deterritorialization' or a 'line of flight' in which it breaks down and becomes otherwise. On the other hand, an assemblage has a molar movement of 'reterritorialization' which stabilizes and fixes things (p. 88). An assemblage is 'machinic' in terms of how its multiple movements connect with other assemblages. An assemblage is conceived in terms of its *function* and what it can *produce*. To properly grasp what an assemblage is in machinic terms involves posing the question (problem) *'how does it work?'* instead of merely asking *'what does it mean?'*

Mobilizing students

Grossberg (1994) conceives the subject in machinic terms for innovating an alternative pedagogy of 'affect'. His critique of the logic of identity is situated in terms of *re-reading* Hall's (1988) 'new ethnicities'. Grossberg attempts to offer a radically alternative premise which rejects identity understood as a 'ground for action', or the '... subsumption of identity within the logic of difference and ... that such structures of identity necessarily belong to a particular subject group' (Grossberg, 1994, p. 98). He inquires, that while cultural identity expresses modes of group organization and that people may act in 'essentialist' ways, it does not necessarily follow that identity should always be the cardinal site which organizes every political struggle over power (cf. Brown, 1995; Nealon, 1998). *Identity demands* are struggles over *representation* – how identities are assigned, who speaks and acts – and are always imbricated by the exercise of power. Power in Deleuzo-Guattarian terms is 'productive' (as well as 'limiting') and operates at every level of the social formation and domains of human life.

> [C]ontemporary organization of power may ... articulate specific fractions of apparently subordinated groups into real positions of power, or into positions in which their 'real' interests lead them into conservative positions within which they seem to embrace their subordination. (Grossberg, 1992, p. 378)

As an alternative strategy against the limits of grounding power in identity and locating political struggle primarily in the 'representation of ideological subjects', Grossberg proposes a practice which attempts to rethink identity as the mobilization of 'affective subjects'. He describes a theory of the 'structurations of power' through an analysis of the relations between a subject-position and political agency (understood as an affective investment). The most basic structures of power regulate specific 'economies of values' which

> organise, constrain, and enable social possibilities and historical struggles ... The various economies of value circulate around, and are articulated to historically constructed systems of social identification and belonging, most commonly in forms of systems of identity and social differences (e.g. race, gender, age, sexuality, ethnicity, class etc.). It is through these articulations that the social formation is organized into relations of domination and subordination. The struggle over power is to deconstruct and reconstruct correspondences between systems of the unequal distribution of values and systems of social identities and differences. (pp. 97–8)

This implies that a specific group cannot be simply defined politically by virtue of its place in a set of social differences (for example, its class or ethnic identity), because it may have access to only certain systems of value. It follows that it is not possible to determine in advance that the identity of a group is articulated to a specific type of politics. Or, as Hall (1992b, pp. 31–2) has highlighted more specifically, '[t]here is no guarantee, in reaching for an essentialized racial identity of which we think we can be certain, that it will always turn out to be mutually liberating and progressive on all the other dimensions'. The difficulty of equating a specific social identity with a (universally progressive) political position gives rise to a complexity for conceiving how pedagogically, cultural identity can be understood and deployed as a resource in the struggle over power for constructing liberatory projects.

If the struggle over power is about contesting the relations between the economies of value and systems of social identification and belonging, it can be grasped as being structured and deployed in the social formation in terms of a 'machinic production' (Grossberg, 1993). Firstly, by a 'differentiating machine' which articulates the production of subjectivity through the normalization of the relations between values and systems of social difference. This type of desiring-machine produces 'discursively (or ideologically) ... differentially valued subject positions', that is, identities (p. 99). However, as Grossberg points out, people take up different identities in a variety of ways, and individuals are not necessarily completely interpellated to prescribed (normative) subject-positions. Notably, that in this account of subjectivity, agency is not located as the failure in the plenitude of identity (as a lack), but as the possibility of being articulated otherwise – the possibility of 'difference' – that is always present because of the failure to be interpellated to a normative subjectivity.[17] It requires identifying a second 'territorializing machine' which does not produce identities, but describes how individuality is constructed through an 'affective investment ... an organisation of places and spaces' (p. 99).

It is from this move to 'deterritorialize identity'[18] that Grossberg attempts to deploy Hall's (1988) re-appropriation of ethnicity in *machinic* terms. Grossberg takes up the challenge of the *production* of new ethnicities by re-describing it spatially through a territorializing machine which generates points of stability in the production of subjectivity. It does not mean the return to the 'original state' of an identity, but rather a recombination of de/territorialized elements and flows into something new, (though its effects can never be guaranteed to be politically progressive). This machinic operation produces a 'structured mobility' which 'maps the possibilities where people can stop and place themselves. Such places are 'temporary points of belonging and identification ... of investments and empowerment' (Grossberg, 1993, p. 100). This site of structured mobility may be struggled over hegemonically at times of social conflict. It attempts to define and circumscribe the moments of stability (identity) and possible mobility (movement between places), and the places of belonging and investment as well as the 'lines of flight' that are made available through a field of power.

Grossberg, more emphatically than Hall, wishes to displace identity as the site of agency. That is, if agency is defined 'by the articulations of subject-positions into specific places (sites of investment)', it follows that a subaltern or marginalized identity, for example, is better understood as a *'statement of power'* rather than a social identity-category (p. 100).[19] Thus, a qualitative distinction needs to be made between an agent and a subject:

> The question of agency ... is how access and investment are distributed within a particular structured mobility. And this suggests that political identity is not the same as subject positions or cultural identity. (p. 101)

Agency is not predicated on a negation of the other in order for a subject's self-constitution. Nor does the spatial-machinic mapping of subjectivity seek to erase cultural specificity. Rather a political-pedagogic agency is a site (set of places) in which specific investments would be articulated and enabled: 'how one can and does invest, and where and how one is empowered, made into an agent' (p. 101).

We should be careful not to read Grossberg's position as an outright rejection of the limitations of an educational strategy based on the politics of border identities. It does not intimate that we ignore how students are already interpellated into particular subject-positions or assigned to specific cultural identities. The compelling pedagogical task is to struggle over the articulation of places and students' affective investments in a bid to move or 'win them over' – by mobilizing their desires (Giroux, 1993) – to another set of places (sites of investment).

> The task of a politically engaged pedagogy is never to convince a predefined subject – whether empty or full, whether essential or fragmented – to adopt a new position. Rather the task is to win an already positioned, already invested individual or group to a different set of places, a different organization of space of possibilities. (Grossberg, 1994, p. 19)

Becoming-other

The possible type of educational practices arising from this affective pedagogy will be explored more concretely in Part II. For the remainder of this chapter, the idea of re-articulating or 'moving' students over to another set of places and possibilities will be examined specifically in terms of an ethical relationship to the other. While Grossberg's account offers a pedagogic standpoint which attempts to dis-articulate political agency from cultural identities, it leaves open the question of what kind of affective investments are made available in a 'structured mobility'. There is good reason for this as they would be situational and site-specific: particular formations of (pedagogic) practices are realized in a given social field of power. It does not follow however, that an ethical agency (the ethical response to alterity) is non-existent, rather as Nealon (1998) contends, it needs to be understood in terms of the site-specific agency of a subject. What is always at stake is the possibility of responding to the other outside of a relationship of appropriation and domination.

Nealon picks up on Judith Butler's thematization of the problematic of theories of intersubjective identity and difference (specificity):

> that elaborate predicates of color, sexuality, ethnicity, class, and able-bodiedness invariably close with an embarrassed 'etc.' at the end of the list. Through this horizontal trajectory of adjectives, these positions strive to encompass a situated subject, but invariably fail to be complete. This failure, however, is instructive: what political impetus

is to be derived from the exasperated 'etc.' that so often occurs at the end of such lines? (Butler, cited in Nealon, 1998, p. 2)

He asks further: 'Why is it so difficult to "situate" and respond to a set of specific others – ethically, politically, or theoretically – and what does the difficulty of doing so teach us about identity politics?' (p. 2). It is this concern which needs to motivate the discussion of the problem of identity and difference in relation to pedagogy: how does one respond to this 'exasperated etc.', to alterity?

A key imperative for this chapter has been that an ethical agency is formative of a critical multicultural pedagogy that refuses 'to thematize difference in terms of the possibility or impossibility of sameness' (p. 3). There has been an acknowledgement by some educationalists of an understanding of ethics which promotes self/other relations that are 'dialogic' rather than oppositional (demanding the submission of the other).[20] These approaches recognize the conflictual 'multi-voicedness' of society through which dominant and subordinated groups 'share' a dialogic existence that is constitutive of their identity relations. It is an attempt to grapple with 'the etc.', the 'irreducible excess' of identity 'as the ethical specificity of the other' (p. 38). Multi-voicedness emphasizes the non-submission of the other through which a dialogical ethics of *response* emerges that may articulate a 'non-appropriative ethical subject position'.

A politics of 'the other' is based on an understanding of ethical agency as a performative subjectivity. Nealon's notion of singular subjectivity emerges from Butler's account which stresses that identities are constituted in the performative repetition of existing social codes or scripts (of gender or 'race' for example). While we cannot resist interpellation (subjection), 'identity carries with it the necessary, structural possibility of its own subversion by other … reinscriptions' (p. 21). There is always the possibility of 'difference' (reinscriptive response) in the performative repetition of the existing codes which interpellate us.

Insofar as identity is always constructed or performed, social norms both provide a script for 'proper' subjectivity and simultaneously offer points of resistance: one is compelled to act in accord with the norm's imperatives, but because one must always repeat the performance of one's subjectivity, the possibility of proceeding otherwise always haunts so-called normative subjectivity. (Nealon, p. 138)[21]

What we experience as the stable identities of 'race' or gender arise from these 'performative effects'. However, Nealon differs from other theorists of performative identity (for example, Butler, Laclau, Bhabha and Connolly) by rejecting the notion that the subject is open-ended because of the failure of the interpellative norm which supposedly inaugurates or 'gives birth' to it.

If the site of agency is the possibility of a reinscriptive response to already given codes, Nealon augments this understanding by utilizing Levinas's account of alterity in order to develop a notion of a performative ethical agency not based on a lack of wholeness. The ethics proposed by Levinas are not static prescriptive or abstract rules to be followed. Rather, ethical relations are constituted in a site-specific dialogic encounter (Levinas, 1979). As Nealon highlights, 'to live and speak in a society is always already to be responding to concrete others' (1998, p. 37). Moreover, the 'irreducible excess' of identity for Levinas is located in the specificity of the other, its uniqueness which is considered to be 'infinite'. In other words, and in contrast to the accounts of identity politics and difference, the other possesses its own positivity and alterity. Levinas promotes an ethical agency which resists positing the subject (self) as the guarantor of its own existence or uniqueness, but instead it is the self which is a 'hostage' to the other. Ethical specificity is not a voluntary act which makes the self as the privileged site of its own uniqueness. 'For Levinas, being able to think or respond in concrete contexts presupposes that one first is open to the other, in a social space ... that is characterized by ... inexorable exposure' (Nealon, 1998, p. 39). It follows that we do not *choose* to respond, just as we have no choice in our subjection (interpellation).

It is important to stress that for an ethical agency there is *always* a response to otherness, which recognizes the continuous 'social dialogue' forged in historical struggles (Falzon, 1998). The appropriation or negation of the other is when there is an attempt to arrest this social dialogue, but it is not prior to the necessity of ethical response. In understanding subjectivity as an ethical response, the singular subject is not simply an effect of difference. Instead of being founded upon a lack of plenitude, it is constituted in (and immanent to) the very act of its performative subjectivity.

> [T]he ethics of performative subjectivity rests primarily not in the recognition or representation of expropriation or failure, but in the production of subjectivities: ethics is mobilized in performative responses to subjection, but these responses are not territorializable before the fact by the constative categories which are their outcomes. (Nealon, 1998, p. 144)

This means that identities are not constituted or territorialized (stratified), prior to the fact of their (ideological) representation. The significance of performativity is most apparent when Nealon stresses that identities need to be comprehended in the Deleuzo-Guattarian sense of 'becoming' (a 'verb') rather than 'being' (a 'noun'). 'Being' describes the hypostatized state of 'molar' (or 'stratified') identities which are territorialized by hierarchical and institutional structurations of power (for example, stabilized identities of 'race', gender or the nation defined by existing social divisions and inequalities). In contrast, 'becoming' is '... the action by which something or someone continues to become other (while continuing to be what is)' (Deleuze and Guattari, in Patton, 2000, p. 78). It is an open-ended, active de-territorializing transformative process which occurs as a 'molecular' movement.

In Deleuzo-Guattarian terms, 'becoming' is tied to power/desire – the capacity of a 'body' to affect and be affected. 'Bodies' as assemblages, which include subjects and social collectivities, are considered machinically in terms of what they are capable of *doing*, rather than their 'being' (what they are).

> Defining bodies in terms of the affects they are capable of is equivalent to defining them in terms of the relations into which they can enter with other bodies ... processes of 'becoming' are precisely such engagements with the powers of other bodies. (Patton, 2000, p. 78)

Paul Patton points out that becoming involves entering into 'alliances' with others, on the basis that it increases the capacity (power) of both parties, rather than the appropriation of the power of the other. While the ethical priority in becoming is one of engaging with the 'outside',[22] to form new connections and relationships with others, 'affects can be active or reactive' (p. 78). An affect is active in a sense that it enables (accelerates) a force of becoming, whereas it is reactive by separating (or decelerating) a force of becoming from what it can do (Deleuze, 1983; Lorraine, 1999).[23] As argued earlier, there is no *a priori* ethical relationship to the other in positive or negative morally prescriptive terms. Rather, it is the performative effects of an encounter which may be politically evaluated (Nealon, 1998; Patton, 2000). Deleuze and Guattari (1987) maintain there are no pre-given liberatory subject-positions to occupy. Moreover, the micro-political activity of becoming has no guarantees of being 'progressive'; it always involves a 'risk'.

We are in a better position to understand Nealon's claim that existing molar or stratified identities of 'being' need to be reconsidered in terms of a performative ethical agency, by their affective capacity and deterritorialized movement of 'becoming'. Following Deleuze and Guattari, the existing marginalized (though stratified) identity of 'black' for example, needs to 'become-black'. Minorities are the privileged agents of becoming in the work of Deleuze and Guattari (1986; 1987), but only when they are no longer a 'definable aggregate' in relation to the majority.[24] This is suggestive of not only investing in a (molar) identity politics which is structured by a norm, but rather activating a 'minoritarian-becoming' which has the potential to challenge and disrupt the norm that defines the majority. A minoritarian politics would constantly seek to diverge from the norm, and offer the possibility of altering minority-majority identities and their relations of power (see Chapter 4).

Becoming-white?

Nealon (1998) makes what is a contentious claim that white people also need to '*become-white*'. In contrast, Deleuze and Guattari (1987) have argued that a becoming-*majoritarian* cannot exist because becomings are minoritarian (molecular) processes, and pass through the subordinate figure in the racialized and gendered dualisms of 'white/black' or 'man/woman' for example. Nealon points out that a conventional anti-racist position concludes that whiteness as a privileged and oppressive social norm is inextricably over-determined by a racist legacy which results in calls for its denouncement and abandonment (see especially Roediger, 1994). However, the strategy of encouraging whites to simply 'become black' can readily lead to the appropriation of cultural otherness, which is increasingly present in contemporary multicultural capitalism (Chapter 3). Nor does the idea of abandoning whiteness confront the powerful (affective) investments and privileges of a white identity. This is particularly crucial in terms of a classroom situation, when we may encounter white students who are more than likely to resist renouncing (and further entrenching) their identity in the pedagogic demand for an anti-racist subjectivity (Cohen, 1992; Gillborn, 1996; Giroux, 1997). By returning to the politically incongruous example of the 'white angry man', the possibilities (and limit) of 'becoming-white' can be interrogated. This subject-position serves as a significant example for multicultural pedagogies, because it offers a means of exploring the ethical agency of whiteness in terms of the im/possibility that it can be productively re-articulated to another set of places.

The 'white angry man' (WAM) is such an awkward case because he exemplifies the logic of *ressentiment* by claiming an injurious identity which is primarily motivated by blame and resentment towards socially excluded minorities (Nealon, 1998). Nealon reconsiders white identity not as a constative identity-category which remains fixed and already determined, but in terms of its performative subjectivity. There is no simple political solution to the WAM, 'a productive intervention would first have to redirect or restage this WAM anger, make it productive of something other than blame and resentment' (Nealon, 1998, p. 149). But is there always a productive place for whiteness to go? The anger of the WAM – its failure in attaining the 'phantasmatic norm' – appears to be oppressive on all fronts. Nealon concludes that 'the question of whiteness would need to be posed somewhat differently: not around what whiteness supposedly *is*, but rather taking up what whiteness does, and what it *can do*' (p. 160). It is in this sense that his claim of the need for whites to 'become-white' may be understood. Nealon reads Deleuze and Guattari (1987) *avant la lettre* when they suggest that an identity would need to deterritorialize itself from where it is already at. To escape from whiteness, if at all possible, does not mean to abandon it, but rather recognize the need to interrogate and *interrupt* whiteness, as otherwise it will remain intact in its normative status.

In terms of challenging contemporary configurations of power and identity, Tamsin Lorraine (1999) and a number of other feminist theorists confront Deleuze and Guattari's specific notion of 'becoming-woman' by arguing that there is always a danger that the male-standard can be left intact in a minoritarian-becoming. Notwithstanding this assertion, Patton argues that we need to conceive Deleuze and Guattari as theorists of 'becoming-revolutionary' which does not necessarily mean the abolition of molar identities, but 'the possibility of redistribution of the molar assignment of differential power and affects' (Patton, 2000, p. 83). It is productive to interpret Nealon's notion of 'becoming-white' in this manner, though we need to note the im/possibility of such a movement.

The kinds of relations or 'alliances' that white identities can potentially make with others, cannot be determined or specified in advance because the reinscriptive responses of an ethical agency occur in a specific context (of power relations). It may be the case that in a particular pedagogic situation, 'becoming-white' has nowhere productive to go, unable to form affective 'alliances' which enhance the capacities of others, as well as itself. We would only be able to judge this in terms of its site-specific performative-political effects. Nevertheless, an affective pedagogy could articulate a white subjectivity outside of itself, one that is 'mobilized otherwise' and follows a deterritorializing 'line of flight' which does not produce appropriating or oppressive effects. 'Becoming-white' offers an opportunity to engage students from an *anti-racist* position that does not naively denounce whiteness.

3
Teaching Difference: Representations and Rhizomes

> Why should pedagogy be of interest to anyone? Few are familiar with the term. Even aficionados gag on its pronunciation and falter in its spelling. (Lusted, 1986, p. 2)

> I sometime feel that teaching ... is like sex – you know other people do it, but you never exactly know what they do or how they do it. (Williamson, 1981/2, p. 83)

David Lusted's droll opening remark about the maladroitness of the term 'pedagogy' overtly registers its restrictive economy. Likewise, Judith Williamson offers a witty, almost throw-away comparison between the '*what*' and 'how' of pedagogy and sex. Although both authors couching their critiques in humour, perhaps belies a substantive problem of the 'repressed' discourse of pedagogy – isn't its opaqueness and regulation in need of liberation? The contention by both Lusted and Williamson that pedagogy remains under-theorized still rings true today, particularly in relation to the antagonisms of cultural difference. In the age of globalization, developments in *multicultural* pedagogy are increasingly being directed towards packaging prescriptive and universalist teaching methods and approaches which pander to the needs of trans-national capital in the creation of new educated class of diversity-aware, information-rich 'flexible workers' (Zavarzadeh and Morton, 1994).

Nevertheless, pedagogy addressing the '*process* through which knowledge is produced' (Lusted, 1986, p. 2) has influenced many contemporary progressive and critical practices, leading to reflexive investigations such as: Whose interests does the production of knowledge serve? What does the empowerment of students seek to achieve? What forms of authority and domination are (re)produced by the practice of emancipatory pedagogies?[1] Lusted's insistence that there are no pedagogies 'in general' does not just echo a post-structuralist desire to avoid positing universalist practices, but also stresses the inseparability of 'how one teaches' from 'what is being taught'. A conceptualization of pedagogy as a site-specific practice of 'knowledge' and 'cultural production' (Simon, 1992) motivates this chapter.

Debates concerning radical pedagogies have become a contested arena amongst theorists and practitioners in the field of education and cultural/media studies. In particular, issues of the bifurcation of theory and practice, teacher authority, the status of student 'experience' and their 'resistance' to a purportedly liberatory curriculum, continue to be debated in many national contexts – see for example, Buckingham (1996; 1998) and Gore (1993). I will avoid rehearsing these debates or attempt to offer any neat resolutions. Instead, these issues serve as vital reference points for thinking through a particular pedagogic practice for alterity. Moreover, to conceptualize an alterity pedagogy outside of questions of its own practice is considered to be theoretically inadequate and limiting. While it will be argued that a universalist or prescriptive practice of pedagogy is problematic, it does not mean that a pedagogy for alterity should remain unspecified or totally contingent.

This chapter is divided into four parts. Firstly, it is maintained that an alterity pedagogy does not involve forwarding a particular teaching method. To realize such a radical practice involves an 'anti-method' (Kincheloe and Steinberg, 1998) of tactics which resist becoming sedimented and neutralized as a set of teaching techniques. The second part scrutinizes the limits of dominant realist pedagogic conceptualizations and curriculum practices of multicultural and anti-racist education (ideology critique). Through the framework of media education, the third part of the chapter will highlight the shift towards teaching approaches that have recognized the limitations of attempting to ideologically demystify students, and instead focuses on the complex processes of knowledge and meaning-production (signification) in the classroom. However, while these approaches move beyond the fallacy of the stability of representations and realist epistemology for pedagogic knowledge production, they can not adequately address the question of alterity in practices of representation. The final part, by drawing on the arguments made in Chapter 2, will describe an alterity pedagogy that collapses the distinction between meaning and 'affect' in order to develop a practice which seeks to mobilize students to other affective sites of investment (and modes of knowing) through the possibility of 'rhizomatic' connections (Deleuze and Guattari, 1987).

Authority and tactics

There has been an increasing examination of the politics of radical pedagogy and its rhetoric of student empowerment and emancipation. A key issue which haunts critical approaches is the possibility of pedagogy to liberate students from the effects of social domination while its own teaching (and institutionalized) practices continue to reproduce authoritarian forms of social control (Lather, 1991; 1994). In the USA educational context the rhetoric of student emancipation played itself out in a 'stand-off' between advocates of critical pedagogy and feminist pedagogy (Luke and Gore, 1992).[2] In Britain, David Buckingham (1996) and Alan O'Shea (1998) echoed some feminist critiques of critical pedagogy and the problem of classroom authority, though the emphasis has been on instigating a critical media/cultural studies pedagogic practice which responds to the complexities of everyday 'messy realities' of the classroom. Jennifer Gore (1993) offered a compelling critique of the limits and tensions within and across both critical and feminist radical pedagogies. Her Foucauldian contention that radical pedagogies' production of their own 'regimes of truth' have been left unacknowledged, leading to the efficacy of their approaches to be highly questionable, and more dangerously, they are liable to reproduce modernist forms of disciplinary control and social regulation in the classroom. The recent work in radical and feminist pedagogies has acknowledged the limitations of emancipatory pedagogies more explicitly (hooks, 2003; Probyn, 2004). Although these issues remain a critical concern for practitioners pursuing radical educational goals, and neither can an alterity pedagogy escape from the necessity of questioning its own practices.

One of the difficulties in assessing the efficacy of radical educational approaches is that they are not easy to delineate, particularly as they can readily overlap (and/or diverge) in their practices. It is therefore useful to identify a number of common progressive pedagogical strategies highlighted by Grossberg (1994).[3] His account of progressive pedagogies is best understood as a series of 'ideal-types' which highlight specific educational activities, though in the classroom situation more than one strategy may be deployed simultaneously. Grossberg begins by first identifying a common teaching strategy as a 'hierarchical practice'. This operates with an implicit assumption that 'the truth' – the *correct* type of knowledge – is known by the teacher and is (seamlessly) transmitted to the student. He considers this approach appropriate in that it may in a particular social context contribute to emancipatory struggles in the classroom. Nevertheless, it remains limited because there is an assumption that *real* meanings of texts or practices, and interests of different social groupings in the classroom are known and understood. It is the teacher who judges what is 'politically correct or incorrect' (Grossberg, 1994, p. 16).

A second pedagogy of 'dialogic practice' aims to allow as far as possible those silenced students to speak. Yet Grossberg argues that this assumes they are already not speaking, or perhaps in a way that is misunderstood or inappropriate. '[It] fails to see that there are often real material and social conditions that have disenabled people from speaking at particular places, in particular ways, at particular moments' (p. 16). We can also add that they are not being 'heard' too (Spivak, 1988a). It points to a pedagogy that cannot be simply based on engendering a 'dialogue' as it must acknowledge the unequal conditions and asymmetrical relations of power that this dialogue already takes place in (Shohat and Stam, 1994). The third pedagogy Grossberg identifies is labelled as 'praxical'. This attempts to empower students by imparting the skills they need to 'understand and intervene within their own histories', which challenge institutional forms of power and connect with broader political struggles. There is much to support in such a pedagogy, and many radical teaching practices advance such approaches (including the pedagogy being outlined for this study). Nevertheless, Grossberg suggests that this strategy assumes that the teacher *knows* what the right skills are, and more significantly these skills are universal, rather than contextually determined. 'There are no universal skills which we can offer independent of the context into which we want to intervene, and, more important, into which our students want to intervene' (Grossberg, 1994, p. 17).

Grossberg's critique of progressive pedagogies highlights the relationship of power between the teacher and students, and questions the 'elitist' nature of radical pedagogies. He also attempts to make explicit the cultural authority assumed by pedagogy, functioning as an institutionalized practice of universalist knowledge production that is embedded in social discourses of power and control. While raising some of the key problems facing radical pedagogies, Grossberg does not specify in any detail what an alternative radical pedagogy might look like in practice, though he rejects a student-centred pedagogy which uncritically celebrates the plurality of student voices and experiences, (see also Cohen, 1991; Mohanty, 1994). Furthermore,

Grossberg does not wish to deny the authority of the teacher or pedagogue, but offers an alternative ethical enunciative position in the practice of pedagogy. As discussed in Chapter 2, a pedagogy of 'risk and possibility' does not claim to know political outcomes in advance or force students to fit into some pre-defined political vision, but neither does it assume that *students know* the answers in advance. It is a contextual pedagogy that seeks to map articulations, and make connections, across the discursive and affective sites occupied by students and their everyday knowledges and practices. However, in a bid to 'win' already positioned students to another set of places and possibilities, Grossberg (1994) acknowledges that this pedagogical approach is not only risky, but it may sometimes *'fail'*. To articulate students to another set of places cannot presuppose that these new places will be necessarily empowering or liberatory, precisely because we do not know in advance what these places and positions are. Although to avoid a 'postmodern' free-play of difference, '… we must collectively articulate a common affective vision of a shared political future based on a politics of practice (what people do, what they invest in, where they belong).' (Grossberg, 1994, p. 20)

The question of teacher authority is however, left open in Grossberg's claim that students need to be articulated by a 'common affective vision'. O'Shea (1998) maintains that this position effectively asserts an 'invisible authority' and assumes that students need to be 'rearticulated' in the first place. He is more comfortable with a pedagogy which stops 'at the point of offering a terrain of debate and tools – analytical skills and knowledge of cultural processes – for whatever students wish to make of them, rather than offering a particular articulation of that terrain' (p. 524). It appears that a tension exists in Grossberg's pedagogy which wants to be both open-ended and 'interventionist' (for a particular political context). Although by returning to the issue of what we can do pedagogically with the figure of the 'white angry man' (Chapter 2), it need not be concluded in advance that this tension is necessarily disabling on these terms. The contention has been that accelerating the active forces of 'becoming-white' may offer this subject a productive place to go – the possibility of a non-racist subjectivity that is not oppressive to others. In the classroom context this could be encountering a white student who (openly) expresses or holds racist sentiments. Of course it would be naïve to suggest that any multicultural pedagogy could simply engender an absolute transformation of a student's racist subjectivity. According to O'Shea (1998, p. 525), a pedagogy 'will not *produce* the student's future identity. It offers one set of understandings at one point in their lives ... [I]t remains one element of many from which students forge their sociality.' Nonetheless, only stopping at offering students the tools to analyse their own identity formation may not be enough if we are to at least attempt to *interrupt* a student's racist subjectivity.

An interventionist (tactical) pedagogy is grounded in and arises from the particular political context it operates in and *responds* to. Moreover, in this situation, pedagogic authority is not denied but neither is it simply determinate. It needs to be reconfigured in terms of an affective power: the possibility of enhancing the capacity to form ethical relationships with others. The dynamic of power between a teacher's authority and a student's subjectivity may be altered and transformed by the forces of becoming. (It does not follow that a student will be successfully re-articulated to a non-racist subjectivity, only that the im/possibility of such a deterritorialization is opened up.) The 'interventionism' of an alterity pedagogy should not be formulaic, prescriptive or reduced to a set of universalistic teaching techniques irrelevant to the existing social conditions both inside and outside of the teaching-learning environment. This does not mean that only a particularistic pedagogy can be valid, but points to the importance of developing a pedagogy attendant to how wider social and political processes and discourses are played out in particular spaces and situations. We can begin to outline such a pedagogy by claiming that it needs to operate 'tactically' as a transmutable practice.

Sleeter and McLaren (1995) distinguish between a pedagogic practice that functions as a 'strategy', in comparison to one that is operationally 'tactical'. This distinction is motivated by Chow's (1993) concern of how intellectuals and their pedagogic practices struggle within a hegemony that already includes and contains them. She contends that most oppositional intellectual or pedagogic practices of constructing a new field of interest (a counter-hegemony) are limited, because existing borders that demarcate the asymmetrical relations of power between the margins and the centre are no longer stable. This instability does not deny that the centre is continually producing marginality through processes of cultural violence and exclusion:

> the margin is the place where the dominant structures exercise their disciplinary control. We are in the midst of the marginalization of the centre: the de-centred dominant is displaced from within the margins, but the power relations between the margins and centre remain intact. (Sharma, 1996, p. 18)

While it follows that it is possible to contest the centre, nevertheless as a strategy, even counter-hegemonic pedagogic practices 'of the margins' are liable to be incorporated back into the centre. This is because, as Michel de Certeau has argued, a strategy is a political project that seeks to construct a practice in order to 'solidify a place or barricade a field of interest' (cited in Sleeter and McLaren, 1995, p. 26). In other words, a strategy as a form of opposition may become congealed into an obstacle unable to contextually adapt or transform its practice, and may result in reasserting what it seeks to overthrow (Chow, 1993). In contrast, a

> tactic is a calculated action determined by the absence of a proper locus... The space of a tactic is space of the other... It takes advantages of opportunities and depends on them, being without any base where it could stockpile its winnings, build up its own position... This nowhere gives tactic mobility... but a mobility that must accept chance offerings of the moment. (de Certeau, cited in Sleeter and McLaren, 1995, p. 27)

It is a notion of tactics as a dynamic practice that is aleatory and opportune: a practice which operates within a hegemonic formation but seeks to counter containment and pacification. An interventionist pedagogic practice of possibility resists becoming sedimented as a teaching method or technique, only to be re-incorporated for maintaining an educational status-quo. A tactical pedagogy would therefore be transformative – both in terms of its *own* practice, as well being site-specific in its educational project. It would be a pedagogy that is situational rather than universalist and responsive to the exigency of the existing structures of domination that impact on the everyday experiences of students.

Teaching 'race' as ideology critique

It is notable that critical discussions of the practices of multicultural/ anti-racist education have been far less significant in comparison to controversies over curriculum content. In particular, the 'culture wars' of USA campuses and the debates over the 'Western canon' focussed more on what was being taught, rather than interrogating the praxis of multicultural pedagogies (Giroux, 2000; Winant, 2004). Notwithstanding the developments towards more democratic teaching approaches and collaborative and peer-learning strategies, it remains

remarkable how relatively little attention has been paid to the theorization of multicultural/anti-racist teaching practice and its epistemological
assumptions of curricular knowledge.[4]

The approaches of conventional liberal multicultural and anti-racist
and education have deployed a particular use of 'ideology critique' in
their pedagogies. In its most elementary application, this is a pedagogy
of 'demystification' which possesses a crude (Marxist) understanding of
the ideology of racism as a form of 'false consciousness' (Buckingham,
1986; Rattansi, 1992). This kind of teaching practice echoes Grossberg's
account of a 'hierarchical practice'. Moreover, as Cohen (1991) points
out, it is invariably the working-class students who are considered as
'passive dupes of racism' and victims of an ideology which works
'invisibly ... behind their backs'. They are in need of 'liberation' by the
(middle-class) teacher who seemingly possesses the necessary knowledge which will 'penetrate the veil of false consciousness, and ... break
with commonsense racist ideology' (pp. 47–8). A more developed
variant of ideology critique – often practised in university seminar
classes (Simons, 1994) – enables students themselves to acquire the
necessary analytic tools and skills to reveal the 'true' (oppressive)
meanings of texts and images deemed to be racist in their intent, for
example by learning semiotic textual analysis. This teaching strategy
can often resort to a notion of the 'dominant ideology thesis'
(Buckingham and Sefton-Green, 1994) by assuming that racist meanings are already embedded in a text, and students need to expose them
for the effects to be counteracted.[5]

The practice of ideology critique seeks to uncover the 'truth' of
racism or the 'reality' of minority cultures: it possesses a reflectionist
or mimetic notion of representation. Curriculum knowledge is governed by a realist epistemology – the possibility of an objective and
accurate representation of reality which is 'mirrored' in the content of
a text. The true meaning of the world (reality) is reflected in the text
which is able to directly represent reality. It means that such a text
possesses a single and fixed *meaning* of reality for the student/reader
(to uncover). This conceptualization of curricular knowledge has most
visibly manifested itself in multicultural and anti-racist curricular
developments concerned with altering content. For both educational
approaches, their strategies have been concerned with the holistic
development of curricular materials which are culturally diverse, non-
Eurocentric and non/anti-racist, with the intention of permeating
across individual school subjects. In schools, there have been curriculum strategies such as the development of a multicultural/anti-racist

science and mathematics which acknowledges the enormous contri-
bution to the development of this subject from non-European cultures
and promoting the 'universality' of knowledge about science (Gill and
Levidow, 1987). Alongside these strategies, it has been recognized that
appropriate curricular materials need to be selected and developed
which are free from racist imagery and negative caricatures of
non-Western cultures, and also that these materials challenge negative
representations (Brandt, 1986).

These strategies have an implicit understanding of 'racist texts' as
producing distorted and false representations of reality – and leading
the reader to hold irrational racist beliefs (Rattansi, 1992). There has
been extensive work in the area highlighting teaching materials which
contain racist negative stereotyping, and instruction in identifying
racism in various forms of media such as textbooks, fiction, newspapers
and television.[6] The identification and purging of offensive racist representations and development of alternative materials with more
'balanced' and 'positive' representations of other cultures and ethnic
groups continues to be considered as a crucial strategy in the development of a more appropriate curriculum for a multicultural society. The
significance of such curriculum strategies should not be under-
estimated. However, the danger that the politically legitimate demands
for 'fair' and 'positive' representations of 'minority' groups in the
curriculum and wider society becomes determinate of the modalities of
pedagogic practice needs to be questioned. The problem being that the
potential of pedagogy is limited to one which has been caught within
the 'race relations discourse of positive/negative images' (Pines, 1988).
This discourse does rightly highlight the absence of representations of
Black images and 'other cultures', and also challenges the negative and
simplistic stereotypical imagery that exist. The strategy here is one of
reversal, countering dominant negative imagery with positive representations of 'other cultures'. In as much gross racist stereotypical representations need to be countered, this strategy nevertheless suffers
acquiescence towards a realist epistemology and should not be simply
conflated with an anti-racist pedagogy.[7] The elementary realist notion
that texts unproblematically reflect the world and carry within them
unitary fixed meanings for students to contest or uncover denies the
polysemic nature of textual meaning and assumes that knowledge (as
truth) exists outside of historical specificity and relations of power
(Hall, 1997a). It embodies a practice of learning which seeks to suppli-
cate students to a predetermined set of truths about reality (racism).
Furthermore, it ignores and is dismissive of students' own cultural real-

ities, experiential knowledge and affective investments. Buckingham remonstrates against the practice of selecting texts

> precisely because of the objectionable ideologies they are seen to contain. Critical analysis consists of detecting this self-evident bias and simply condemning it. Although students may be encouraged to reach their own conclusions, in practice there is often little opportunity for them to generate their own reading, or to explore the contradictory pleasures such texts may afford. It is as if potentially dangerous meanings and pleasures have to be policed out of existence by rigorous, rational analysis. (Buckingham, 1993, p. 147)

The 'positive images' discourse has the effect of imposing limitations and boundaries to the form of pedagogy and content of curriculum materials. It can result in black individuals as 'role models' or 'other cultures' being represented in essentialist terms: either depicted only in a positive light or merely reduced to an inverted response to racist representations.

> It is a model in which unitary subjects learn about their true origins and destinies through certain strategic images which narcissistically mirror back them their own preferred identities. Positive role models represent certain essential defining characteristics of Blackness, Jewishness or whatever – a simple inversion of the racist proposition. (Cohen, 1991, p. 56)

Before acknowledging the theoretical challenges and pedagogic alternatives to the practice of ideology critique described so far, it is worth considering the limitations of such an anti-racist and multicultural practice in terms of the 'resistance' it may provoke from students. It becomes apparent that for the case in Britain, the educational interrogation of 'theory' has been largely conducted in relation to classroom practice (Buckingham, 1993). The question of 'representation' (for example, structuralist theories of ideology and the subject) occurred most significantly in relation to developments in British media education and film/cultural studies. In particular, during the late 1970s and early 1980s the work in the journal *Screen Education*, and of the *Birmingham Centre for Contemporary Cultural Studies* (CCCS) – both influenced by continental philosophy – were leading the discussions of ideology and subjectivity.[8] While media education (and cultural studies) remained marginal in school and university curricula during this period, it has become more prominent in the 1990s. Moreover, the question of *representation*, or rather its *'crisis'* emerged as a key problematic for animating many of the debates in contemporary media/cultural theory. In particular, questions of the politics of 'race' and cultural difference have been increasingly framed by the problem of 'representation'.[9]

It is not possible here to trace the complex genealogy of theoretical work which has informed anti-racist and multicultural pedagogic practices. Notably, the marxist shift in the 'new sociology of education' during the mid-1970s was influential for later developing anti-racist concerns which highlighted that curriculum knowledge was indeed a site of ideological struggle (see Whitty, 1985; Harris, 1992). Although, as David Harris (1992, p. 52) points out, 'the false consciousness approach was to haunt much of the later' work in radical pedagogy, and especially within *anti-racist* educational practices. This dominance of the 'demystification approach' seems perplexing given that developments in theory from the mid-1970s and 1980s challenged and became increasingly dismissive of crude structuralist notions of ideology and the subject, particularly from the influence of continental philosophy characterized in terms of the 'linguistic/cultural' turn in marxism (Davies, 1995). Perhaps the different operations and demands of 'theory' and 'practice' in education (Williamson, 1981/2), and the focus on empirical classroom situations in Britain resulted in a situation of radical pedagogy being insulated from these significant theoretical developments.[10] For anti-racist pedagogy nevertheless, it could be argued that a context of institutional racism determined its teaching practices, and especially given the political dictates for inclusive Black representation (Hall, 1988).

It was the journal *Screen Education* during the late 1970s and 1980s which seriously considered questions of representation in relation to the practice of pedagogy. Judith Williamson's (1981/2) article, *How does girl number twenty understand ideology?* was particularly formative, because it interrogated received theories of ideology and subjectivity by reflecting on concrete classroom situations. Some of the concerns raised by Williamson remain relevant issues for pedagogy. One of her key contentions was against a rationalist and moral approach to teaching about oppression in society. She argues it is when the 'personal experiences' of students are acknowledged and engaged with that students may begin to 'see' the significance of ideology – deconstructing their common-sense thinking in terms of their *own* identity formation and frameworks of reference. Otherwise, students are liable to mimic the radical expectations of the teacher. She cites the example of a group of boys presenting from a feminist perspective in their discussion of sexist representations, and remarks that their abstract analytical and moral account 'meant nothing to *them*, it didn't *affect* them'. Williamson concludes that students learn best 'when it becomes in their own interest – when they are actually caught in a contradiction, believing things which are directly hindering their own well-being or wishes, or which conflict with a change in experience' (Williamson, 1981/2, p. 85).

Williamson's example highlights that students can 'learn' and echo back what they perceive to be the 'politically correct' moral and rationalist teaching discourse expected in the classroom, without it affecting their own subjectivities (cf. Cohen, 1991; Buckingham and Sefton-Green, 1994). Cohen (1991; 1992) has highlighted a comparable situation for those anti-racist pedagogies which present predictable narratives of 'racism' that are produced by expunging the discontinuities of historical developments and contradictory ideological struggles. He comments on how the limit of such a reductive pedagogic discourse is revealed when a student replies cynically, 'I know Sir, it was racism what dunnit' (Cohen, 1991, p. 26).[11] Cohen also points out that students can be 'reasonable' about 'race' when facing a teacher, while actively holding onto racist beliefs and behaviour beyond this situation. Moreover, white students can resist such 'politically correct' anti-racist/multicultural discourses by purposefully making offensive racist statements or jokes in order to 'wind up' the teacher. The disruption of the moral and rationalist discourse of racism or the tenets of multicultural harmony can lead to challenging teacher authority, thereby resulting in widespread policing of racist expression and disciplinary control measures being imposed in the classroom. 'The regime of reason is revealed as a regime of surveillance and punishment' (p. 50) which can vindicate a student's racist beliefs and entrench their standpoint even further.

The characterizations of strategies of pedagogy underpinned by a method of 'ideology critique' have been rather crude, and in practice more sophisticated variants would operate in a classroom or seminar situation. Nevertheless, the intention has been to make explicit some of the key underlying assumptions which govern anti-racist and multicultural pedagogies. The limitations of these teaching approaches have come under intense scrutiny, and much of the critique has emerged from the fields of media, film and cultural studies.

Cultural and media studies: the pursuit of signification

The educational focus on popular culture as a legitimate area of study has been significant for thinking about pedagogic *practice* and developing a more 'student-centred' pedagogy and curriculum (Epstein, 1993; Buckingham and Sefton-Green, 1994). Buckingham and Sefton-Green emphasize that the move beyond the demystification approach of ideology critique for pedagogy has taken place because of more attention towards students' experiences and their 'active' engagement with (popular) media culture, and a much greater consideration of the actual learning situations in the classroom.[12] Their stress on *learning* seeks to understand how students acquire so-called 'critical discourses' and thus challenging conceiving texts as directly socializing passive learners into the dominant ideology and values of the wider society. It has led to media educationalists such as Buckingham (1996), Lusted (1986) and Ferguson (1998) to consider ideology 'as a lived relationship rather than a set of beliefs which are shared and imposed' (Ferguson, 1998, p. 44). Such an approach rejects the notion of a unitary subject of ideology, and as Ferguson maintains, critical analysis should not be reduced 'to a game of recognizing the ideology in the message and, in effect, prescribing a given reading to a given subject' (p. 44).

The move beyond a pedagogy of demystification stresses the *contradictory* nature of the processes of ideology, especially in relation to how the reader/students are 'positioned' by, or 'negotiate', media texts. Texts may make available a range of positions and offer 'solutions' to non-unitary subjects (Walkerdine, 1990). There are a range of sophisticated and divergent theoretical perspectives explicating the relationship between a text and the reader. These perspectives have varying notions of how a text functions, how the subject may be ideologically positioned or discursively produced, and how a text may be 'read' or negotiated.[13] For the question of pedagogy, it is unsurprising that no unique theoretical position for the reading of (media) texts has emerged, though it is possible to identify a general perspective which rightly emphasizes the *textual encounter*; meanings are not simply already given within a text, but are 'the result of a "circulation" between social formation, reader and text' (Belsey, 1980, p. 69).

There is a shift away from merely identifying the (hidden) meanings of a text, to one of exploring the process of *signification* – the making or production of meanings in the textual encounter. Madan Sarup (1986) was one of the few early anti-racist educationalists to recognize the importance of developing pedagogic strategies beyond the ideological practices of censoring materials and correcting racial bias. He argued that it would be more useful to facilitate students to develop critical skills enabling them to recognize how meaning are produced through representations. '[They] should be given the opportunity to develop the desire and capacity to control the apparatus of meaning-production, of which school knowledge is on one aspect' (p. 52).[14]

The interventionist educational research by Cohen (1991; 1992; 1998) is one area of radical multicultural/anti-racist pedagogy which has attempted to innovate this kind of practice in schools. Cohen has explored the importance of tackling what is described as the 'common sense racism in pupil cultures' which rationalist anti-racist teaching approaches have failed to adequately engage with. Alongside other media educationalists, his approach utilizes popular culture by accenting its contradictory nature and as a site of students' emotional investments. Against the limitations of the teaching of 'positive images', he has used stories of the 'anti-heroic' West African trickster figure of 'Anansi the Spiderman' in classroom research. He argues that this complex figure acknowledges the 'contradictory, many faceted aspects of ethnic identity, which arise from the anxiety of influence which all diaspora communities experience. It is just a model which most effectively undermines the reductionist structures of a racist imagination' (Cohen, 1991, p. 59).[15]

Cohen (1998) offers another instance of a radical multicultural teaching practice which endeavours to account for the complex negotiations of identity by a small group of ethnically mixed female pupils in a primary school setting. Through a collaborative image-based work activity the group draw a fantasy female figure, labelled by Cohen as 'the Indian Cowgirl Warrior'. He perceptively comments on the multiple processes, interactions, and points of solidarity as well dissonances between the pupils in the *making* of the figure. From the girls' conversations during their activity, Cohen interprets the 'warrior' character as a response to the racial hostilities and sexist taunts experienced by the girls in the playground. Although it is the process of the production of the figure that is of most significance:

For *en route*, they have to grapple with a whole series of contradictions related to gender, class and ethnicity. Members of the groups are continually shifting their positions vis-à-vis each other and the issues under debate. In the process they are setting their own agenda and staking out areas for further work. My job was to support what might emerge in this potential space of representation, rather than foreclose it through any irritable reaching after fact or interpretive intervention ... [W]e are directed towards a more complex theory of subjectivity and meaning, one which focuses on the unconscious process of representation. (p. 173)

This anti-racist pedagogy exemplified by Cohen's work maintains that racialized and ethnic discourses are contextually produced and situationally deployed, contradictory and ambivalent in their effects. Racism is theorized intersectionally which strives to account for other differences of ethnicity, class and sexuality (cf. Rattansi, 1992; Hall, 1988). Furthermore, the non-unitary subject is understood in terms of multiple subject positions that are available to individuals in racialized discourses. Subjects are conceptualized as being discursively produced and 'contradictorily and ambivalently positioned' by the 'irrationality of popular racism' (Rattansi, 1992, pp. 29–30).[16] It is clear that this kind of understanding recognizes that teaching about racism and cultural difference is an entangled and fraught terrain to negotiate.

The educational standpoints of border difference (as articulated by Cohen and Rattansi above) and the 'other', while predicated on alternative ontological grounds, can nevertheless respectively share similar pedagogic practices. Although, it was maintained that the standpoint of the border is unable to adequately conceive and respond to the alterity of the other, thus possibly limiting its scope and effectivity (Chapter 2). This however, does not mean that pedagogies arising from such a standpoint cannot operate successfully in terms of the context and aims of a teaching situation. It is important to reiterate that there is no simple one-to-one correspondence between a theorization of identity formation and the practice of pedagogy, (and this is not only because often educationalists deploy and engender more than one notion of identity production). Cohen's example of the 'making of the Indian Cowgirl Warrior' is a case in point. He uses a 'weak' psychoanalytical model in attempting to interpret the pedagogic intervention and situate pupil subjectivities – a perspective which in conclusion stresses the 'unconscious process of representation'. Although much of Cohen's account also elaborates upon the multifarious *negotiations* between the pupils, something that could be (better?) recognized as an articulation of their *affective* investments.[17] The pupils appear to be making open-ended, rhizomatic connections in drawing the 'cowgirl warrior' montage figure – an 'assemblage' that engenders new ways of knowing and affects (as opposed to only its polysemic and contradictory sign-ificatory value). The multiple-identity productions of the 'cowgirl warrior' assemblage may interrupt and *reconfigure* any stable class or ethnic affiliations in the movements of the pupils 'becoming-other'. The consequence of conceiving the pedagogy of the 'cowgirl warrior' in such a manner enables an exploration of its site-specific performa-tive effects. It provides the conditions to actualize the production of pupil subjectivities by acknowledging and affirming the ethical responses to alterity, rather than deliberating over the contradictory negotiations and ambivalence of identity-differences.

The work by media educationalists in Britain has been at the fore-front of developing practices which conceive the activity of pedagogy in terms of the *production* of classroom knowledge. A comparable deve-lopment in the USA has taken place in the work of critical pedagogy and its call for media literacy – see especially Giroux (1993), McLaren and Hammer (1996) and Kellner (1995).[18] While the fields of cultural and media studies have developed in different historical and institu-tional contexts in Britain and the USA, there is a shared educational conviction that (popular) media culture is central to pedagogical engagement in the everyday lives of students. These fields of study rec-ognize the multiple sites students occupy, and the kind of knowledges and practices that circulate in the sites of media culture which struc-ture students' points of belonging, and play a significant role in the formation of their identities.

The radical multicultural pedagogy being developed in this book likewise shares an outlook that begins with where students 'are at' (by selecting 'popular' film texts for a classroom practice). It seeks to engage with the everyday knowledges and practices that students are articulated by – the range of structuring and mediating sites such as agencies of the state (including education and schooling), the family, the community, peer groups, and most importantly the media artefacts operating in the spaces of everyday and popular culture (Grossberg, 1992; McLaren and Hammer, 1996). This per-spective of sublimating 'the everyday' challenges the legitimacy and relevance of conventional classroom and curriculum knowledge (Wexler, 1987; 1992). Moreover, it acknowledges that an increas-ingly information/media-based contemporary culture is becoming the dominant multiple-site in discursively shaping, and making available, the *everyday* for students. Wexler urges that the shifts towards an information society requires that we reassess the role of pedagogy, and recognize that a competing mass information discourse has become the key educational relation for identity formation in contemporary society.

> Where the forces of production become informational/communica-tional, semiotic and the formation of the subject occurs significantly through mass discourse, then it is that relation which is the educa-tional one. The mass communications/individual relation now already better exemplifies the educational relation than does the school. (Wexler, 1987, p. 174)

Wexler perhaps over-states the demise of the school as a site for pro-ducing the everyday in relation to subject formation. Nonetheless, he rightly highlights that the key influences on identity lie outside con-ventional or official educational/school knowledge. More specifically, an ever-expanding 'media culture' (print, music, photography, cinema, television, video, multi-media, and the internet for example) has become pervasive in constituting the everyday in the lives of many stu-dents in Western societies (McLaren and Hammer, 1996; Kellner, 1995). Although this media culture does not only simply constitute the everyday, and as Kellner maintains, nor is media culture unequivocally hegemonic. Rather, it can be conceived as a discursive site through which subjectivity is formed in lived social relations, and that media culture operates as a *(re)source* for a pedagogy of the everyday. McLaren and Hammer make this point more explicitly:

> A critical media literacy recognizes that we inhabit a ... culture in which the proliferation of photographic and electronically produced images and sounds serves as a form of media catechism – a perpetual pedagogy – through which individuals ritually encode and evaluate the engagements they make in the various discursive contexts of everyday life. (McLaren and Hammer, 1996, p. 106)

A number of educational theorists from Britain and the USA for example, have stressed that a critical media literacy needs to be deve-loped in order to engage with the everyday lives of students, and to enable them to understand and analyse how their own identities and subject-positions are formed by a prevailing media culture. My work is not aiming to develop such a general educational approach for study-ing media culture as there already exists a well established 'media and cultural studies' literature offering a variety of useful approaches.[19] The intention here is rather more specific in outlining a *tactical pedagogy* that interrogates the production of cultural difference and otherness. The development of such a pedagogy however, is not determined by a distinctive teaching approach or subject matter.[20] The approach being advanced here is attentive to the production of the everyday and identity formation in relation to exploring issues of cultural difference and alterity. Giroux points to a pedagogic practice

> which does not simply tell the student how to think or what to believe, but provides the conditions for a set of ideological and social relations which engender diverse possibilities for students to produce rather than simply acquire knowledge, to be self-critical about both the positions they describe and locations from which they speak from, and the make explicit the values that inform their relations with others. (Giroux, 1993, p. 39)

A pedagogy beginning from where students 'are at' recognizes that they are already governed by normalizing, identitarian subject-positions. The pedagogic task is to struggle over these identity-sites in order to mobilize students to speak/act from a different set of places and possibilities (Chapter 2). The mere acquisition of knowledge is insufficient to deterritorialize students to new sites of affective investment. Giroux attests to the necessity of conceptualizing pedagogy as a 'critical practice' which enables students to *produce* new knowledges and accomplish a self-reflexive practice about their own constructed sense of identity and subjectivity. It begs the question, what types of pedagogic practice can be identified that provide students with the conditions to 'produce' new ways of knowing and identification?

We can begin by taking pedagogy as a form of 'cultural production' (Simon, 1992; Giroux, 1993) which strives to implode the distinction between official educational knowledge and everyday knowledges by legitimizing specific media texts as being capable of fostering new positions of belonging and identification for students. Particular media texts – understood as forms of cultural production and practice – can be read and deployed as *performing* a pedagogy of the everyday. Conceiving pedagogy as a practice realizes the site-specific nature of student deterritorializations: the dialogic encounter between the 'irreducible materiality' of a text (Chapter 4), the student and the classroom institutional context is a site where new modes of knowing and subjectivities may be produced.

Using media texts for pedagogy is hardly a new type of learning activity. Much educational work, especially multicultural and anti-racist approaches, have utilized particular kinds of texts for teaching. But there is always a danger that these kinds of activities reduce social relations to a form of textualism which as a consequence, make the other a 'knowable' ethnographic object of fascination and appreciation (Carby, 1992). The pedagogical practice being outlined is committed to understanding how forms of domination seek to secure their hegemony through particular representational strategies of cultural difference. It points to the need to *situate* specific media texts within on-going social struggles. As noted by Giroux (1993, pp. 39–40): 'cultural texts can be understood as part of a complex and contradictory set of ideological and material processes through which the transformation of knowledge, identities and values takes place'. While the text/reader encounter as the site of meaning-production and affect is at the heart of a radical pedagogy, it does not mean that media texts possess the same pedagogical function.

> This means not only reading media culture in a socio-political ... context, but also seeing how the internal constituents of its texts either encode relations of power and domination, serving to advance the interests of dominant groups at the expense of others, or oppose hegemonic ideologies, institutions, and practices or contain a contradictory mixture of forms that promote domination and resistance ... [M]edia culture is a contest of representations that reproduce existing social struggles and transcode the political discourses of the era. (Kellner, 1995, p. 56)

Kellner working from a neo-Gramscian perspective argues that the representational strategies of media texts are not arbitrary in their social significance and political effects. Acknowledging that media texts are embedded in sets of historically determined political struggles and social discourses is significant, as well as uncovering and interpreting their meanings and highlighting contradictory elements.

The type of pedagogy forwarded by Kellner can rely on the assumption that revealing the social contradictions of a text will give us a 'better' access to 'reality'. A variation of this approach – derived from a more elaborate Foucauldian position eschewing notions of an underlying reality – seeks to expose the operations of power that discursively produce particular 'regimes of truth'.[21] While one of the functions of a text is to produce meanings, the pedagogic activity of only interpreting or exposing a text's contradictory meanings within existing hegemonic frameworks of cultural knowledge can result in blocking, or closing down ethical modalities of knowledge production from being articulated. To question that pedagogic practices governed by interpreting (hidden ideological) meanings of a text and exposing a text's contradictions or discursive operations are limited activities, does not suggest that such practices should be abandoned. Nevertheless, a text's pedagogic performativity – what does it '*do*' – needs to be also considered.

What does knowledge do?

It is useful to briefly probe an influential essay by Hall (1997a), *The Spectacle of the Other* as it exemplifies some key concerns which continue to inform much of the theoretical and educational 'race' work in cultural/media studies.[22] Hall interrogates the representational practices of racial otherness circulating in contemporary (popular) culture. One of the central concerns is the possibilities and practices of contesting and changing dominant racialized regimes of representation. He acknowledges that the question of representation 'engages feelings, attitudes and emotions and it mobilizes fears and anxieties in the viewer' (Hall, 1997a, p. 226); and employs a psychoanalytical approach (via the concept of fetishization) in attempting to account for the fascination of 'black' bodies. Much of the analysis of racial imagery is governed by a now familiar post-structuralist proposition 'that meaning can never be finally fixed' (p. 270). The practice of 'trans-coding' – the counter-strategy of challenging existing racialized representations in the making of new possible meanings – is understood in terms of this fundamental semiotic insight. The upshot of such an approach is made evident via Hall's utilization of the politically indeterminate position expressed by Mercer (1994). Mercer examines the aesthetic strategies of Robert Mapplethorpe's photography of black gay men, and interestingly offers a 'double-take' (more than one reading) of this work. For Hall this powerfully intimates the semiotic struggle over meaning:

> Which of Mercer's two readings of fetishism in Mapplethorpe's work do you find most persuasive? You won't expect 'correct' answers to my questions, for there are none. They are a matter of interpretation and judgement. I post them to drive home the point about the complexity and ambivalences of representation as a practice, and to suggest how and why attempting to dismantle or subvert a racialized regime of representation is an extremely difficult exercise, about which ... there can be no absolute guarantees. (Hall, 1997a, p. 276)

Hall offers a compelling account of how we can understand the politics of representation of racial or cultural otherness in terms of 'a struggle over meaning which continues and is unfinished' (p. 277). His analysis offers a pedagogy of signification which stresses the acts of *interpretation* and *judgement* in the reading of contradictory and always contestable racialized representations. The limits of such an approach is not that this deconstructive reading practice is a purely rational exercise (which it is not), but rather that the *exposition* of the ambivalences of textual meaning-production tends to be the dominant pedagogic mode of engaging with racialized representations.

In terms of classroom practice, there is an implicit assumption that by highlighting and problematizing the politics of representations of racial and cultural difference, students are offered the analytical tools to explore and contest dominant racialized imagery. This type of pedagogy hopes that students will grasp these analytical tools for such purposes, though it cannot be assumed that students undertaking this type of analysis necessarily learn to see and experience the world differently by embracing an 'anti-racist' perspective. The problem is that *exposing* social contradictions and *disagreements* over textual meaning can become the principal student activity (cf. Simon, 1992; Sedgwick, 1997). Hall implicitly situates his approach in Bakhtinian terms which acknowledges that the struggles over meanings 'are not simply struggles over the sign – what a given text means – but actually struggles over how people's identities will be constituted and history lived' (Simon, 1992, p. 116). Yet what is *pedagogically* underplayed in his account in the final analysis is not only the grounds on which knowledge-production – a particular interpretation, judgement or exposition – takes place, but also what this knowledge 'can do'.

Eve Sedgwick pushes at the limits of the pedagogical pursuit of 'knowledge' when she asks:

> What does knowledge *do* – the pursuit of it, the having and exposing of it, the receiving-again of knowledge what one already knows? *How*, in short, is knowledge performative, how best does one move among its causes and effects? (Sedgwick, 1997, p. 3)

She claims that contemporary critical practices (and we should add radical pedagogies) are governed by a 'hermeneutics of suspicion' which have an 'extraordinary stress on the efficacy of *knowledge per se* – knowledge in the form of exposure' (p. 8). She argues that knowledge of 'an unmystified view of systemic oppression' or in our case, that racialized representations are a product of regimes of power-knowledge 'does not *intrinsically* or *necessarily* enjoin on that person any specific train of epistemological or narrative consequence' (p. 4). Sedgwick maintains that 'cynicism or "enlightened false consciousness" – false consciousness that knows itself to be false' – means that for what could be called a 'knowing' student, highlighting how ideologies are contradictory, meanings unfinished or that identities are discursively constructed, gives no guarantee of producing emancipatory knowledge effects.

> [S]uch popular cynicism, while undoubtedly widespread, is only one of the heterogeneous, competing theories that constitute the mental ecology of most people. Some exposés, some demystifications ... do have great effectual force (though often of an unanticipated kind). Many that are just as true and convincing have none at all, however; and as long that is so, we must admit that the efficacy and directionality of such acts reside somewhere else than in their relation to knowledge per se. (p. 9)

Sedgwick makes the further point that the dominant method of the 'hermeneutics of suspicion' present in social and cultural theory has disavowed and mis-recognized 'other ways of knowing' which are actually practiced *at the same time*. The pedagogies of signification discussed above may concurrently have other knowledge practices operating (perhaps unintentionally), which do not conceive classroom knowledge in purely 'representational' terms.

In asking about the pedagogic possibilities of 'knowing the other' outside of extant hegemonic representations, the possibility of an ethical relation may occur if normative racialized representational strategies are transgressed. This is clearly a difficult task, not least because pedagogy is only one site of identity production. Nor is there a pre-existing pedagogical blueprint for an alterity teaching practice. While it is not expedient to delineate any kind of a universal pedagogy, it is still feasible to outline a specific type of tactical practice – one that would not claim to work outside its own particularity but seeks to open up the site-specific possibilities of engendering non-appropriative ethical relationships with otherness. The pedagogy to being developed in this book is based on utilizing Black/Minority film as it offers a critical practice which articulates such possibilities (cf. Mercer, 1994; Marks, 2000). But before exploring the expressive cultural politics of Black/Minority film in Part II, these cultural productions need to be situated in terms of a materialist rhizomatic 'reading praxis' (Fernández, 1993) which advances the workings of an affective pedagogy of becoming and possibility.

It becomes apparent that my pedagogy for alterity is articulated by two inter-dependent elements. Firstly, the pedagogy is actualized by a specific operation and movement of a (de/territorializing) 'reading praxis' which deploys Black film as a cultural production. Secondly, in terms of identifying the singularizing force of Black film, that is, how it functions expressively as a 'minor' text which may challenge and interrupt normative racialized representations. The performative effects of these films in a teaching situation would be site-specific. Whether they do engender 'new subjectivities' in creating the possibilities of a non-appropriative relationship with alterity cannot be known in advance. It is important to stress that the pedagogic practice being proposed is not unique, but rather needs to be considered as a tactical intervention (as indeed should any critical pedagogy).

A rhizomatic reading praxis

In beginning to think through a pedagogy that seeks to mobilize other ethical ways of 'knowing', we first need to acknowledge that any practice of pedagogy encounters the limits of what can be 'known' in the classroom. Elizabeth Ellsworth has asked:

> What would it mean to recognize not only that a multiplicity of knowledges are present in the classroom as a result of the way difference has been used to structure social relations inside and outside the classroom, but that these knowledges are contradictory, partial and irreducible? They cannot be made to 'make sense' – they cannot be known, in terms of the single master discourse of an educational project's curriculum or theoretical framework. (Ellsworth, 1992, p. 112)

Ellsworth raises the aporia of the 'unknowable' in relation to the discursive production of classroom knowledges. She points not only to the multiplicity of other ways of knowing which cannot be wholly contained or rendered by existing master discourses, but also that pedagogic practices are confronted by and contingent upon the extra-discursive – the 'outside' which lies beyond existing frameworks of (representational) knowledge.[23] What are the implications for how we envision a radical pedagogical practice? At the very least, it compels us to be 'modest' in our ability to conceive the kinds of knowledge that are engendered in the classroom situation because we can never wholly 'know' its limits, operations and 'origins'. In this respect, the issue of ascertaining the 'success' of a radical pedagogy is further problematized and made less relevant. In fact, the success of any radical pedagogy is perhaps more contingent upon the 'outside' than we would like to admit. We find that it points to an open-ended pedagogy which seeks to make connections and mobilize students' becomings, rather than compelling them to acquire 'emancipatory' knowledge by occupying prescribed 'radical' subject-positions – a practice that would often fail.

The 'reading practice' being developed in this book, while still acknowledging the relevance and utility of exposing or interpreting the meanings of a particular text, focuses on the site-specific production of these meanings and *affects*, and how they come to be articulated in the first place. Josep-Anton Fernández (1993, p. 109) suggests it would be a reading *praxis* which considers the text in 'machinic terms; the question to ask is not "What does it mean", but "How does it work?", "What does it produce?" and "Where does it go?"' Or in the words of Claire Colebrook (2000, p. 3), how 'one *inhabits* a text: ... follow its movements, trace its steps and discover it as field of singularities (effects that cannot be subordinated to some pre-given identity of meaning)'. The act of inhabiting a text allows us to establish a 'non-normative' reading praxis which is *rhizomatic*, rather than framed by 'arborescent' (hierarchical and centralized) systems which organize our knowledge and social practices (Deleuze and Guattari, 1987).

A rhizome functions in terms of 'connection and heterogeneity', and is like a mobile line which at any point 'can be connected to anything other ... [It] has no beginning or end; it is always in the middle, between things' (1987, pp. 7, 25).[24] The rhizome is a highly elaborate concept in the work of Deleuze and Guattari and it is important that we grasp its potential for understanding how an alter-representational pedagogy may work (especially because the term has been inappropriately universalized in recent cultural theory). A rhizomatic practice does not reject the significance of meaning or interpretation, rather it dwells on the connections between things (that are not necessarily related), and looks at the relations of forces between things that are constitutive of the structural organizations of meanings, knowledges and identities. The rhizome is defined by a constitutive 'outside'. It '... does not conform to a pre-defined structure of movement, and we can never identify all its elements involved since they do not resemble one another' (Short, 2000, p. 6). In terms of conceptualizing the 'outside', this involves rethinking the relations of the inside/outside (or identity/difference) from a non-dialectical standpoint. That is, from a position which places both the inside/outside in the same field of immanence. The outside (difference) is not a function of the inside (identity), rather *difference* makes the inside possible and is conceived instead as a 'multiplicity' that is irreducible and singular. The philosophical theory of multiplicities is at the heart of the Deleuzian project and is not easy to summarize. It is a consideration of difference as immanent which conceives identity (or unity) in terms that are not identical to itself. 'Difference is the fundamental term on the basis which the identity of all phenomena must be understood. As such, difference never refers back to a primary identity but only to further differences' (Patton, 2000, p. 39).[25]

For understanding the 'outside' as already within the 'inside' we can turn to how Deleuze deploys Bergsons's concepts of the 'virtual' and the 'actual', and distinguishes them from the 'possible' and the 'real'. Both the 'virtual' and the 'actual' are *real* (they both exist), but are different because the virtual is structured differently from the actual: the virtual actualizes itself. In contrast, the possible does not exist, but may become real: the possible mirrors the real (May, 2004).[26] Jon Short further elaborates these complex concepts:

> if the possible is the not-yet-real, the possible in becoming real depends on the conditions of resemblance and limitation. Resemblance demands that the real resemble the possible out of which it is derived ... [However] the possible does not and cannot explain the real, but rather, through the backward projection, it is the real that explains the possible ... [B]ecause the possible is simply a derivation or particular configuration of the real, there is no actual difference between them ... The outside, as immanent variability, *subsists* as a potential difference within the inside, such that the inside is always threatened from within. This can happen because unlike the possible/real, both terms of the actual and virtual are equally *real* ... as Deleuze puts it 'the actual ... does not resemble the virtuality that it embodies'. (2000, pp. 5–6)

The rhizome as a multiplicity can be understood as the passage from the virtual to the actual (or the actualization of the virtual) in terms of the production of a 'proliferation of non-resembling differences'. To put it more simply, it accounts for how something new might be produced (beyond systems of arborescent or hegemonic knowledge). A rhizome makes connections between elements which are *qualitatively* different, it is an open, non-hierarchical system whose unregulated movements cannot be defined (by reducing it to something else) or be known in advance. As Nealon (1998) suggests, it means that the movement of open-ended rhizomatic transformations ('becomings') do not go from 'either/or to both/and', as this is still a movement of 'difference to assimilation'. He offers the example of how 'gangsta rap' music has been *either* understood as an authentic expression of black 'ghetto life' *or* merely a commercial ploy for white suburbia. To simply claim instead that gangsta rap is 'both/and' these things assumes we know enough about both the original terms under consideration – it leads to conflating the relations between them and erasing black otherness. Rather, the 'specificity of the difference' (of gangsta rap) may be enacted by the movement from 'either/or to either or or or or ...' (Nealon, 1998, p. 123). This can lead to a consideration of the multiplicity of gangsta rap outside of its hegemonic terms of reference.

The antinomies and *irreducibility* of the multiplicity of classroom knowledges which Ellsworth alludes to may now be considered in rhizomatic terms. This offers a way of thinking about a reading tactic which does not seek to produce knowledge already governed by existing hegemonic practices. Most importantly, neither does it conceive of a practice which makes the unknowable ('the outside' or difference) something that is a function of what is already, or can be, known ('the inside' or identity).[27] Moreover, the concept of the rhizome perhaps enables us to begin to map and even harness the unruly multifarious events of knowledge-production that actually occur in and pass through the classroom.

A pedagogy with a rhizomatic trajectory would be open-ended and tactical – an active force attempting to 'unfold' and 'refract' the unknowable (multiple singularities) in the classroom. In more concrete terms, students would be encouraged to be exploratory, and creatively *make* and *multiply* connections beyond their everyday common sense experiences and knowledge – connections which may appear unexpected, anomalous or even aberrant (cf. Grossberg, 1994). It would be a pedagogy which neither seeks closure or is determined by a single strategy or method. As a deterritorializing practice it attempts to offer more than positing that ideological knowledge is contradictory and that meanings are to be uncovered, interpreted or only struggled over within our existing frameworks of cultural knowledge. As Deleuze and Guattari (1987, p. 90) claim, 'a social field is defined less by its conflicts and contradictions than by the lines of flight running through it.' A rhizomatic reading praxis tries to activate the affective capacities of students by making connections that offer the potentiality of other (ethical) ways of knowing and living in the world. It would be an unfinished, somewhat 'imperfect' and 'experimental' pedagogy; and one which as Grossberg (1994) has pointed out, is about 'risk' as well as 'possibilities'. It does not mean that pedagogy necessarily becomes a purely 'experimental' or 'avant-garde' activity. We would need to consider how the everyday institutionalized activities of assessments for example could be harnessed for a rhizomatic pedagogy (Chapter 6). After all, the practice of pedagogy as a process of knowledge-production operating within institutionalized contexts is unlikely (and indeed antithetical) to proliferate rhizomatic connections for new ways of living with difference.

The mechanisms of a pedagogic reading tactic have so far been outlined without much attention to how a text may be conceived and what type of texts could be put to use. Fernández considers the text by relating it to Sedgwick's (queer) reading practice that attends to the 'performative aspects of texts, their "reader relations", as sites of definitional creation, violence and rupture in relation to particular readers, particular institutional circumstances' (Sedgwick, cited in Fernández, 1993, p. 109). He carefully situates the *pedagogy of a text* in terms of its site-specific performative effects when he maintains that this reading practice 'places the text and the multiple conditions of its production, distribution and consumption in the same field of immanence'. In other words, the encounter between a text, reader and (institutional) context is considered as the site of pedagogy, which raises a further set of questions:

> 'What are the desires, the becomings articulated in and by this text?', 'What are the desires and becomings that I articulate through my reading?', 'To what broader universes of reference are both my text and my reading, and the multiple conditions of their production related?' ... 'How does my reading practice modify, at a micropolitical level, the institutional relations that frame it?' (Fernández, 1993, p. 109)

These issues are useful in deciding how a text could be deployed in the classroom, what we could ask about it and do with it. Such a tactical reading praxis would not maintain a universal practice, but mutate in relation to the site-specific nature of the teaching situation (for example, the type of texts used, course of study, the diversity of the student body, and the kind of teacher-student relationships, as well as the broader institutional context). Nevertheless, in asking about the 'affective capacities' of texts – what they can 'do' in terms of creating linkages and connections, articulating and mobilizing becomings – in a concrete sense it involves taking into account 'the material grounds and discursive practices that make such texts intelligible in the first place' (Simon, 1992, p. 116). The multiple and multifarious rhizomatic conditions of the production of classroom knowledge would need to be considered. As Simon suggests, knowledge production in the classroom exceeds asking whether the meanings of a text are racist or not for example, because it 'is not so much a matter of recognizing the abstract truth value of a text as it is assessing how well a text performs desirable functions for particular people at particular times' (p. 118).

Part II
Multicultural Praxis

4
Reading Racial Crisis

'[R]ace' has lost much of its common-sense credibility, because the elaborate cultural and ideological work that goes into producing and reproducing it is more visible than ever before, because it has been stripped of its moral and intellectual integrity, and because there is a chance to prevent its rehabilitation ... It is therefore all the more disappointing that much influential recent work in this area loses its nerve in the final furlong and opts to remain ambiguous about whether the idea of 'race' can survive a critical revision of the relationship between human beings and their constantly shifting social nature. (Gilroy, 2000, pp. 28–9)

This is a crucial moment for those of us who teach about race and racism. People, we are experiencing a crisis of racial meaning. In the classic definition, a crisis is a situation in which 'the old is dying and the new cannot be born'. That is the situation in which racial pedagogy finds itself at the start of the twenty-first century ... New racial formations have developed from processes of confrontation and accommodation, of conflict and reform that swept across much of the world over the past few decades. Changing racial dynamics are in part effects of antiracist movements and the achievements of democratic reform in the latter half of the twentieth century. They are linked as well to patterns of globalization, to the unsteady and unfulfilled postcolonial situation that obtains across the world's South, and to the tremendous international flows of people, capital and information. (Winant, 2004, pp. 69–70)

While we incessantly remind ourselves that race is a social construct, in determining 'what must live and what must die' (Foucault, 2003, p. 254), can the force of its 'reality' ever be denied? An emergent 'post-race' discourse championed by Gilroy does not refuse the reality of racism, though it seeks to displace the essentializing power of race. The exigency of raciology for Gilroy offers an opportunity to do away with the debilitating concept of race – the scientific, philosophical, political and representational 'truth' of race can no longer be countenanced. Both Gilroy and Winant emphatically point to the *crisis* of race, but they diverge in their objectives. Gilroy's manifestly utopian project of a post-racial 'planetary humanism' differs from Winant's insistence of the intensification of a 'racial globalism' in post-colonial times.

The changing political and cultural dynamics of race and racism frames this chapter. It explores how shifts in a globalizing racial hegemony pose a critical challenge for a pedagogy of race and multiculturalism. The crisis of race which Gilroy underscores appears to offer an opening for its erasure from human thought. However, and more crucially, the instability of race also marks the struggle for its *renewal* as Winant highlights. What continues to haunt us is the question about the essential representational 'truth of race' and its relation to the 'real'. How would an alterity pedagogy represent difference outside of racialized regimes of truth?

The problem of race and representation remains a significant concern for Gilroy (2000). Interestingly, he (re)invokes the articulation of race with fascism in his analysis of contemporary media and visual culture. The allure of race is conjoined with the seductions of fascism. Gilroy targets conservative elements of black popular culture (especially rap and hip hop) for posturing a pseudo-rebelliousness – a 'revolutionary conservatism' – which is disturbingly ultra-nationalist, pro-capitalist and misogynist. The proliferating spectacle of an essential 'blackness' in media culture has fascistic overtones in terms of its feigned trangressive zeal.

In relation to the circulation of fascist desire, the complexity of contemporary racial politics and multicultural representation is not easy to contend with. Its pervasiveness also can be considered in 'molecular' terms:

> ... fascism is inseparable from a proliferation of molecular forces of interaction, which skip from point to point, before beginning to resonate together ... What makes fascism dangerous is its molecular or micropolitical power, for it is a mass movement: a cancerous body

rather than a totalitarian organism ... It is too easy to be antifascist at the molar level, and not even see the fascist inside you, the fascist you yourself sustain and nourish. (Deleuze and Guattari, 1987, pp. 214–15)[1]

For any readers seduced by the seemingly liberatory force of the molecular (Chapter 3), Deleuze and Guattari remind us that the molecular does not necessarily harbour a freedom to discover or a line of flight to activate. If the molecular is about virtual potential, the flow of unstructured desire, there are no guarantees its actualization will produce emancipatory anti-fascist or anti-racist effects and practices. These authors do not merely connect fascism with the molecular, but contend that the molecular and molar are thoroughly entangled: fascist desire permeates every level of the social before resonating together and solidifying into the fascism of the state, the workplace, school and (black) popular culture. To their question, 'why does desire desire its own repression?' Deleuze and Guattari respond by maintaining that the masses 'do not passively submit to power' and 'nor are they tricked by ideological lure' (1987, p. 215). Rather, micro-fascist affective investments can merge with molar ideological commitments and macro-political perspectives to engender oppressive modes of power.

Chow also invokes fascism not as a common 'floating signifier' of collective denunciation in liberal culture, but instead deploys it for challenging Western (intellectual) culture's relentless fascination (desire) for otherness in the name of multiculturalism.

The myth, in the days of territorial colonialism, was that (white) consciousness had to be established in resistance to captivity – even when whites were holding other peoples and lands captive – so that white cultural origins had to be kept pure. In the postcolonial era, by contrast, the myth is that (white) consciousness must itself 'surrender to' or 'be held captive by' the other – that (white) consciousness is nothing without this captivity called 'otherness.' In both cases, however, *what remains constant is the belief that 'we' are not 'them,' and that 'white' is not 'other.'* This belief, which can be further encapsulated as 'we are not other,' is fascism par excellence. (Chow, 1998, p. 31)

Her re-working of fascism echoes Deleuze and Guattari's stress on the 'positive' machinic operation of fascism at the molecular level. The turn to the other is emblematic of what Chow calls a 'new liberal fascism' in the Western academy – the positive desire for an *idealized* other. Her provocation highlights the contestation of imploding racial boundaries in the shift towards a post-colonial neo-racism. She links contemporary multiculturalism with a 'fascist' desire for (a disavowed) other – an imagined projection, a 'pure' other, devoid of history or agency. I do not directly pursue an elaboration of contemporary fascism in this chapter, but examine the consociation between the crisis of race, whiteness and neo-liberal multiculturalism in relation to an emergent neo-racism.

This chapter acts as a bridge between an analysis of racialized representation in popular (film) culture and the practice of an alterity pedagogy. The 'truth' about race is synonymous with the domestication of racial and cultural difference, and the epistemic violence of representing the other is a key challenge facing an alterity pedagogy. Endeavours to innovate a multicultural pedagogy and curriculum invariably involve including texts marked by ethnic or racial difference. Concerns of curriculum content and inclusion regulate multicultural curricular developments, yet they are structured in a manner which continues to produce a domesticated otherness. Pedagogic practices of multicultural inclusion fail to reckon with the problem of racialized representation, most especially in relation to students' affective investments (Chapter 2). The pedagogy being advanced deliberately deploys popular film as it resonates with, and is formative of contemporary student subjectivities. Moreover, racialized popular media culture offers a significant challenge to pedagogies of alterity, because the contested sites of media culture play an influential role in producing everyday racialized affects, knowledges and representations about otherness. Racialized representations are never innocent in (post-)colonial discourses. They have been burdened by an excess of meaning and affects and subject to the voyeuristic gaze of whiteness.[2]

Conventional critical reading strategies of multicultural/anti-racist pedagogies have been governed by the need to discover the 'truth' of a text – demystify its ideological obfuscations and posit its real meanings (Chapter 3). The assumption is that a text is reducible to its essential (hidden) ideologies, as if the text is an expression of something else, an exterior reality (Montag, 2003). This chapter opens up the question of pedagogically engaging with racialized texts by introducing a 'materialist' reading practice. A text is situated in terms of its historical determinations, rather than simply mirroring reality. A 'symptomatic' reading eschews substituting one truth about race over another, which reduces pedagogic engagement to acts of ideological demystification, or a matter of accenting multiple meanings or adjudicating between competing audience interpretations. It has become commonplace to claim that racialized texts of popular culture are contradictory, polysemic, and elicit multiple readings; their ambivalence is reduced to textual or interpretative indeterminacies. A materialist reading practice avoids proffering an authoritative reading, even if it is to highlight the contested multiple meanings of a text. Instead, it aims to account for the *political ambivalence* of a multicultural text by grappling with the antagonized racial discourses it is part of. And the ambivalence and conflicting meanings of contemporary racialized texts being examined need to be situated in relation to the crisis of race: the struggle for the renewal of race in a post-colonial age of multicultural globalization.

   Three films have been selected for this chapter on the basis that they are replete with complex racialized representations, and draw on conventions of popular media culture. These films offer a challenging multicultural terrain for developing a critical practice for an alterity pedagogy. The first two texts, *Menace II Society* (1993) and *La Haine* (1995) share what could be described as a 'ghetto aesthetic'. They are used to introduce the entangled relationship of racialized representation and the 'real' in which race acts as the marker of authentic knowledge about otherness. The third text, *The Matrix* Trilogy (1999; 2003)[3] differs from *Menace* and *La Haine* as it associated with a genre of science-fiction and has a more globalized multicultural outlook, rather than a localizing 'ghetto realism' of the former films. Nevertheless, *The Matrix* shares similarities in as much as its subtext is concerned with questions of race, and projects an affective multicultural aesthetic. It is in the analysis of *The Matrix* where much of the substantive arguments of the chapter will be made.

Ghetto aesthetics: reading *Menace II Society* and *La Haine*

Caine Lawson: Went into the store just to get a beer. Came out an accessory to murder and armed robbery. It's funny like that in the 'hood sometimes. You never knew what was gonna happen, or when. After that I knew it was gonna be a long summer. (*Menace II Society*)

Voice-over: It's a story about a guy falling from a 50-storey building. As he falls, he tries to reassure himself by repeating: so far so good, so far so good ... It's not the fall that matters ... it's the landing. (*La Haine*)

There are striking similarities between *Menace II Society* (1993, Albert and Allan Hughes) and *La Haine* (1995, Mathieu Kassovitz). Both films are centred on groups of young males from racialized minority backgrounds. Their lives are precarious and mundane, with a sense of hopelessness pervading everyday existence. The stifling 'ghettoized' urban spaces they occupy constrain their life-chances and movements, and subject them to daily oppressions. The films vividly portray the nihilistic violence these youth perpetuate, and the deadly violence they are subjected to. The preoccupation with violence and masculinity has become a common characteristic of youth films depicting the 'realities' of 'ghetto life' during the 1990s (Diawara, 1993; Denzin, 2003). In this respect, both *Menace* and *La Haine* are committed to presenting an *authentic* account of life for marginalized urban youth who are effectively 'voiceless' and excluded from self-representation.

The Hughes brothers claimed that *Menace* '... is based on true, day to day life in Watts' (cited in Gormley, 2005, p. 104). The inclusion of old black and white television news footage of the 1965 Watts civil unrest adds a flavour of authenticity to the film's opening scenes. *La Haine* goes even further than *Menace* in its reality claims. Kassovitz made the film partly as an indictment against the racist violence of an encroaching police-state in France. The director uses a comparable opening strategy, with film scenes being interspersed with real-life contemporary news footage of rioting youth responding to the police murder of a young French-Arab male, of whom the film is dedicated to. Kassovitz unequivocally maintains:

> You can't be disturbed by this film, it would be disturbing if it portrayed something as real that was not. But nobody can claim that this film tells anything but the truth. If anything the film takes the situation and tones it down. The government said the movie was not very good, but they couldn't say it was not the truth. (Cited in Deussing, 1996)

The ambition of both sets of directors to depict the 'reality' of marginalized young lives is not straightforward, however. The critical and commercial success of *Menace* and *La Haine* (as relatively low budget 'independent' films) has been contingent on the films being constructed as compelling accounts of urban life by the directors, critics and audiences alike. Manthia Diawara (1993) identifying the emergence of USA films focussing on the quandary of young African-Americans males labels these films in terms of a 'New Black Realism'.

'The new realism films imitate the existent reality of urban life in America', particularly in their foregrounding issues of gang violence, crime, drugs, racism, exclusion and everyday survival (pp. 24–5).[4] Nevertheless, the acceptance of these films as authentic social commentaries requires viewers to connect the on-screen representations with 'real' life.

> Urban realism imagines and interpolates its audience through the construction of a consciously foregrounded relationship between what is represented on screen and its corresponding reality. The success of this stage depends on the coincidence of what the audience understands to be real and what they see on screen. (Schroader, 2001, p. 148)

The reality claims expounded by the directors is not a conviction to a naïve ideology of realism. While they trade on propagating a filmic realism for authenticating the 'truth-telling' function of their texts, we will find that the realism presented is cogently aestheticized and embellished with a self-conscious stylization. The films extensively draw on existing elements of hip hop culture, style and linguistic vernaculars for establishing a tactile urban realism (Gormley, 2005).

In the use of newsreel footage, both films invoke a sense of urban racial crisis from the very beginning. The viewer experiences this crisis most intensely in *Menace* by the unpredictable violence that is randomly unleashed. Its 'rites-of-passage' story is in similar vein to other so-called 'hood films. The story is centred on the character of Caine Lawson after his high school summer graduation. He lives in Watts, a post-industrial decaying part of South Central Los Angeles. In the opening sequences of *Menace* we witness Caine entering a grocery store with his friend O'Dog, who decides to commit armed robbery. To his horror, Caine witnesses O'Dog callously shooting dead the Korean store-owners after only a minor verbal exchange during the robbery. The crisis expressed in *La Haine* while of a different quality to *Menace* is 'realistically' conveyed with equal force. The film charts a period of 24-hours after anti-police riots in the lives of the three troubled figures: Hubert, Vinz and Saïd (of 'Black African', 'Jewish' and 'Arabic' background respectively). They reside on a crumbling estate (*banlieue*) on the outskirts of Paris, spending much of their time aimlessly gathering, hustling and evading daily police brutality. The unfolding of the narrative is recurrently interrupted by an on-screen ticking clock, which counts down towards an impending tragedy. The anxious repetition of the phrase 'so far, so good ...' in *La Haine* captures the trepidacious 24-hours before the calamitous event of a police officer shooting dead Vinz at the end of the film.

The crisis articulated in both *Menace* and *La Haine* is not a simple device for advancing the storyline. More knowingly, it is a 'structure of feeling' which pervades the texts throughout, and drives the viewers' experiences. The directors of *Menace* and *La Haine* display a 'mastery of cinematic technique' (Massood, 1993) which has made their films credible for both critics and audiences. It derives from an intimate knowledge of media culture, ranging from *avant-garde* cinema to contemporary black popular culture. In *Menace*, the scene of explosive violence in the grocery store is not immediately shown to the viewer, but captured on a CCTV video recording, which O'Dog removes in an attempt to ensure he will not be implicated in the crime. Although, later in the narrative, O'Dog obscenely brags about his exploits by showing the video footage to his fellow 'home-boys'. The grainy footage mimics scenes from the copious 'reality' police shows (perpetually populated by black suspects) that litter USA television scheduling. The Hughes brothers reflexively play with the affective power of 'reality television' – the turn to the 'real' for immediacy and authenticity in our increasingly mediated culture (Sharma and Sharma, 2000). The representation of the murder of the Korean store-owners through the CCTV surveillance video footage in *Menace* establishes a reality effect which is in fact highly aestheticized. And as Massood (1993) has highlighted, the bird's-eye perspective of the Watts district in the opening scenes of *Menace* gives it an absorbing documentary and ethnographic quality. Similarly, Kassovitz establishes a documentary-feel by mimicking the style of *cinéma vérité* (originally associated with low-budget French film-making in the 1960s). His use of hand-held cameras, 'naturalistic' lighting and acting, location filming in the banlieue adds to producing a stark, convincing reality effect. In particular, the presentation of what comes across as an 'un-scripted' dialogue, with acerbic exchanges between the three protagonists, instils a powerful filmic authenticity.[5]

The style of film-making of both *Menace* and *La Haine* actively draws upon the aesthetics of black popular culture, especially hip hop stylization. There are few post-industrial spaces whose youth cultures have escaped the influence by black popular culture today (Lipsitz, 1994). It has become the global style and soundtrack of everyday urban life for many marginalized youth. The hip hop ethos of 'keeping it real' (in spite of being commercially exploited via gangsta rap) has served to authenticate these films. The rap soundtrack of *Menace* is seamlessly woven into the film's narrative, to the point that without it, *Menace* would be found wanting. In the French youth context, Kassovitz purposefully reflects the hybridization of North American hip hop in *La Haine*. One of the most memorable scenes of the film is sutured by an evocative mixed hip hop track. We witness (the real-life) *DJ Cut Killer* cueing up a record in his bedroom on a housing estate. A booming rap sound of the French group *Supreme NTM* echoes across the banlieue as the camera sweeps through it: *NTM's* lyrics '*Fuck the Police*' are cut up with American rapper, *KRS1s* '*Sounds of da Police*' alongside a fêted sample of Edith Piaf's '*Non, je ne regrette rien*'.

Menace and *La Haine* have both received critical acclaim for their potent portrayal of marginalized urban youth. The respective viewing in both the USA and France by governmental authority figures in a flailing bid to comprehend the 'youth problem' of racial dissent and violence undoubtedly reflects how the films have been (conservatively) read as *true-to-life* social commentaries. However, both films have been rebuked for a contrived authenticity because of an excessive aestheti-cization of their representations of everyday urban life (Elstob, 1997/8; Schroader, 2001). But from a pedagogic perspective, the multiple readings which these films engender open up critical questions of the status of these texts in terms of their historical determinations. *Menace II Society* has been subject to significant analysis and review, and the remainder of this section will focus on its reception.[6] It transpires that the film has been either admonished or celebrated for its authenticity, and an *in/ability* to eschew a voyeuristic racializing gaze. However, to reduce these readings to a matter of the polysemy of popular texts or the multiple interpretations of critics and audiences, fails to engage with the social forces which gives rise to these contrary readings in the first place.

In his scathing review of the 'New Black Realism' genre of 'hood films, Norman Denzin condemnation stands out amongst the critics. He reads *Menace*, amongst other 'hood films, as perpetuating a naïve 'racial realism' of essentialist, authoritative representations of black life.

> Their invisible cameras offered detailed, close-up images that filled the screen. This was an authentic realism that was everywhere, but no where more visible then in the blood-soaked stains that spilled across the sidewalks after drive-bys ... This social problems-based cinematic realism demanded the viewers react in horror to senseless, youthful genocidal violence ... Paradoxically, they sought to do this,

even as they resisted mainstream Hollywood and its racist, cinematic apparatuses. But they were using the same codes, methods,
techniques, and conservative racist story lines as mainstream
Hollywood. (Denzin, 2003, p. 28)

Denzin's attack on 'hood film-makers, including the Hughes brothers,
leaves little room for contemplating the possibility their film advances
a highly aestheticized subversive practice of realism, operating on the
contestable terrain of popular culture (where meanings are politically
ambivalent). bell hooks offers a more insightful analysis of *Menace*, by
noting that the Hughes brothers seek to advance a critique of the
innate violence of white American society, of which black 'gangsta
culture' is a symptom of. She highlights the scenes where we find
Caine and O'Dog avidly watching classic American gangster movies,
wanting to emulate the violent pathological figure of the 'white gangster'. hooks concludes however, that *Menace* is ultimately a 'reactionary
film' because it nihilistically imagines no future for black youth, only
to abandon them as victims of white supremacy.

The ambivalence of *Menace* is also picked up in Paula Massood's
(1993) review. She identifies its unconventional narrative and stylistic
devices. The anti-hero figure of Caine destabilizes the conventional
identification with the central protagonist via the authority of the
(male) narrator's 'voice-over' in mainstream Hollywood films. Caine
proves to be highly unreliable as the film's narrator in his contradictory accounts that offer no explanation of his actions, which are
shown to be different from his claims. Similarly, Massood highlights
that in *Menace*, the patriarchal father figure as a site of moral authority
(found in other 'hood and mainstream films) is clearly absent.
Nevertheless, she finds *Menace* unable to completely break free from
mainstream voyeuristic representations of violence. In the final scene,
we witness Caine being riddled with bullets in a drive-by-shooting, and
according to Massood (1993, p. 45) the film '... falls prey to the same
stylistic conventions the Hughes claim to work against.'

While the readings by hooks and Massood point to a political
ambivalence in *Menace*, this does not prevent them from taking issue
with the film's racially suspect representational strategies and nihilistic
drive. On the hand, Paul Gormley (2005) considers these readings of
Menace limiting because they valorize ideological representation and
meaning, and overlook the aesthetic-*affective* force of the genre of
'hood films. Gormley contends that we need to conceive these films
primarily in terms of how they deploy images of blackness for creating

a 'new cinematic affect and immediacy'. He situates 'hood films as contesting the 'white American cultural imagination' – a site of fear and desire generated by the threat of blackness.

> Films like ... *Menace II Society* ... contain a politicised 'black rage' at the way white cultural identity and the American dream has been founded on the marginalisation and oppression of African-Americans. The films express this rage by miming and signifyin' the aesthetic structures of Hollywood cinema in a way which reanimates the affective impact of the action film. (Gormley, 2005, p. 35)

Mimesis for Gormley, whether as filmic realism or the 'violent white gangsters' of classical Hollywood, is filled with the possibility of subverting existing hegemonies of cultural authority and representation. He draws on Michael Taussig's work, by arguing that mimesis can add another dimension to the object it invades. Mimesis also signals contagion and tactility 'where the differences between the white cultural self and the "other" are always "polluted" by that "other" ... [W]hiteness in the US is always affected and altered by agency of black culture to the point where the racial boundaries between white and black have become blurred and difficult to determine'. (p. 31) To read 'hood films only in terms of an objectivist realist authenticity, misses how their affective mimesis of dominant culture can assault the 'senses of white audiences and shocking them in a way to provoke a reassessment of the boundaries of racial identity' (p. 79). Caine as an unreliable narrator in *Menace* is also highlighted by Gormley as a significant example of disrupting the truth-telling authority of conventional cinema. He goes on to argue that the use of gangsta rap music in *Menace* and the associated difficulty that white viewers may experience in discerning its lyrical meanings reflexively 'exposes their desire to know otherness' (p. 88). For this author, *Menace* actively seeks to prevent granting the voyeuristic pleasures of black images in dominant culture by not allowing the 'hood to become an easily consumable object of knowledge for audiences.

What is most striking about *Menace* as Todd Boyd has remarked, is that it 'refuses to give an ideological explanation for the violent culture that it represents' (1997, p. 101). Gormley, rather than finding this wanting, reconsiders the question of violence in terms of how the white cultural imagination resists acknowledging its own racial rage against black communities and its complicity in producing the horrifying conditions of the 'hood. Instead, authenticity attributed to images

of blackness functions as the 'real' in the white cultural imagination –
the 'hood as a site of meaningless, incomprehensible violence.

> The 'hood then becomes a place of senseless violence for the white
> cultural imagination, because to ascribe meaning to the violence of
> black rage would be to destabilise the authority of white American
> cultural identity while accepting that this identity has been built on
> white racial rage. The film plays on this repressed sense of guilt by
> its constant allusions to the violence which constitutes the cinema
> and culture of white America. (Gormley, 2005, p. 116)

The reading of *Menace* Gormley presents is not necessarily incon-
testable, though it differs from that of Denzin, hooks and Massood.
Gormley is not merely offering another interpretative reading of the
'hood films. His specific project is to *situate* these films in relation to an
emergence of a new kind of affective cinema, which is concerned more
with mapping the development of cinematic regimes, than historiciz-
ing the emergence of new regimes of racism. Gormley offers elements
of what can be identified as a materialist reading, which attempts to
reckon with the singularity of a text (in his case, its immanent affective
force). The pedagogic problem of the political ambivalence of racialized
popular texts such as *Menace* or *La Haine* is then not simply a matter of
highlighting contradictory representations and conflicting textual
meanings, or deciding upon multiple interpretations.

In the second part of this chapter, an analysis of *The Matrix* is
presented which develops the practice of a materialist reading to
explore the historical determinations of an emergent post-colonial
racism. The aim is to think through how an alterity pedagogy may
account for and engage with the contradictions and conflicts of a
racialized text, without being limited to adjudicating between
alternative interpretations of textual meanings.

Exit The Matrix?

> *Morpheus: The Matrix is everywhere, it is all around us. Even now, in this
> very room. You can see it when you look out your window, or when you
> turn on your television. You can feel it when you go to work, or when go to
> church or when you pay your taxes. It is the world that has been pulled
> over your eyes to blind you from the truth.*
>
> *Neo: What truth?*

Morpheus: That you are a slave, Neo. Like everyone else, you were born into bondage, born inside a prison that you cannot smell, taste, or touch. A prison for your mind. Unfortunately, no one can be told what the Matrix is. You have to see it for yourself.

This is your last chance. After this, there is no turning back. You take the blue pill and the story ends. You wake in your bed and believe whatever you want to believe. You take the red pill and you stay in Wonderland and I show you how deep the rabbit-hole goes. Remember – all I am offering is the truth, nothing more. (The Matrix, 1999)

The commercial and critical success of *The Matrix* (1999, directed by Andy and Larry Wachowski) ostensibly defined a new cinematic genre for the millennium. While the subsequent *Matrix* sequels added little to the original film, the series was not only unique for its innovative 'bullet-time' special effects and spectacular set-pieces; its appeal exceeded the genre conventions of commercial Hollywood or the narrow demographic of a 'science-fiction' film. The trilogy of films, alongside the noteworthy *Animatrix* DVD, a series of short features and documentaries, an *Enter the Matrix* computer-console game, numerous comics, merchandising and an official website whatisthematrix.com, spawned a multimedia 'Matrixology' (Romney, 2003) which offered audiences labyrinthine inter-textual encounters without simple narrative closure.

In the original movie, the hacker-by-night *Neo* (or Thomas Anderson when in his mundane day job) is confronted by the possibility that his life up until this moment has been a falsehood, an ideological screen of mere appearance. *The Matrix* has been nothing less than a fake or virtual reality; a collective mind-prison for docile humans, created by the 'sentient machines' in order to feed on the energy of cocooned human bodies. *Morpheus*, representing the resistance of a relatively small number of beleaguered humans who exist 'outside' the Matrix, offers *Neo* the chance to experience reality as it really is. *Neo* learns to overcome the panopticon power of *The Matrix*, and rouses the final human battle against the machines. The Wachowski's Matrixology has generated a plethora of writings, with collections such as *The Matrix and Philosophy* (Irwin, 2003), *Taking the Red Pill* (Yeffeth, 2003) and *The Gospel Reloaded* (Seay and Garett, 2003). There have also been numerous student-friendly down-loadable essays and protracted discussions on internet forums fanatically devoted to the trilogy. The official *Matrix* website shrewdly includes a 'Philosophy' section, replete with high-brow articles authored by notable theorists concerning themselves with cybernetics, artificial intelligence and phenomenology, consciousness, existentialism, Christian Gnosticism and Buddhism. There has been much discussion about the coloured pills in *The Matrix*, referred to in one of the most memorable scenes of the film in the epigraph above.

During the USA-led invasion of Iraq in 2002, *Not in Our Name* anti-war campaigners distributed flyers to cinema-goers attending *Matrix Reloaded* (the second of the trilogy). The leaflet boldly encouraged the audiences to 'Take the Red Pill' and '... Join the Resistance.' It echoed the slogan of many alter-globalization protestors by proclaiming, 'Another world is possible and we pledge to make it real.' In spite of the inventiveness of the leaflet, it appears that many Americans have kept on taking the blue pills. Although, from the moment when *Neo* (Keanu Reeves) was spotted clutching a copy of Baudrillard's *Simulacra and Simulation* in the original *Matrix*, the film's political and philosophical pretensions about the nature of lived reality in the late-twentieth century were staked out. Popular film has become legitimate fodder for serious academic scrutiny and the screen writers-directors, the Wachowski brothers' references to Greek mythology, religious doctrine and social theory were designed to invite critical attention and celebration.

Contemplating the ontology of (virtual) reality and existence has attracted and preoccupied many commentaries about *The Matrix* series. The original film's cinematic trailer, in the form of a tantalizing slogan-question of 'What is *The Matrix*?' was masterly in defining both the essential appeal of the film and much of its subsequent commentary. However, rather than being led by the film's own *maxim*, I wish to raise an alternative pedagogic problem of 'How to read *The Matrix*?' The question of the nature of reality that *The Matrix* plays on is thus displaced, and the task instead is to consider the film's own relationship to the 'historical reality' it is part of. The problem of reading is not one in general of textual interpretation, but specifically concerned with the palpable multicultural representations of *The Matrix* trilogy and its symbolic racial politics. The intention is to eschew advancing a normative critique of the film that compensates for the relative lack of attention paid to its racial subtexts.

A pedagogy which situates *The Matrix* series as a 'multicultural text' is confronted by what appears to be a problem of counter-posing interpretations. We find that the films may be read as either propagating a neo-liberal, Orientalizing multiculturalism (exemplified by the underground miscegenated human society of *Zion*, outside of *The Matrix*), or as a text acknowledging the extant racial conflict in society (present in the depiction of the 'white' *Matrix* world itself). To make an interpretative move and suggest that both readings of films are legitimate does not resolve the issue of multiple readings, and fails to account for the racial determinations of the films. Concluding that *The Matrix* series is a contradictory text exhibiting the ideological tensions of 'race' (or gender) has now become *de rigueur* in cultural-media studies analysis of popular culture texts. A pedagogic practice revealing textual contradiction governed by a set of counter-posed readings can engender an indifferent 'so what?' student response, for whom the experiences of such 'contradictions' can be a state of everyday precarious postmodern life (see Giroux *et al.*, 1996). Or worse still, the racial antagonisms which the film is situated in are transformed into only textual ideological tensions. Consequently, audience agency is reduced to an ability to 'decide' upon the efficacy of alternative filmic interpretations.

The next section offers two 'opposing' readings of *The Matrix* which highlight how the film may be interpreted in more than one way: as a text espousing a liberal multicultural ideology, and/or forwarding a critical anti-racist standpoint. The problem with offering such counter-posed readings leaves open the question of why such textual contradictions arise, as well as obfuscating a more profound concern of the text's own historically circumscribed interpretative possibilities (Althusser and Balibar, 1997; Montag, 2003).

Multicultural *vs.* anti-racist Matrix?

The Matrix trilogy presents a storyline devoid of explicitly employing racial or ethnic difference as a narrative device, yet its array of on-screen multicultural representations and references is remarkable. While it would be improper to label or describe it as a 'multicultural' or 'black' film, its (problematic) representational ideology of multiculturalism is plainly evident. The film actively draws on the conventions of Hong Kong cinema for example, and the multi-ethnic casting of *The Matrix* trilogy was unique for a Hollywood production unconcerned with racial/ethnic issues in its plot. *Morpheus*, played by the African-American actor Lawrence Fishburne was prominently present in the 'Matrixology' publicity. He had a central role in all three films, playing the captain of *The Nebuchadnezzar* ship with its multi-ethnic crew, and especially as leading the human resistance. In *Matrix Reloaded*, we also see that crew of the second craft, *The Logos*, consists of many 'non-white' actors, and in this case captained by a female African-American actor, *Niobe* (Jada Pinkett Smith). Although often overlooked, the somewhat enigmatic figure of hacker-messiah *Neo* was likely to be enhanced by Keanu Reeves's own mixed-Hawaiian ethnicity. Moreover, the key characters in the trilogy in the form of 'rogue' Matrix programmes aiding human emancipation from the machines were significantly played by a non-white, multi-ethnic cast: the mystic *Oracle* (Gloria Foster) was represented by an elderly African-American women; both the characters *Seraph* (Collin Chou) as the *Oracle's* bodyguard and the *Keymaker* (Randall Duk Kim) who offers access to the backdoors of *The Matrix* were of Southeast Asian ethnic origin; and the fleeing *Sati* (Tanveer Atwal) along with her 'parents' (whom *Neo* meets at the train station in *Matrix Revolutions*), were all played by actors of South Asian background. The ruling body of *Zion* was similarly a multicultural mix of individuals, which conspicuously included a (in)famous cameo by Cornel *'Councillor West'*.

The Wachowskis intentionally employed a multi-ethnic cast; and it remains a challenge to name another film with comparable worldwide commercial success that has so purposefully included a diversity of actors with such prominent roles. Although to read this as expressive of a progressive multicultural politics of representation is rather simplistic. Notwithstanding Keanu Reeves's ambiguous ethnicity (which will be explored later), in the final analysis, the 'white' actors – Keanu Reeves (*Neo*), Carrie-Anne Moss (*Trinity*) and Hugo Weaving (*Agent Smith*) – attracted the most significant Hollywood stardom and global recognition. And needless to say, the mere inclusion of non-white actors does not un-do the institutionally racist structures of Hollywood cinema production. While such an 'anti-racist' demand would burden any film, it would also be a mistake to read the inclusion of 'non-white' actors as the only multicultural gesture of the Wachowskis. Notably, the narrative of *The Matrix* trilogy involves many ordinary on-screen 'black-on-black' heterosexual relationships, for example, between *Morpheus* and *Niobe*; a mainstream 'non-black' Hollywood film depicting just one of these relationships remains a relatively rare occurrence. Nevertheless, these characters were in the shadow of the central 'white' relationship between *Neo* and *Trinity*.

The convergence of multi-ethnic casting and the plot was most discernible in the peopling of the underground, post-industrial city of *Zion* itself. *Zion* was massively populated by what appeared to be thousands of actors, of whom the majority were 'non-white'. A key scene in *Matrix Reloaded* begins with *Morpheus* delivering a rousing speech to the subterranean inhabitants of *Zion* celebrating their promised freedom, and ended with an intense synaesthesia of erotically-charged, 'misce-genating' bodies dancing to a deep, hypnotic musical bass-line. The scene was astonishing for the sheer ethnic-cultural diversity of the crowd that defied racial categorizations. *Zion* ideologically represents to the viewer a future world of equality, without racial conflict. Its multi-cultural imaginary is one of cultural hybridization exempt from the dehumanizing practices of racism. The representational realization of such multicultural idealization in the film begs to be questioned, however. What is striking is how the celebrated *Zion* scene is predicted upon the ethno-racial otherness of the dancing bodies. The pathology of these racialized bodies as disavowed yet desired sites of 'primordial' sexualized agency has been a persistent theme of Western representa-tions of racial difference (Gilman, 1985; hooks, 1992). The spectacle of the frenetic dancing crowd was pointedly juxtaposed against the cou-pling white bodies of *Neo* and *Trinity* in the 'private' space of the bedroom (their relationship being sublimated to a crypto-religious significance in the story-line). This attempt to evoke heightened sexual pleasure between the lead actors while evading clichéd representations of white heterosexual romantic love-making, relied on its imbrication with the racialized differences of a mass of indistinguishable 'others'. The alternative life-world of *Zion* – represented as *our* multicultural future – seeks to include cultural differences, yet appears to obscure the grounds on which these differences are othered. Furthermore, the ide-ology of cultural miscegenation which the film supposedly advances can be found to be suspect in relation to the representations of hetero-sexual associations. While the 'black-on-black' heterosexual couples are given some recognition in the narrative, no such representations are displayed for 'black-white' inter-racial coupling. It appears that an inter-racial representational taboo persists in *The Matrix* trilogy, in contrast to its celebration of inter-cultural mixing.

The valorization of cultural difference can be found most readily in the Southeast Asian themes referenced throughout the trilogy by the Wachowskis. The Japanese comic-book, anime origins of *The Matrix* are well documented and used to secure a credibility beyond a cinematic presence. Although it is the engagement with the martial arts action genres of Chinese cinema which gained *The Matrix* trilogy much popular acclaim and recognition. Through the deployment of expert martial arts choreographers directly from Hong Kong, the Hollywood directors garnered an unrivalled authenticity for the spectacular fighting scenes in the films. The relatively recent turn to the 'East' by Western directors – whether mediated by the Wachowskis or Quentin

Tarantino, or more directly by film-makers such as John Woo – nevertheless raises questions of cultural commodification, appropriation and the hegemony of the Orientalizing gaze. Arguably, *The Matrix* legitimated and made palatable the exotic spectacle of extended, unadulterated martial arts sequences in mainstream Hollywood cinema. When *Neo* audaciously declared 'I know Kung-Fu' upon entering a Matrix training programme which instantaneously downloaded this vast corpus of corporeal knowledge, didn't his gesture objectify and appropriate a whole gamut of variegated kung-fu systems, each with their own complex lineages, 'ways of life' and genre-specific filmic representations? *The Matrix*'s martial arts authenticity effectively reified kung-fu into a generic, universalized fighting style for effortless western spectacle and consumption.[7]

The foregoing discussion of *The Matrix* offers a reading which highlights how the text expresses a suspect liberal multicultural ideology. The film's celebration of cultural diversity is governed by a racialized structure of representation, manifested most visibly through a neo-Orientalist gaze. However, such an interpretation of *The Matrix* does not appear to exhaust other alternatives. It is also possible to highlight a contrary reading, which contends that *The Matrix* sub-text projects an 'anti-racist' consciousness, beyond most mainstream Hollywood productions.

The world of *The Matrix* set in the late-twentieth century actually suffers the very same social inequalities and racial ideologies of our current age (Lawrence, 2004). In the first film, *Agent Smith* enlightens a captured *Morpheus* by revealing that humans in the virtual reality world of *The Matrix* have been only able to successfully function in states of social hierarchies and perpetual modes of subjugation. It is not difficult to appreciate how the liberal-capitalist 'end of history' thesis is being exposed for its implicit Euro-American inequities by the Wachowskis. The corporate world that Thomas Anderson/*Neo* occupies is emphatically represented as a white world in *The Matrix*. All the figures of authority are white males, especially the police and the Agents themselves. The cloned Agents as Matrix programmes (infinite in their capacity to reproduce) are emblematic of the power of white privilege in North America. Such representations of *The Matrix* world are starkly contrasted with the 'non-white' characters occupying *Zion*. To the audience, multicultural *Zion* embodies an ideal future vision of a world without racial inequalities. In the film, the constant threat and attack against *Zion* by the machines is suggestive of the 'real' precarious status of multicultural ways of being today.

The two starkest film scenes in *The Matrix* which make explicit reference to racialized power are those involving *Morpheus*. After being captured by *Agent Smith* in a violent encounter, the defeated *Morpheus* is sadistically assaulted by a dozen white riot police officers. No longer able to defend himself, the visceral spectacle of a prolonged beating invokes the infamous scene of the brutalization of Rodney King in the hands of police officers in 1991 (Cunningham, 2003). The recurring public playing of the King video footage capturing the scene led to it being inscribed in the racial consciousness of America. The over-head point-of-view shot of the immobilized *Morpheus* being repeatedly beaten in *The Matrix* – positioning the audience as knowing viewers – sought to establish its reality effect as a primal scene of extant racial conflict (cf. Butler, 1993b).

What remains as the pivotal scene of *The Matrix* trilogy which this section's epigraph begins with is *Neo's* first encounter with *Morpheus*. While much attention has focussed upon this scene's revelation of the ontological problem of determining the real, an alternative extra-diegetic historical determination is also present. When *Morpheus* points out that *Neo* is a 'slave ... born in bondage', isn't this a deliberate acknowledgement of a history of slavery which America has been born out of? The articulation of this expunged knowledge by the 'black' *Morpheus* to the bewildered 'white' *Neo* is not simply an oft-repeated necessary history lesson, but rather a summoning towards a racial consciousness for the viewer. Moreover, it is surprisingly easy to syntactically substitute the term 'whiteness' for the titular '*The Matrix*' in almost all of *Morpheus'* dialogue in this whole scene: '[Whiteness] is everywhere, it is all around us ...'.

Reading materially

As stated earlier, the counter-posed readings of *The Matrix* are not meant to be exhaustive, nor be used to make increasingly banal claims of ideological indeterminacy or contradiction as an *a priori* condition of all texts of popular culture. On the contrary, it is the pedagogy of the text that is being pursued here and in particular, why such readings arise and on what grounds. In this respect, both the 'multicultural' and 'anti-racist' readings of *The Matrix* have their basis of explanation in terms of an external origin. But situating the film in this manner actually fails to fully grasp the text's own complex multicultural determinations. *The Matrix* explicitly read as expounding a liberal multiculturalism is structured by a normative critique revealing the film's hidden meanings, and thus aiming to restore it to the reality of its racialized ideological origins. The work of a pedagogue-theorist (or the critical student) is to penetrate the surface of *The Matrix* in order to discover its 'real', possibly contradictory, meanings. The uncovering of veiled racial ideologies in *The Matrix* highlights that the film is a product of these ideologies, and/or reflects the tensions of liberal multiculturalism – *Zion* exhibits both a desired future of cultural/racial miscegenation and a myth of 'racelessness' (cf. Goldberg, 2002). In either case, the film is liable to be admonished for denying the operations of societal racialized power.

The alternative, 'positive' reading of *The Matrix* is similarly determined by an external origin, but in this case through the anti-racist 'intention' of the directors. It is the Wachowski-*auteurs* who artfully imbue the text with references to extant racial conflicts. In their desire to critique the inequalities of neo-liberal capitalism, they highlight a racialized panopticon power operating which maintains hierarchies of difference and social subjugation (see Cunningham, 2003). Although, the intention of the text need not be so naively advanced vis-à-vis an auteurist stance. From a structuralist perspective, textual determination is an effect the 'anonymous authoring' of the ideological structure itself. The counter-hegemony of *The Matrix*'s racial sub-text reflects particular marginalized anti-racist discourses which circulate in the contested sites of commodified popular culture today.

The problem with these kinds of reading practices is that they are compelled by an interpretive act unable to duly account for the film's own racial historical determinations and singularity. The attempt to restore the text to an external origin renders it as a mirror or representation of something 'more real' than itself (Montag, 2003). The resulting possible multiple interpretations of a text are explained away in terms of textual indeterminacy, rather than reckoning with the conflicting forces of history a text is produced in.

Warren Montag's insistence of the 'materiality of the text' rejects an interpretive tradition which seeks out a deeper concealed truth existing outside of the text, or reducing it to a set of hidden ideological meanings to be exposed. Following Spinoza, Montag contends that the text does not have an inside/outside, otherwise it is constructed as merely reflecting or expressing reality, standing outside of history.

> To regard the work as irreducible is to begin to recover the way in which the work exhibits a multiplicity of meanings, the way that it, unbeknownst to itself, diverges from itself, to produce absolutely conflicting meanings. Its faults, inconsistencies and contradictions,

then are not signs of artistic failure but of the historical necessity
that made the work what is and no other. (2003, p. 60)

His alternative reading strategy, one that intimates more open-ended
politico-pedagogic possibilities, extends Althusser's method of reading
a text *symptomatically*. The act of reading for Althusser and Balibar
(1997) is an act of (pedagogic) knowledge production. Their original
contention that there are 'no innocent readings' and that texts have
'already been read' for us, lays emphasis on how (dominant) interpretations are widely shared or circumscribed because of particular relations of power, and nor would our own reading practice stand outside
of these forces. Montag's intercession, which stresses the *irreducible*
materiality of the text, leads to the supposedly inveterate Althusser
being unchained from the vestiges of structuralism, and instead, the
deconstructive influences of Spinoza and Macherey are accentuated in
Althusser's work.

In *Reading Capital*, Althusser and Balibar raised the problem of how
to account for the structured absences of a text – the 'outside' of the
text – not in terms of what it seemingly excludes, but how it refuses to
see what is always *already* present (visible, but made invisible).

> The invisible is defined by the visible as its invisible, its forbidden
> vision: the invisible is not therefore simply what is outside the
> visible ... the outer darkness of exclusion, but the inner darkness of
> exclusion, inside the visible itself because defined by its structure ...
> In other words, all its limits are internal. (Althusser and Balibar,
> 1997, pp. 26–7)

Althusser's practice of reading symptomatically underlines how a text
offers answers to absent questions. Macherey, as Montag highlights,
elaborates this point: a text says more than what it wants to say, or can
say.

> In this sense ... to produce knowledge of the work is to grasp not
> only what it says but what it does not and cannot say: the absent
> conjunctions (whether of addition or opposition) between divergent
> meanings, that are not hidden even if the silences that separate
> them render certain of them illegible, the empty spaces ... that
> divide the work from itself, that separate it into a multiplicity ... It is
> not external to history but part of it, thrown up and torn asunder by
> its conflicts. (Montag, 2003: 60–1)

A symptomatic reading of *The Matrix* offers the possibility of engendering a critical pedagogy able to encounter the film's own historical racialized determinations and account for its multiplicity of conflicting meanings. Thus, the contention is that the counter-posed readings presented of *The Matrix* cannot properly fathom the antagonized multicultural discourses they are part of. We shall discover that the structured absences of *The Matrix* is of *whiteness* itself – the operations of a neo-racism which is extant (visible) but denied (invisible).

Unravelling whiteness

I wish you could see this. It's so beautiful. (*Neo, Matrix Revolutions*)

The key protagonist of *The Matrix* trilogy is hacker-messiah *Neo*, whom *Morpheus* celebrates as 'The One'.[8] *Neo*'s destiny to liberate all of humanity from the sentient machines appears to be ultimately a matter of faith in terms of the somewhat perplexing crypto-religious narrative elements of the film. Although what stands out is that only *Neo* is able to *transcend* the simulacra of reality created by *The Matrix*, he literally sees through its essential binary computer code. Consequently, *Neo* realizes his innate 'supra-human' qualities inside *The Matrix* (for example, dodging bullets, overcoming the Agents, defying gravity and taking flight, and even saving his lover *Trinity* after she has 'died').

The ability of *Neo* to 'escape' *The Matrix* world is central to Douglas Cunningham's provocative reading of the film's 'anti-racist' sub-text. Interestingly, he poses the significance of the diegetic and extra-diegetic characteristics of *Neo*/Reeves, and questions whether *Neo* is represented as simply a 'white' figure in *The Matrix*.

> Is Neo, in fact, a character of mixed blood? Although traditionally coded as white within his films, the actor behind Neo – Keanu Reeves – in fact hails from a rich racial heritage (part Chinese-Hawaiian, part Caucasian [sic]) that uniquely suits him to play this role ... [T]he film does seem to rely heavily on the physical hints of 'otherness' personified by Keanu Reeves in order to set *Neo* apart as somehow separate from his Matrix and 'real world' human colleagues. His dark eyes and dark hair contrast sharply with his pale skin and high cheek bones, as if to suggest that he is, in fact, the human amalgam of two (or more) collided worlds. (Cunningham, 2003)

The racial-cultural hybridity of *Neo*/Reeves embodies a trangressive quality for Cunningham, able to disrupt the white-black master binary of racist ideology. By also reading *The Matrix* as a racialized panopticon power, Cunningham contends that the character of *Neo* threatens its rule of whiteness.

> Despite his ability to 'pass' as white – whether intentionally or not ... he represents difference on both the diegetic and extra-diegetic levels. As *Neo*, Reeves personifies a type of 'neo'-multiculturalism that stands as a threat to the stark whiteness of authority and normalcy within the Matrix, and his place with the crew of *The Nebuchadnezzar* sends a clear message that the future of humanity will not fall into easy categories of black or white. (2003)

The persuasiveness of Cunningham's account hinges on concatenating the character of *Neo* with the 'mixed-race' characteristics of the actor Reeves. The ambiguous 'white but not quite' status of *Neo* resists *The Matrix* as a racializing regime of power. *Neo*'s ability to evade the panoptic Matrix means that he is capable of fashioning an alternative subjectivity outside of the hegemonic discourses of racial domination. Cunningham writes:

> When acting within the Matrix, [*Neo*] stands apart from its categories and proscriptions to define his own sense of self and identity. He ceases to act as a subject of the system, rejects its technologies of domination, and becomes instead a subject of his own construction ... The ambiguity of Neo's racial identity, then, serves as at least part of his liberating potential as 'the One'; he upsets the perpetuation of racial conflict because he represents the potential independent, self-definition and for collective human resistance to machine power. (2003)

What appears compelling in Cunningham's reading is how *The Matrix* represents the contemporary real world forces of racial subjection and division. He lays emphasis on the film's racial signifiers in critically exposing the authority of whiteness. The suggestion that *Neo* possesses the capacity to transcend *The Matrix* advances a particular conception of a '*neo*-multiculturalism' which according to Cunningham threatens to un-do the structure of whiteness.

The problem with such an anti-racist reading is that while it conceives whiteness as a technology of racializing power (Hesse, 2004), it forecloses how whiteness actually remains an ex-nominated (invisible) structuring force in the text. Critically exposing whiteness relies on deploying the apparently transgressive subjecthood of hybrid *Neo*, an alternative 'neo-multiculturalism' that does not however address the *differential* 'integrating' force of contemporary whiteness. In other words, Cunningham's reading is in danger of disarticulating whiteness from a modality of a *neo-liberal* multicultural racism. We shall find that he does not properly consider and situate *The Matrix* in the circuits of a contemporary global multicultural capitalism. Moreover, to claim that *Neo* can transcend *The Matrix* belies the operation of what will be argued to be an 'inclusive' neo-racism which valorizes cultural hybridity and excludes through *containment* (cf. Goldberg, 2002; Hage, 2003). To read the character of *Neo* as escaping *The Matrix* recognizes the possibility of breaching whiteness, but fails to come to terms with the hegemonic operations of *whiteness in crisis*.

The Matrix needs to be considered in terms of a racialized text 'divided against itself' (Montag, 2003) – a text symptomatic of racial crisis. The film is indicative of how whiteness is responding to the encroachment of globalizing multicultural difference, yet cannot advance a veritable articulation of its own antagonized response. Reading *The Matrix* symptomatically leads to grasping an *unravelling* of whiteness in the age of globalizing multiculture: making visible the force of whiteness and reckoning with how it is *un/able* to attest its own apparatus of power. It is worth stressing that the unravelling of whiteness does mean to suggest that its supremacy is waning. Rather it highlights how whiteness is at once being increasingly exposed as a (paranoiac) normalizing regime of power, and at the same time is ever more compelled to maintain and intensify its structure of authority.

In order to elaborate the relationship between globalizing multiculture and whiteness, Hardt and Negri's (2000) provocative thesis of *Empire* can provide a useful point of departure. Their account of Empire has attracted as much criticism as praise, though the aim here is not to scrutinize its overarching validity. Instead, I utilize elements of their work in relation to conceiving a contemporary integrating modality of multicultural racism (instrumental to an unravelling of whiteness). Hardt and Negri's grand thesis is neatly captured by the oft-cited passage in their introduction:

> ... Empire establishes no territorial centre of power and does not rely on fixed boundaries or barriers. It is a *decentred* and *deterritorializing* apparatus of rule that progressively incorporates the entire

global realm within its open, expanding frontiers. Empire manages hybrid identities, flexible hierarchies, and plural exchanges through modulating networks of command. (2000, p. xiii)

Empire marks the emergence of a new post-imperialist political consti-tution of world order (what they label as 'imperial power'). The authors insist that fixed boundaries and the maintenance of impervious borders are no longer the defining features of Empire. Conversely, movement, flux and the breaching of all limits characterizes an Empire of porous borders, increasing mobility of people, labour, commodity flows and the proliferation of multiplicities of difference.

This operation of a new deterritorializing power and rule – a global postmodern sovereignty – is contrasted with the earlier essentializing power of imperialism and the nation-state. The rise of the modern nation state was conjoined with the production of bounded identities anchored to territory. Notions of a common descent, language (and 'blood') defined the boundaries of the nation, and were intimately tied to ideologies of racial exclusion. The colonizing nations of Europe attempted to 'manufacture homogeneity' amongst its own popula-tions, and steadily divided its citizens from foreigners (others). This was distinguished from the regulation of heterogeneity for colonized nations, in the will to manage racialized others through colonial terror and domination. In terms of post-imperial racial rule and the waning of the influence of the nation-state, Empire marks a shift from European nations 'exteriorizing race' (as being outside of civilized soci-eties), to a practice of 'internal containment' (Stoler, 1995; Goldberg, 2002). The accelerated movements of racialized others, especially after decolonization in the twentieth century, led to existing boundaries of nation, culture and identity progressively becoming more unsettled. The racism of Empire appears to decouple 'race' from nation in the production of 'differential hierarchies' and through the reification of globalized 'hybrid subjectivities', compared to the bounded primordial ethno-racial identities of colonial racism.

Nevertheless, this shift towards a post-colonial racism of Empire should not be conceived as a simple displacement of earlier modes of racialization because racism appears '... renewed and new at the same time' (Stoler, 1995, p. 89). The Manichean division between an emer-gent Europe and its abject Other has always been a precarious bound-ary for the colonizer: that which was excluded and negated gave birth to a positive identity for the European colonizer (Said, 1978). Edward Said cogently argued that the inverted absolute and essentialized

104 Multicultural Encounters

difference of the other was crucial for the possibility and maintenance of a superior Occident. However, the requisite other was not what was merely excluded, but had to be acknowledged at the same time. The policing of the racial/cultural boundary has been a profound site of anxiety for white Europeans, though in reality, its transgression (and violent consequences for the other) was the norm rather than the exception (Fanon, 1986). The ineluctable necessity of upholding and sustaining the besieged boundary of absolute difference has been an 'impossible', but necessary project, for the making of colonial white privilege.

Whiteness as a structure of privilege of power emerged from the development of a racialized European identity. 'Racial whiteness' as Alastair Bonnett points out was forged in '... new mass political identities based on the distinctions between coloniser and colonised, dominant and subject peoples' (2000, p. 17). The maintenance and investment of a racial whiteness has nevertheless been a fraught project. The 'demands' of whiteness (purity, morality etc.) have been ironically denied to the mass of populations riven by social divisions and ambiguous ethnicities.

> Whiteness, both as the ultimate symbol of superiority and as the legitimising authority and mobilising ideology for national imperial and colonial enterprises, must simultaneously be made available to all Europeans and denied to those deemed unfit or unwilling to carry its burden. Thus the excessive nature of European construction of whiteness, its exclusionary zeal, brings about its own impossibility: most whites are unworthy of whiteness. (Bonnett, 2000, pp. 21–2)

Whiteness as an im/possible ideal paradoxically has served to further enhance its subjectifying force. The absolute racial division between white/black has underpinned colonial practices of racism, yet as we have seen, it has been a boundary under threat of constant transgression. In the age of Empire, whiteness has mutated towards a neoracism of 'inclusion' and 'integration', rather than a binary exclusion. It has become more an issue of degrees of (deviance from) whiteness than merely exclusion. Hardt and Negri stress this point when they accuse 'post-colonial theory' as deconstructing and challenging essentialist racial binaries of modernity. It is rebuked for employing anachronistic dialectical notions of colonial power that can only seek to displace a *binaristic* hierarchy, through the postmodern incantation of cultural hybridity and difference. Notwithstanding their wildly reductive characterization of 'post-colonial theory', the authors of *Empire* contend that positing the condition of hybridity as a transgressive, anti-racist condition obfuscates contemporary hegemonic operations of whiteness. For Hardt and Negri, the failure to fully grasp the new modality of a decentred and deterritorializing global power – which feeds on hybridities and fragmented subjectivities – means that post-colonial theory marks a shift towards Empire, rather than being able to challenge its form of rule.[9]

The bifurcating racialized structure (inside/outside, inclusion/exclusion, self/other) of colonial racism appears to be at odds with the subsumption of difference in Empire, vis-à-vis the new imperial or neo-racism. 'Real subsumption,' according to Hardt and Negri, has no 'outside' for the expansion of capitalism. It does not exclusively lead to the exclusion or obliteration of difference; rather, it can equivocally produce differential hierarchies and multicultural hybrid subjectivities in the incorporation of all forms of life. They argue that the racism of Empire is a *cultural* neo-racism of segregation, which primarily integrates others (as the management and ordering of difference). This is distinguished from the colonial racism of division and hierarchy, which takes place across the racial boundary of self/other (as the exclusion and negation of difference). Following Deleuze and Guattari, they contend that cultural racism needs to be conceived as a 'strategy of differential inclusion,' as opposed to the absolute exclusion of the Other.

White supremacy functions ... through engaging alterity and then subordinating differences according to degrees of deviance from whiteness. This has nothing to do with the hatred and fear of the strange, unknown Other. It is a hatred born in proximity and elaborated through degrees of difference of the neighbor ... Subordination is enacted in regimes of everyday practices that are more mobile and flexible but that create racial hierarchies that are nonetheless stable and brutal. (Hardt and Negri, 2000, p. 194)

While these authors properly maintain that a contemporary racism 'rests on the play of differences' instead of a Manichean bio-racial divide, Alain Policar has cautioned that the two formulations 'easily flow into each other and so that they cannot be found in a pure state' (1990, p. 100). The issue is not just one of historical specificity, as the practice of Western racisms have been irrevocably imbricated with culture (see Young, 1995). For instance, contra Hardt and Negri, Orientalist discourses have interweaved both colonial and cultural racisms.

Said observed a shift in the regime of colonial power during the nineteenth century which 'turned the Orient from an alien into colonial space' (1978, p. 211). This materialization of power over the 'Orient' attempted to *penetrate* its '... cultural, temporal, and geographical distance ... expressed in metaphors of depth, secrecy and sexual promise ... the 'veils of an Eastern bride' or "the inscrutable Orient"' (p. 222). The closing down of distance between the West and its Others in the actual encounter with the spaces and bodies of the 'Orient' did not result in existing boundaries melting away. Colonial governmentality has been onerously preoccupied with maintaining a racial and cultural divide. For the colonizer, the ambivalent coupling between racism and sexualized desire for the Other was undoubtedly the most de-stabilizing and perverse to police. And the popular colonial tales of Westerners 'going native' or insane in exotic foreign lands were thinly disguised warnings for not getting too close to the other (McClintock, 1995; Root, 1995).

It is notable that contemporary modes of cultural racism, including a neo-Orientalism, appear less troubled with the danger of going native (and even miscegenation) in their relation to otherness. This may account for the 'frisson' of difference being harder to sustain now, and its novelty less significant in popular culture. Moreover, the encounter with the other is no longer only one of a distant place or mediated through racialized representations; it has become an everyday occurrence in the Western multicultural metropolis. Nevertheless, while the racism of Empire has shifted towards a differentialist inclusion, the preservation of 'the proper distance' from the other has become ominous. Cultural racism is one of proximity to a normalizing Whiteness. The deterritorializing global capitalism of Empire furiously traverses national, cultural and racial borders, paying little heed to place, yet its multicultural ideology seemingly appreciates (requires) the difference (distance) of the Other.

The spatializing characteristic of contemporary racism has also been cogently highlighted by Slavoj Žižek. His polemical critique against a 'cultural studies' complicit with neo-liberal multiculturalism, does however adversely screen out the operations of a normalizing whiteness. Žižek writes:

> Multiculturalism is a disavowed, inverted, self-referential form of racism, a 'racism with a distance' – it 'respects' the Other's identity, conceiving the Other as a self-enclosed 'authentic' community towards which he, the multiculturalist, *maintains a distance* rendered possible by his privileged universal position. (1997, p. 44, my emphasis)

It is the 'empty point of universality' of multiculturalism which enables it to respect the specificity of the embodied other by maintaining the proper distance and asserting its own superiority. In Žižek's account, the so-called respect and tolerance of the difference of the other is deeply hostile to all actual Others. The other of liberal multiculturalism is an idealized other (cf. Chow, 1998). It is an experience of otherness deprived of its own alterity, which can be known, represented and consumed – the other of a global multicultural capitalism.

Žižek castigates what is sweepingly labelled as 'cultural studies' for naively championing the multicultural differences of minorities. Its desire for a rainbow coalition cultural politics has countenanced the forces of global capitalism which structure all contemporary social relations and formations of identities. Moreover, he argues that it is not enough to merely expose the (false) universality of multiculturalism as harbouring Eurocentricism in the masking of its own particularity. Instead, he asserts, that the 'particular cultural background or roots which always support the universal multiculturalist position ... conceals the fact that the subject is already thoroughly 'rootless,' that his true position is the void of universality' (Žižek, 1993, p. 44). His own reading of *The Matrix* is disappointed with the film because it does not go far enough in questioning the ontology of the subject. When *Neo* is about to meet the Oracle for the first time he is confronted by a child able to psychically twist a spoon. The child tells *Neo* that it is not about convincing myself I can bend the spoon, but convincing myself the spoon does not exist. Although Žižek (1999) contends '... what about MYSELF? Is it not that the further step should have been to accept the Buddhist proposition that I MYSELF, the subject, do not exist?' To contest the myth of the unitary subject is a significant conceptual operation for coming to terms with the effects of hegemonizing power, but it does not necessarily overcome the politics of culture and identity. In an attempt to legitimate demands for *universal* socio-economic justice, Žižek's critique of multiculturalism wishes to do away with recognizing cultural difference altogether on the grounds that it only can lead to reification of particular identities. For Žižek, rather than pointing out the particular characteristics of the universal subject (white, male, heterosexual etc.) which subordinate difference, 'identifying universality with its empty point of exclusion' (1993, p. 51) will challenge extant capitalist hegemony. The problem is that such a claim results in erasing the agency of the other, who becomes an exclusionary structural *effect* of the machinations of global capitalism. When Žižek laudably declares that we should all claim to be 'immigrant workers', cultural specificity as well as the singularity of the other is all but erased. Furthermore, if the contemporary neo-racism of Empire operates by an assimilative hegemony (which has no 'outside'), it begs the question, 'what' occupies the void of universality?

The analysis of multiculturalism offered by Žižek is mirrored by what remains absent (repressed) in *The Matrix*. He falls short of marking the empty place of the universal as a positionality of *Whiteness* itself. The multicultural universal, or the universal of post-modernity is governed by whiteness, otherwise 'race' is written out of the history of modernity (Gilroy, 1993). Marking whiteness does not aim to identify the particularities of Whiteness, because its own inscription has no content. Whiteness as an 'absent presence' seeks to stand for, and be a measure of, all of humanity. It operates as a universal point of identification that strives to structure all social identities. In this respect, Whiteness functions like an 'empty signifier' (Laclau, 1994), such that it needs to fill or hegemonize the empty place of the multicultural universal in order to uphold its authority and suture its identity.

The crisis of whiteness – its unravelling – reveals how it is increasingly threatened by the encroachment of otherness, though at the same time is compelled to desire, integrate multicultural difference. Historically, as Goldberg insists, whiteness has needed to project itself anew in the face of the presence of racialized others in heterogeneous urban spaces and metropoles, for example the Irish, Jews and even the working-class. '... [T]he renegotiation of whiteness recreates no straightforward homogeneity but a troubled hierarchy of internally differentiated and differentially privileged "white races"' (Goldberg, 2002, p. 183). The neo-racism of Empire is however, not simply figured on the inclusion/exclusion of others. It uniquely marks the irruption of the boundaries of whiteness itself, which has led to what may be perversely identified as a 'multicultural whiteness' – a whiteness whose empty universality (hegemonizing power) is governed by the differences it seeks to desire, disavow and domesticate, or exclude through containment; a condition of its own im/possibility. To read *The Matrix* symptomatically makes present an absent desiring multicultural whiteness that the text is determined by. Cunningham's claims that the figure of *Neo* is able to un-do the racializing power of *The Matrix* – on the basis of *Neo*/Reeves's miscegenated ethnicity transgressing the bio-racial divide – does not grasp how the messiah-hacker is a product (symptom) of an assimilative multicultural whiteness.

Moreover, neither Cunningham nor Žižek are in the position to fathom the paranoiac response to racial/cultural difference which *The*

Matrix unfaithfully attests. Žižek can only identify a generalized paranoia about the loss of self-hood/agency in a virtualized late-modernity
which the film exploits: 'Is not the ultimate American paranoiac
fantasy that of an individual living in ... a consumerist paradise, who
suddenly starts to suspect that the world he lives in is fake ...?' (Žižek,
1999). *The Matrix* also harbours a *racialized* paranoia. Cunningham has
highlighted the seemingly Foucauldian practice of self-fashioning
when *Neo* becomes 'a subject of his own construction' within the
Matrix. His analysis misreads the pathology of contemporary whiteness. The structural anxiety of whiteness, a fear of losing its privilege
and authority has intensified in the age Empire, and transformed into a
paranoid response towards alterity. The breaching of the racial divide
has meant that the fear of otherness at the white/black boundary has
become a generalized fear of otherness *everywhere*. The other has progressively threatened to abscond its racialized idealization and designa-
tion. It is no longer remaining in its proper place (no longer 'other'),
and the policing of the racial-cultural border is no longer limited to the
boundary of its transgression. Thus, Cunningham's contention that
the miscegenated *Neo*'s practice of self-transformation threatens to un-
do whiteness misses the point. *Neo* is symptomatic of a multicultural
whiteness manifestly penetrated by 'non-white' elements, increasingly
less capable of expressing its superior civilizational values and distinctiveness (cf. Hage, 2003). The re-making of the self that *Neo* exhibits
(recall his spectacular 'I know Kung-Fu' corporeal transformation), does
not express the Foucauldian practice of ethico-critical reflection which
potentially opens itself up to otherness. To the contrary, it is symptomatic of the white Western subject's paranoid response to an
encroaching global multi-culture in the face of its incessant claim to
universality. The unravelling of whiteness, the crisis of its universality,
is being managed by a compulsion to integrate and stratify all others.[10]

Re-reading the racialized text

The duplicity of *The Matrix* revolves around the film seemingly
acknowledging racial conflict, but unable to articulate the hegemony
of a contemporary multicultural whiteness. In this respect, the contradiction of the text has not been figured on the supposedly irreconcil-
able 'positive' anti-racist and 'negative' liberal multicultural elements
of the film. Reducing the text to such a reading elides the imbrication
of whiteness with multiculturalism – symptomatic of the 'fascist' desire
(neo-racism) of Empire.

A pedagogy of the Matrix attempts to avoid simply condemning the text for any ideological shortcomings; its complicity with, and inability to, expose the contemporary power of whiteness and neo-liberal multiculturalism. Rather, the aim is to read the text symptomatically as a condition of a contemporary antagonized liberal multiculturalism. What becomes apparent is that the multicultural antagonism of *The Matrix* is governed by a 'constitutive double-bind' (Hesse, 2004) of racism. Hesse argues that the modern conception of racism has been predicated on a particular set of European experiences, namely Nazi persecution of the Jewish population. These experiences of racism have been taken to be paradigmatic, and *universalized* to include 'non-white', 'non-European' racial others.

> A conceptual logic emerged where what become foregrounded (exclusion, discrimination, ghettoisation, exterminations) supplied the conceptual resources to translate 'other' experiences into the vaunted paradigmatic template. However, what was simultaneously foreclosed ... were aspects of 'other's' racialised experiences that appeared inassimilable ... and threatening to the privileging of the paradigmatic experience (e.g. colonial inclusions, orientalism, exoticism) ... [T]he concept of racism is doubly bound into revealing (nationalism) and concealing (liberalism), fore-grounding (sub-humanism) and fore-closing (non-Europeanism), affirming (extremist ideology) and denying (routine governmentality). (Hesse, 2004, p. 14)

Hesse is careful to point out that this double-bind does not invoke a contradiction or a paradox, but is a *constitutive* antagonism of the modern concept of racism. And it is precisely this antagonism of racism which a symptomatic, materialist reading practice is able to engage. *The Matrix* raises the spectre of racism for the viewer, and its subtext highlights the normalizing panopticon power of whiteness. But this is the ruse of the text – seemingly making visible whiteness, yet denying its subjectifying, assimilative force.

This chapter has raised the thorny of issue of how to read a racialized text. An analysis examined three 'popular' films, *Menace II Society*, *La Haine*, and especially *The Matrix*, which were selected on the basis of their complex racialized and multicultural representations of difference. My aim has been to interrogate orthodox reading strategies of these types of films that invariably highlight their conflicting meanings or multiple interpretations. By failing to situate a text within its own historical determinations, its pedagogy cannot adequately account for why particular contested readings arise in the first place. In relation to classroom practice, such an approach is liable to generate a pedagogy which stresses textual indeterminacy in the contested terrain of racialized popular culture, rather than exploring the social forces that the text is part of. Although a materialist reading in itself does not simply generate a 'correct' reading of a racialized text. Nevertheless, through such a reading practice we have moved towards developing a pedagogy which engages with how texts work, rather than only in terms of what they mean.

5
Critical Practice: 'Minor-Popular' Film

The potential use of what will be identified as 'minor-popular' film for an alterity pedagogy will be explored in this chapter. It turns to a particular cinema of popular, diasporic 'British-South Asian' film. This cinema does not neatly fit into the artistic characterizations of 'minority ethnic' cultural productions (Mercer, 1994), though they need to be read against these works. In relation to minority cinema, much of the critical attention has focussed on the independent sector, and its pursuit of innovative practices which interrogate, subvert and often counter conventional and popular representations of racialized difference. Laura Marks labels this as an 'Intercultural Cinema'

> characterized by experimental styles that attempt to represent the experiences of living between two or more cultural regimes of knowledge, or living as a minority in the still majority white, Euro-American West. The violent disjunctions in space time that characterise disaporan experience – the physical effects of exile, immigration and displacement – also, ... cause a disjunction in notions of truth. (Marks, 2000, p. 1)

While intercultural cinema is not limited to any specific national formation, Marks notes that the work of 'Black British' film-makers (which includes those of African-Caribbean and South Asian descent) has been one of the most significant sites of development. These cultural productions have been understood as grappling with the politics of difference (Hall, 1988; Mercer, 1994; Willeman, 1994). Their critical practice has been understood as having a 'pedagogic' function which seeks to open up difficult questions of identity, belonging and otherness (Shohat and Stam, 1994; Kaplan, 1997). This is not to naively claim that Black film is able to innately perform a radical pedagogy that autonomously produces new (ethical) subjectivities. Although on occasion, the readings and claims made of these films do suppose a 'modernist' aesthetic textual practice in relation to an unspecified 'ideal' viewer. In contrast, a 'materialist' analysis would need to situate these texts in the social contexts and political struggles they inhabit (Chapter 4).

A key contention of this chapter begins by conceiving Black British film as a 'minor' cinema (cf. Deleuze and Guattari, 1986). The expressive cultural politics of these cultural productions attempt to interrupt and deconstruct normative racialized representations and nationalist exclusionary discourses, and seek to connect with other 'becoming-sites' of deterritorialization. Conceiving Black film in such a manner enables the possibility of uniquely identifying it as a critical practice (otherwise we would be unable to delineate the *singularizing* force of Black film). However, we cannot necessarily determine this cinema's political effects in advance, nor in the ways it could affectively mobilize audiences/students to new ethical sites of investments. A pedagogic and performative distinction needs to be made between identifying the affective capacities of these films, and what they actually do in a particular teaching situation (their performative effects). It is not possible to determine *a priori* the performative effects of these filmic texts – as this involves exploring a site-specific pedagogic encounter in the classroom (Chapter 6) – yet the potential deployment of Black-British (South Asian) cinema for identifying an alterity practice can be explored, which is the aim of this chapter.

I begin by exploring the specificity of Black film in terms of its expressive cultural politics, though it worth noting that the label of 'Black British film' is inadequate for at least three reasons. Firstly, the signifier 'Black' itself has long been a contestable (unifying anti-racist) 'political' identity-category for African-Caribbean and South Asian groupings in Britain (Hall, 1991b). Its utility nevertheless will be retained for distinguishing some of the shared characteristics of this body of filmic work. Secondly, the label fails to capture the complexities and heterogeneity of a range of *diasporic* cultural productions. In this respect, Black British film can be thought of as a radical multicultural, diasporic cinematic practice which is not contained by its national specificity (Willeman, 1994). Finally, some of the work of British-South Asian film-makers is not experimental or adheres to an *avant garde* critical practice which has characterized much of the 'independent' intercultural/Black British Cinema sector.

The body of work primarily being referred to as 'Black film' emerged during the 1980s in Britain from the state-subsidized 'Black workshop' movement (for example, *Sankofa, Black Audio Film Collective* and *Retake*), and similarly the 'Independent' sector (most significantly, through the support of *Channel Four* television's commitment to 'minority' programming). The films do not exhibit one kind of genre, aesthetic representational strategy or mode of address. They have ranged from the 'formal experimental' type works such as *Handsworth Songs* (1986, John Akromfrah), *The Passion of Remembrance* (1986, Isaac Julian and Maureen Blackwood), *Looking for Langston* (1989, Isaac Julien), and *Kush* (1991, Pratibha Parmar), which have been largely a product of the workshop movement, to the more 'popular' narrative based films of the independent sector, for instance, *My Beautiful Laundrette* (1985, Stephen Frears), *Young Soul Rebels* (1991, Isaac Julien) and *Bhaji on the Beach* (1993, Gurinder Chadha).[1] It will be maintained that while Black film has been usefully analysed as a deconstructive practice of a 'diaspora aesthetics' (Mercer, 1994) and occupying a position of 'marginality' (Willeman, 1994), its politics of alterity has remained rather muted. This requires making a further move by conceiving Black film more explicitly as a 'minor cinema'.

The actual films being pedagogically deployed are 'popular' British-South Asian texts. This work is made up of mainly 'semi-commercial' narrative-based films such as: *My Beautiful Laundrette* (1985), *Sammy and Rosie get Laid* (1987, Stephen Frears) and *My Son the Fanatic* (1998, Udayan Prasad), all written by Kureishi; *Bhaji on the Beach*; *Wild West* (1999, written by Harwant Bains); *Brothers in Trouble* (1996, Udayan Prasad), *East is East* (1999, written by Ayub Khan) and *Bend It Like Beckham* (2002, Chadha). Unsurprisingly, most of the theoretical and political claims about Black film as a deconstructive practice and intercultural cinema have been implicitly directed towards the 'experimental' works, rather than the more 'popular' narrative films. The second half of this chapter will position these films specifically in relation to a rhizomatic pedagogy operating on the contested terrain of the '*popular*'.

Popular representations of diasporic South Asian 'culture' have recently figured prominently in multicultural celebrations of cultural diversity in Western nations. While this makes British-Asian films such as *East is East* and *Bend It Like Beckham* especially meaningful as they are capable of resonating with everyday representations of diasporic 'Asian culture', they are equally politically ambivalent because these films ambiguously inhabit the contradictory racialized sites of popular culture. Using these texts in a teaching situation is likely to be a risky activity because their filmic representations continue to be regulated by a discourse of an Orientalized authentic Asian-Other. Nevertheless, when these types of films are redeployed in terms of a *'minor-popular'* critical practice, their utilization for an alterity pedagogy becomes possible.[2]

Black British film

It is by no means accidental that Black film has been selected as a (re)source for developing a critical multicultural pedagogy. Hall (1988) situated contemporary Black artistic cultural productions in terms of their critical explorations and rethinking of Black identity (politics) beyond the limitations of the 'essentialisms' circulating in the projects of anti-racism and liberal multiculturalism in Britain. By re-inflecting the term 'ethnicity' (Chapter 2), he highlighted that the politics of difference – the multiple differences and contestations within, between and across a diasporic identity – marks a shift in Black cultural politics. This was intimately tied to the question of representation by identifying a movement away from a struggle over the 'relations of representation' to a new phase of the 'politics of representation itself'. Hall was anxious not to characterize the shift as a binary opposition, but rather to think of it in terms of Black cultural strategies which assume new forms of struggle. The key aspects which defined the earlier strategies of the 'relations of representation' have been the issue of access for black cultural workers to the 'rights of representation', and the *'contestation* of the marginality, the stereotypical quality and fetishized nature of images of blacks, by the counter-position of a "positive" black imagery' (Hall, 1988, p. 27). It is not so much that the demands for Black representation and contesting the dominant regimes of representation are no longer politically relevant, rather that the struggle over the politics of representation points to new cultural strategies and representational practices for exploring the alterity of Black identity formation. Hall's claim of 'the end of an innocent notion of the essential black subject' acknowledged the contested politics of difference for new practices of artistic cultural production, especially within Black British film.

Mercer (1994) locates the development of Black film in the 1970s and 1980s in terms of two key processes. Firstly, its formation has involved a diverse range of cinematic practices such as oppositional 'Third World' documentary, counter-informational community

orientated newsreels, Euro-American art cinema and formalist experimentation. Secondly, he highlights that the anti-racist contestations
and political alliances amongst South Asian and African-Caribbean
people around the signifier 'Black', as a political category (rather than
as a naturalized fixed racial identity), situated the cultural struggles of
Black film as an emergent 'counterpractice' against essentializing
representations of Black subjects.[3] It is from these concurrent arenas
of new representational practices in relation to the interrogation of
the politics of diasporic Black British identities that we can begin
to conceive Black film as a critical practice. The shift from the 'relations' to the 'politics of representation' gave rise to questions of new
aesthetic practices of Black film.[4]

Cameron Baily captures the political strategies of the earlier moment
in Black film in the 1960 and 70s when he stated:

> Social issue content, documentary realist in style, firmly *responsible*
> in intention – [the cinema of duty] positions its subjects in direct
> relation to social crisis, and attempts to articulate 'problems' and
> 'solutions to problems' within a framework of centre and margin,
> white and non-white communities. The goal is often to tell buried
> or forgotten stories, to write unwritten histories to 'correct' the
> misrepresentation of the mainstream. (Baily, cited in Malik, 1997,
> pp. 203–4)

Following Baily, Sarita Malik characterized films such as *Pressure*
(1975, Horace Ové) and *Step Forward Youth* (1977, Menelik Shabazz) as
a 'cinema of duty' – films with a radical political content which neces-
sitate a 'realist' representation of Black subjects in the demand for
racial equality. Earlier Black productions such as *Pressure* have been
scrutinized by Jim Pines (1988) and Mercer (1994) for attempting to
articulate a counter-discourse against the dominant regimes of representation, but 'at the level of film form and cinematic expression
these films often adhere to the same aesthetic principles as the media
discourses whose authority and ideological effects they seek to resist'
(Mercer, 1994, p. 84). Mercer claimed that the documentary realism
and linear narrative of *Pressure* reproduced the pathologization of
black identity 'in crisis' that circulates in the classic 'problem' orientated race-relations discourse. Similarly, the struggle to retell stories of
the antinomies faced by Asian youth in Britain was pursued vis-à-vis a
realist 'authenticity' in the narrative fiction film *Majdhar* (1984,
Ahmed Jamal). The representation of an Asian female subject as

'caught between two cultures' articulated 'identity' as the site of the problem of cultural difference.

For Mercer (1994), the film *Passion of Remembrance* (1986) by *Sankofa* was a 'turning point' by breaking out of the 'master-codes of the race-relations narrative'. In the film, narrative continuity is disrupted by inserts of a dialogue taking place in an abstract space, and actual video footage of political demonstrations is cut into the domestic drama of the film. *Passion* tries to rupture the supposed homogeneity of the black community by poetically exploring the plurality of black identities. Alongside the 'non-realist documentary' texts of *Territories* and *Handsworth Songs*, these films self-consciously deconstructed the aesthetic strategies of documentary realism and were reflexively aware of their own cultural construction.

In terms of identifying the critical function of Black film as well as the mode of its critique, it is the Bakhtinian recognition of the 'materiality of the sign' that informed much of the practice of the workshop sector. The struggle over the filmic sign is the site of cultural struggle and political intervention. For example, observe how Mercer describes the film *Territories* as not simply about the Nottinghill Carnival, but exploring the complexities and political meanings of 'representing' this popular event by its performative and reflexive mode of address. He writes:

> The choral refrain of – 'we are struggling to tell a story/a history, a herstory' – underlines the fact that its story does not arrive at a point of closure, and this deferral of any authoritative resolution ... implies that the spectator shares active responsibility for making semantic connections between the multiaccentuated elements of the image flow ... Of the many readings the film allows, it can be said that *Territories* is a film about black identity ... because the ambivalence of its images ... is directional; its multiaccentuality is strategically anchored to sense of location in order to raise questions about the dialectics of race, class ... gender, and sexuality. (Mercer, 1994, p. 60)

Mercer valorizes the 'creolizing' or 'hybridizing' tendencies of Black film by its capacity to (re)appropriate elements from dominant master-codes, and attempts to implicate the audience in the performative moves of Black film towards the production of new languages of the representation of black subjectivity. While he adroitly recognizes the significance of the audience in his dialogical conceptualization of Black film, the critical function of these texts is seemingly determined by their innovative aesthetic representational strategies. It raises the question of whether it is only the formal experimental and avant-garde qualities of Black film which enables the possibilities of new representational practices of otherness to emerge? The danger of setting up a dichotomy between the new 'experimental' workshop sector (as non-realist, formalist, and avant-garde), against the earlier moment of Black film as 'conventional' or the independent production sector as more 'mainstream' (ostensibly realist, linear with narrative closure etc.) has been recognized (McCabe, 1988; Williamson, 1988). Mercer too, refuses to set up such a dichotomy within Black film when he insists that both moments

> are implicated in a critical dialogue with the discourses and representations whose power and hegemony they contest. The point was ... to historicise the shared problematic in which black film-makers have struggles to 'find a voice'. (1994, p. 74)

Parenthetically, it can be noted that Gilroy (1989/90) in his call for a 'popular modernism' for understanding Black cultural productions claimed contentiously that a meaningful Black audience does not exist for the avant-garde films of the workshop sector. Mercer's (1990) response accused Gilroy of advancing a populist class-based agenda which homogenizes Black communities, trades on notions of authenticity and reproduces the burden of representation for Black practitioners. It is possible to read the debate between Gilroy and Mercer in terms of their divergent attempts to locate the political *effects* of Black cultural productions. In a crude polarization of their positions, arguably Gilroy wishes to situate these effects firmly in terms of 'mass' Black audiences, while Mercer considers a key critical function of experimental Black film as operating in, and attempting to transform the Eurocentric cultural spaces that Black practitioners find themselves working in. How it functions in other spaces and audiences for Mercer, is similarly contextually determined and cannot be simply known in advance in terms of a pre-given Black 'working-class' audience. Mercer does not claim that experimental Black film is liberatory, while the independent sector is still caught up in and determined by the dominant regimes of representation. Such a line of reasoning would assume that the critical function of these texts operates outside of any socio-cultural context – as if performative avant-garde Black films simply 'do' political work by innately possessing a radical cultural praxis. Mercer does still appear to privilege a 'diaspora aesthetics' of 'montage', 'brico-lage' and 'hybridization' in defining the new representational strategies of Black film, even if they are not considered to be exclusively deter-mined or articulated by a modernist Euro-American formalist practice found in experimental films.[5] What Mercer fails to do is adequately address the ambivalent politics of the 'popular' in relation to Black cul-tural productions. (This omission will be taken up in the final section of this chapter when examining British-Asian films.)

When we consider Black film as a deconstructive practice which articulates a 'minoritarian politics', its critical function becomes most apparent and productive (and without it being reduced to relying solely on formalist or avant-garde aesthetic strategies). This approach begins by acknowledging that the 'restricted economy of ethnic enun-ciation' (Julian and Mercer, 1988) is symptomatic of the marginality of Black subjects and their cultural productions within a hegemonic culture. But this marginalization is not governed by fixed centre/ margin power relations. Rather it is the binary structure itself in the hegemonic boundary maintenance of majority/minority relations which appoints Black subjects to a subordinated racialized subject-position (for example, through the process of stereotyping) that becomes the site of cultural struggle.

Mercer recognizes that while Black cultural practices remain a marginal activity, their de-marginalization is occurring at a time when the 'centred' Eurocentric discourses of cultural authority and legitima-tion are becoming de-stabilized and de-centred – and this has been commonly understood as a 'postmodern crisis' of Western cultural hegemony, (or alternatively as a 'crisis of race' – Chapter 3). Black film is characterized as a 'minor cinema' in the following way by Mercer:

> as it expands and gets taken up by different audiences in the public sphere, it becomes progressively de-marginalized, and in the process its oppositional perspectives reveal that traditional structures of cultural value and national identity are themselves becoming increasingly fractured, fragmented and in this sense decentred from their previous authority and dominance. (1994, p. 74)

It is through an appropriation of Bakhtin's theory of 'dialogicism' in relation to questions of national formation that marginality is recon-sidered in the practice of Black film (see also Willeman, 1994). The expressive cultural politics of Black film embodies a 'critical dialo-gicism' that not only reveals the binaristic relations of hegemonic boundaries, but actively seeks to undermine and overturn them by proliferating 'critical dialogues' both within and across the various 'imagined communities' of the nation (Mercer, 1994, p. 65). These critical dialogues open up questions of the multiple differences of gender and sexuality as well as 'race' and class in relation to the discursive formation of both national and diasporic identities.

Mercer employs the term 'hybridization'[6] for discussing the transformative nature of Black expressive practices:

> the project of hybridization as 'something happening to the English whether, they like it or not,' the point is to recognize that black cultural politics becomes hegemonic to the extent that it affects and involves not only black people, but white people as well. (1994, p. 26)

He points to the possibility that the normative status of whiteness may be disrupted in the de-centring of majority/minority relations, which is most intensely experienced in the 'potential displacement of nation as the basis of collective identity' (p. 27). In Chapter 1, it was maintained that the impossibility of full national representation haunts discourses of multiculturalism. The incongruity between identity-differences and the national space is predicated on the series of inclusions/exclusions that operate in nation formation. It is this very terrain that diasporic Black film traverses in contesting hegemonic national culture. As Mercer writes, 'the national peculiarities of Britain's post-imperial condition provided unique conditions of possibility for diasporic ways of seeing that sought to move beyond "nation" as a necessary category of thought' (p. 24).

Paul Willeman has further elaborated an understanding of the national specificity of Black British film by considering it vis-à-vis a Third Cinema framework. It is useful to examine Willeman's position as it can be read as deploying a nascent minor politics. While Black film does not neatly fit into a Third Cinema schema, it still can be conceived as a 'diasporic cinema' that builds on and interrogates the conventions of Third Cinema (Shohat and Stam, 1994). From the mid-1980s the discourse of Black film gained a greater degree of coherence in terms of the questions being asked about where it ought to be located, and how it should be understood, as a cultural production (Ross, 1996). As Ross notes, situated as a counter and oppositional political practice in the 'developed' West, a concordance was coveted alongside the militant film-making of other 'developing countries'/'Third World'. The expression 'Third Cinema' originally emerged from the revolutionary cultural politics and film-making of Latin America in the 1960s (Gabriel, 1989). One of the principal characteristics of contemporary Third Cinema 'is really not so much where it is made, or even who makes it, but rather, the ideology it espouses and the consciousness it displays' (p. 40). The evolution and meaning of the Third Cinema is of course complex, and the account presented by Willeman (1994) remains one of the most accomplished in respect to extending our understanding of Black film in Britain, and the concomitant questions of cultural marginality and difference.

Willeman usefully identifies two key characteristics of Third Cinema: (i) its status as 'research category' – an 'experimental' or 'imperfect' cinema. A practice which is in constant need of adaptation in order to resonate with the changing social processes and social struggles; and (ii) Third Cinema in contrast to mainstream cinema

attempts to speak a socially pertinent discourse [and] ... seeks to articulate a different set of aspirations out of the raw materials pro-vided by the ... complex interactions and condensations of which shape the national cultural spaces inhabited by the film-makers as well as their audiences. (1994, p. 184)

Willeman holds onto a notion of Third Cinema as not being located outside the West, though he is equally keen to ensure that different filmic practices across the globe are not homogenized under the label of Third Cinema. He brings to attention two con-ceptual elements to assist making the analysis of Third Cinema films more discernible and culturally specific. Firstly, he draws on the Bakhtinian term of 'chronotopes [as] ... time and space arti-culations characteristic of particular, historically determined conceptions of the relations between human, the social and the natural world, that is, the ways of conceptualizing social existence' (Willeman, 1984, p. 189). It allows films to be understood in terms of their spatio-temporal features which structure different narrative possibilities and evoke a life-word that is outside of the formal aes-thetic qualities of a text. It is not so much the issue of whether films using 'Western', avant-garde or mainstream aesthetic strate-gies are acceptable as Third Cinema texts, but rather *how* particular deployments of time-space relations produce alternative, possibly counter-hegemonic ways of experiencing reality.

Drawing upon a chronotopic analysis, Willeman maintains that Black British film

> can be seen as organising time-space relations differently from ... dominant ... British cinemas, and this complex differentiation from its immediate industrial-social-cultural context is a more pertinent (over-)determining process than, for example, any reference to black African cinema. Moreover, within black British cinema, there are further important distinctions to be made between films drawing on Asian and on Caribbean cultural discourses and histories. (p. 190)

His claim for a more distinctive analysis to be made of Third Cinema texts focuses on the specific filmic language deployed and the socio-political and national cultural context these films inhabit. (The next chapter will highlight how popular British-Asian films project a spatio-temporal life-world inflected by a diasporic South Asian cultural presence in Britain.) Not only can this rupture exclusivist narratives of 'race' and nation that seek to marginalize minority groups, but it offers alternative pedagogic possibilities for re-imagining (racialized) *British* identities. Nevertheless, Willeman advances an understanding of Black film which presupposes a deconstructive *pedagogic* function, but gives insufficient attention to their site-specific performative effects.

Willeman however, does stress the related question of 'the national' in his characterization of Third Cinema. This issue has customarily been framed for films of 'Third World' countries promoting a discourse of national liberation against forces of (neo-) colonialism for the creation of a new national culture. Willeman connects this to a Third Cinema in Britain, beginning from the critique of a liberal multiculturalism which insists on the discreteness of 'othered' ethnic groups existing in bounded cultural zones within a nation-state. While avoiding an essentialist standpoint, he highlights the importance of the notion of cultural specificity in relation to the extent that national socio-cultural formations determine particular (filmic/artistic) signifying practices. At stake here is the separation of a discourse of nationalism (which is an imperial political project) with the issue of national specificity. As Willeman points out, Black film is able to articulate a British specificity outside of a debilitating racialized nationalistic discourse. (Hall's argument for the New Ethnicities has made a similar assertion.) Furthermore, Willeman urges that we should not confuse the concern with national identity with the specificity of a cultural formation for understanding how Third Cinema films work.

'The specificity of a cultural formation may be marked by the presence but also the absence of preoccupations with national identity. Indeed, national specificity will determine, which, if any, notions of identity are on the agenda' (1994, p. 210). His contentions characterize Black film practice as interrogating alternative narratives of British national specificity undergoing profound cultural transformations, by expressly invoking the disruptive presence of *diasporic* identities.

Willeman's account of Third Cinema recognizes that many of these texts (especially Black British film), operate from a position of 'otherness'. We can note that he echoes Bhabha's (1994) position, when he draws upon a Bakhtinian notion of liminality and cultural difference, and relates it to the practices of Third Cinema. Willeman points out that Third Cinema is made by intellectuals who as film-makers seek to achieve in their work 'the production of social intelligibility' (1994, p. 200). And its pedagogy of producing a social intelligibility for cultural difference is fulfilled through the accession of a 'creative understanding' from a position of marginality or 'outsideness'. That is, 'one must other oneself if anything is to be learned about the meanings of another culture, of another culture's limits, the effectiveness of its borders, of the areas where … "the most intense and productive life of culture takes place" (Bakhtin)' (Willeman, 1994, p. 214). For Willeman, it follows that the position of outsideness of Third Cinema arises because of a consequence of its 'non-belonging' and 'non-identity' to the dominant culture. It does not mean that these films' site of enunciation is simply exterior to this culture, rather 'it is possible to be "other" in some respects and to be "in and of" the culture at the same time, the fact remains that it is in this disjuncture, in this in-between position, that the production of social intelligibility thrives' (p. 201).

The condition of liminality as a site of social intelligibility where new ways of understanding and knowing are engendered is commensurate with Bhabha's 'third space' of cultural/border difference (which is to be anticipated as both theorists rely on a Bakhtinian framework). We need not rehearse the problem of conceptualizing outsideness as a site of agency predicated upon a 'lack', which may lead to proscribing the singular politics of alterity as discussed in Chapter 2. Although relying on a perspective of border difference does not readily invalidate Willeman's insightful claims (as he is attempting to establish an agency for the other). Rather, it is the basis upon which his claims operate upon that are limiting. Instead of concluding that the condition of cultural hybridity or liminality 'as a positional necessity is the precondition for a critical-cultural practice in Britain, as witnessed by the work of black film-makers' (p. 201), we can rework the contentions of Willeman and Mercer through a Deleuzo-Guattarian practice of a 'minor politics' (Rodowick, 1997) for further understanding the expressive cultural politics of Black film. Moreover, this framework will be applied to popular British Black (South Asian) films, a cinema which both Mercer and Willeman have not addressed.

British-Asian film

The motives for selecting specific British-South Asian films are principally two-fold. Firstly, these manifestly 'popular' films have appealed to diverse multi-ethnic, transnational audiences; and secondly, their subject matter of so-called diasporic South Asian 'culture and identity' resonates closely with the recognition of a (new-found) multicultural diversity in Western nations.

Over the last two decades, a significant number of British-South Asian films have been produced by the 'independent' sector, and partially financed by terrestrial television such as Channel Four and the BBC, in addition to organizations like the British Film Institute. In many respects these independent films can be considered also as 'semi-commercial' productions (Malik, 1997; 2002). Furthermore, a handful of these films such as *My Beautiful Laundrette* (1985), *Bhaji on the Beach* (1993), and more recently, *East is East* (1999) and *Bend It Like Beckham* (2002) have achieved 'mainstream' box-office success, as well as receiving international acclaim. What makes them distinct as minority film practice is not only that they explore a diasporic 'Asian' cultural identity in Britain, but that they mainly draw on popular narrative and fiction formats, particularly a comedic genre. In terms of their aesthetics of representation, they appear to articulate a range of 'popular pleasures', rather than operating as formalist 'pedagogic' works which explicitly employ experimental or avant-garde strategies.

While these films appear to be more 'conventional' in their representational form (in comparison to experimentalist intercultural cinema), they do not rely on countering or inverting 'negative' Asian stereotypes that circulate in dominant culture. We shall find that what makes these films politically 'ambiguous' and even 'risky' is that they do not resort to employing a naïve social-realist perspective, or attempt to exhaustively represent and tell the 'whole truth' about Asian culture – a demand for ethnic authenticity. At the same time though, their use of 'popular' film genre and language means they also operate ambivalently within, as well as struggle against, the master-codes of 'race' and ethnicity.

My Beautiful Laundrette written by Hanif Kureishi was the first independent British-Asian film to gain relative commercial success in terms of appealing to a more 'mainstream' audience, rather than being confined to the art-house sector.[7] It has proved to be an emblematic example for highlighting the ambiguities of both the expressive politics and reception of these texts.[8] *Laundrette's* 'unconventional' story-line focussed on a youthful gay love affair between a white, working-class ex-fascist and a more middle-class Asian male. Partly through the genre of comedy as well as narrative fiction, *Laundrette's* iconoclastic quality contested the limited repertoire of stereotypes about Asians without being determined by the discourse of positive images. Hall argued that the film raised controversy because of 'its refusal to represent the black experience in Britain as monolithic, self-contained, sexually stabilized and always ... and only positive' (1988, p. 30). Kureishi himself commented on the need to confront the complexity of identity formation and forgo the *idealization* of 'minority culture'.

> If there is to be a serious attempt to understand Britain today, with its mix of races and colours, its hysteria and despair, then, writing about it has to be complex. It can't apologise or idealise. It can't sentimentalise and it can't represent only one group as having a monopoly on virtue. (Kureishi, cited in Hall, 1988, p. 30)

It could have been anticipated that *My Beautiful Laundrette* would be subject to sharp polemic. Contrary to Hall and Kureishi, Mahmood Jamal considered the film as caricaturing and reinforcing stereotypes of Asians 'for a few cheap laughs'. He wrote:

> What is surprising about the film is that it expresses all the prejudices that this society has felt about Asians ... that they are money grabbing, scheming, sex-crazed people. It's not surprising therefore, that it was popular with European audiences. It says everything they thought about us, but were afraid to say. (1988, p. 21)

For Jamal, the film's distasteful liberalism makes the viewer sympathize with the 'paki-bashing' white unemployed youth, and the sexual relationship between the two gay protagonists occludes the social contradictions of a racist British society. Moreover, it projects a neo-Orientalist perspective by dangerously setting up a simple dichotomy between Asians who 'assimilate as goodies. Those who don't and carry on with their "dirty habits" are the baddies' (p. 21).[9]

It has been argued that Jamal's objections rest largely on 'reading' *My Beautiful Laundrette* in a conventional social-realist manner. Julian Henriques maintained that,

> the success of the film was that it breaks with a realist tradition. The souped up laundrette and the rest of the film were to me a fantasy expressing the feelings, contradictions and imaginations of the characters, rather than any attempt to reflect reality ... [W]hat the imaginative contradictory world of *Laundrette* points to is the possibility of change. It is only when reality is taken up as being full of contradictory tendencies and forces ... can there be any place for struggle. (1988, p. 19)

A problem however remains that while Henriques's claims are compelling for moving beyond the straight-jacket of realist strategies for exploring questions of racial and cultural difference in Black artistic practices, it does not displace a possibility that films such as *Laundrette* still can be read in 'realist' terms by a range of audiences. Nevertheless, this does not simply validate the claims made by Jamal and negate those of Henriques. One is tempted to conclude that gauging the film's politics is therefore a matter of judgement or interpretation, but what remains crucial is the context and grounds on which this takes place (Chapter 4). Henriques's legitimate demand for displacing the problematic of realism, which delimits the representational politics of Black film, is made in relation to acknowledging the distinctiveness and autonomy of Black artistic practices in exploring *new* languages of representation. While he does not attend to the question of audiences (cf. Williamson, 1988), we should avoid reducing the politics of representation to a question of realist/non-realist aesthetic practices for Black film (Young, 1996), or think that 'mainstream' audiences are incapable of reading 'non-realist' texts. It is evident that Jamal's negative evaluation of Laundrette for propagating negative stereotypes is caught up within a realist problematic, but it also too quickly forecloses a more profound question of the *representational* politics of a racialized 'Asian' culture in Britain.

'Authentic' Asians

The signifier 'Asian' in Britain has become a popular umbrella term for more specific identifications predicated on overlapping national, regional, or religious social groupings of the South Asian diaspora. An account of the genealogy of the term 'Asian' is too complex to delineate here, although according to Harry Goulbourne (1993) it has been principally an imperial/colonial construction originally used to describe certain groups from the Indian subcontinent (and sought to distinguish between 'Europeans' and 'Africans' in a tripartite racial categorisation).[10] Within colonial discourse, the usage of 'Asian' was founded upon a racial-geographic characterization, but it is notable, as Robert Young (1995) points out, that racialized identities have always been articulated by, and imbricated with, culture.

The identity-category 'South Asian' has been specifically othered in terms of being imbued with an excess of 'culture', and its particular mode of racialization has been played out through an *Orientalizing* discourse (cf. Said, 1978).[11] Said cogently argued that colonial operations of power produced and legitimated how 'the West' has come to conceptualize and construct the figure of the 'Oriental' as an absolute other.

> The Oriental was linked ... to elements in Western society (delinquents, the insane, women, the poor) having in common an identity best described as lamentably alien. Orientals were rarely seen or looked at: they were seen through, analysed not as citizens, or even people, but as problems to be solved or confined, or – as the colonial powers openly coveted their territory – taken over. (Said, 1978, p. 207)

The discourse of Orientalism installs a regime of truth which produces the Orient as a object of knowledge. This process of 'othering' is animated by a complex interweaving series of essentializing stereotypes such as an eternal, authentic and unchanging culture, mystical religiosity, the 'feminine' exotic, irrational, pathological and disorderly.

In relation to the production of knowledge of South Asian identity, the multifarious regional, linguistic, religious, class and gender differences have been homogenized and essentialized, leading to caricatured and culturalist descriptions of post-colonial South Asians in Britain. Asian patriarchy, cultural conflict and identity crisis within the pathology of the Asian family have been the dominant representations of Asian culture (Lawrence, 1982; Parmar, 1982). Institutional, academic and popular discourses of Asianess seek to tell the 'truth' about these identities – their plethoric 'culture' – through the master trope of *ethnicity*. Asianess as wholly other (alien) appears to lie outside of the civilizing processes of modernity. Its absolute ethnic otherness has been traditionally constructed as 'pre-modern', unassimilatable and in opposition to British cultural values and a modern way of life. The fixity of Asian culture in post-war Britain has been personified by the popular thesis of a 'second generation' of Asian young people experiencing a crisis of identity because they are 'caught between two cultures' (Parmar, 1982).

More recently, a greater visibility and positivity has been attached to the signifier 'Asian'. In contrast to an earlier period of 'invisibility' in the spaces of the public sphere and popular culture (Sharma, 2006), it has increasingly become difficult to ignore the rise of a range of differentiated Asian cultural practices in the realms of art, music, film, fashion, comedy and literature that claim a legitimacy and presence in British culture. For example, the rise of a 'new Asian dance music' in Britain and its global impact (Sharma *et al.*, 1996), has led to artists such as Talvin Singh and Nitin Sawhney receiving international acclaim. Likewise, the BBC television comedy sketch shows, such as *Goodness Gracious Me* and *The Kumars at No. 42*, have been celebrated as a new wave of multicultural entertainment.[12] Conceived in terms of their *British*-Asianess, these cultural productions not only appear to challenge the racial exclusivity of national identity, but also seem to contest notions of an essentialist Asian identity burdened by a primordial ethnicity. It is notable that the visibility of new 'hybrid' Asian culture occurred during the moment of a tacit acknowledgement and approval of a multicultural diversity in Britain. A Blairite Labour government has embraced a liberal agenda that endorses the *cultural* contributions and influences of abiding minority cultures for adding to the richness of an evolving Britishness (*The Guardian*, 20/02/1999).[13]

The celebratory constituents of multiculturalism such as the impact of popular Asian dance music or the declaration that the 'Indian Curry' is Britain's national dish (*The Guardian*, 31/10/1999) hardly designates that Asian culture has been finally liberated from its Orientalized status. The recognition of all things 'multicultural' cannot be divorced from the concurrent intensification of the fetishization of ethnic otherness in contemporary Western culture. The very formation of Western modernity is intimately tied to the colonial processes of othering cultures prescribed as 'non-western' (Said, 1978). The fetishized consumptive relationship to these cultures has ranged from 'disavowal' (annihilation, violence, abjection and fear) to 'desire' (domination, fascination, appropriation and spirituality). What we are witnessing now, fuelled by the expansion of global consumer capitalism, is the acceleration of a fetishized commodification of ethnic otherness (see Chapter 3). The charged terrain of global popular media culture has proved to be a pivotal site for advancing this process. The ubiquitous pop-star Madonna's conceited appropriation and vacuous aggrandisement of 'Eastern culture' (Kalra and Hutnyk, 1998), exemplified a contemporary multicultural moment of neo-orientalism which inaugurated a new found fascination and idealization of what can be labelled as a 'postmodern hybrid' ethnic authenticity. Mercer (1999/2000, p. 56) identifies this process as 'a new and wholly unanticipated predicament of "hypervisibility."'

The new found hypervisibility and popularity of 'hybrid' Asian fashion, music and comedy, summed up by the specious label 'Asian Kool' (created by a style media, especially magazines like *The Face* and *i-D*) signifies a splitting of Asian cultural representation in terms of a 'postmodern hybrid' against a traditional, ossified culture.[14] For example, talented musical artists such as Talvin Singh and Nitin Sawhney, or writers like Meera Syal and Hanif Kureishi received popular critical *recognition* primarily because of their syncretic ability to draw upon 'Eastern' and 'Western' cultural elements. These new hybrid forms of Asianess are seen to represent a kind of (usually middle-class), 'kitsch' or 'avant-garde' in dominant culture: fashionably and effortlessly fusing translatable elements from the 'East' with a 'modern' Western way of being. They are considered at the cutting edge of cultural innovation (while leaving behind the discordant untranslatable elements of their 'traditional' and unassimilable parental culture). It is notable that such forms of hybridity, especially the bodily consumption of style, fashion and jewellery, are highly gendered, and continue to echo the Orientalist desire for exotica (Puwar, 2000). Assimilatory hybridity is celebrated because it represents a kind of 'postmodern future' of mixing and fusion, different cultural elements coming together and creating something novel in Western culture. Ossified cultures are abandoned, boundaries are fractured as new multicultural practices and hybrid identities enter into the *smorgasbord* of contemporary culture. Such an idealized assimilatory Asian hybridity fails to address the grounds on which the political antagonism and dissonance of cultural difference are played out in a racialized dominant culture. Arguably, it still remains regulated by a neo-Orientalist discourse of 'postmodern' ethnic *authenticity* (Banerjea, 2000; Sharma, 2003).

Chow (1998) takes issue with the current hypervisibility and idealization of otherness which is represented 'through mythification ... no matter how prosaic or impoverished, as essentially different, good, kind, enveloped in a halo, and beyond the contradictions that constitute our own historical place' (p. xx). This idealism is anchored in processes of (epistemological) violence, domination and appropriation, and is present in contemporary academic discourses such as cultural studies, as well as the terrain of popular culture. It effectively proscribes the articulation of the alterity of the other. Chow highlights that the current enthusiasm for celebrating 'minority' artistic practices neatly fits in with the pedagogical tenet of teaching about 'other cultures' operating in liberal multiculturalism. While these works and the identities of artists that produce them are complex and multi-faceted, they are still 'primarily identified as targets of "ethnic" information' (p. 99). She contrasts this with the stark absence of not hearing about the 'ethnic origins' (and we can add, the 'hybridity') of iconic white figures such as Madonna or Bart Simpson.

More specifically in relation to film, the reception of the diverse range of texts made by 'minority' film-makers are primarily defined in terms of being 'ethnic films' and often reduced to the pedagogical function of trying to discover their ethnic origins. Chow does not want to deny the right for 'minority' practitioners to explore their own histories, rather she highlights how these works are circumscribed and contained by dominant culture. This is in contrast to the normative status of white Western texts and identities which are unfettered in their universalist pretensions, and unencumbered by ethnic particularity.

> In terms of the conventions of representation, the West and its 'others' are thus implicitly divided in the following manner: the West is a place for language games, aesthetic fantasies, and fragmented subjectivities; the West's others, instead, offer us 'lessons' about history, reality, and wholesome collective consciousness. This division has much to tell us about the ways 'ethnicity' functions to produce, organize, and cohere subjectivities in the 'multicultural' age. (Chow, 1998, p. 100)

She makes an interesting theoretical juxtaposition of the significance of ethnicity in the age of multiculturalism against Foucault's argument about the discursive construction of sexuality in Western culture. The discourse of ethnicity is compared to that of sexuality which has prolifically circulated in society, yet was considered to be something repressed in need of liberation. Ethnicity is now also a 'repressed truth' which needs to be revealed through processes of confession, (auto)biography and storytelling. The marking of subordinated ethnic identities do have a subversive potential in relation to a politics of recognition, and similarly, the recognition of new hybrid ethnicities disrupt exclusivist accounts of national identity. Nevertheless, their institutional and popular mobilizations also can lead to a disciplinary subject formation. Chow inquires:

> Would it be far-fetched to say that precisely those apparatuses that have been instituted for us to gain access to our 'ethnicities' are at the same time accomplishing the goal of an ever-refined, ever-perfected, and ever-expanding system of visuality and visibility, of observation and surveillance, that is not unlike Bentham's Panopticon ... which Foucault used to summarize the modern production of knowledge? (p. 102)

Chow alerts us to the hypervisibility of ethnically marked identity-differences in a globalizing multiculture. The panopticist interrogating gaze of an invisible 'multicultural ethnicity apparatus' demands that the other narrate the truth about themselves – in our case, vis-à-vis the binarism of a 'pre-modern traditional' or 'postmodern hybrid' Asian identity – which is invariably framed by the question: 'How *authentic* are you?' (Chow, 1998, p. 103, my emphasis). It suggests that in a racialized dominant culture, the representation of Asian-Otherness is an 'im/possibility', but does it follow that the 'Other' can never escape this problem of representation?

'Minor-popular' British-Asian film

I have maintained that an alterity pedagogy needs to innovate alternative practices other than only the interpretation and judgement of a text. There is a need to move beyond only examining the content and meaning of cultural representations, (see Chapters 3 and 4). The exigency of such a practice becomes most evident in relation to the question of the representation of the other; and this is not an abstract ontological question of the im/possibility of knowing the other. If a contemporary multicultural gaze produces 'Asian cultures' as both hypervisible and ethnicized knowable objects (outside of the operations of power and historical struggles that produce them), a pedagogic practice seeking to reveal the differences or explicate the complexities of Asianess can never simply succeed. A pedagogy attempting to transgress or overturn Orientalist representations and stereotypes of Asianess invariably promotes a counter-positive imagery or exposes the racialized structures of representation. (Indeed, the utility of both strategies should not be dismissed out of hand.) However, the problem is facing the im/possibility of representing Asian otherness outside of racialized multicultural regimes of representation: Can Asianess be 'known' or represented beyond a primordial or 'hybrid' authentic ethnicity? How can we understand the representational practices of popular British-Asian film in confronting this issue? Even a radical pedagogy which seeks to complicate or pluralize Asian identities and culture – presenting the multiple identity-differences across Asianess as one way of reading and using these films – is not a *solution* to the problem of representing otherness. The accretion and multiplication of representations does not necessarily escape extant neo-Orientalist frameworks of cultural knowledge which return the multiplicities of Asian culture back into a prior structure of representation – as an *authentic* ethnic-other. The supposedly radical cultural content and complex meanings of British-Asian film do not ensure that these texts escape the problem of racialized representation.

While one can 'neither deny or escape the structuring force of identity and difference, self and other' (Kawash, 1998, p. 132), turning to the practice of a 'minority discourse' opens up the possibility of writing an agency for the other and articulating an *alter*-representational politics of alterity (JanMohammed and Lloyd, 1990). Deleuze and Guattari's (1986) study of *Kafka* as a 'minor literature' has been influential for formulating the constitutive characteristics of a minority practice. Firstly, these theorists argue that 'a minor literature does not come from a minor language; it is rather that which a minority constructs within a major language' (p. 16). They refer to the 'deterritorialization of language' by a minor practice which works within and against dominant culture. The second characteristic is 'the connection of the individual to a political immediacy' (p. 18) which stresses that individual concerns are always imbricated with other social forces and political operations of power. The final characteristic of a minor literature is that 'everything takes on a collective value' (p. 16). A writer is inseparable from the membership of the variegated communities s/he addresses. Their work seeks to break down the division between production and consumption as it expresses a politicized immediacy, which urges an involvement and response – 'a collective enunciation' – from its readers. While the account offered by Deleuze and Guattari can appear too schematic, it offers a useful way of characterizing a deconstructive Black film practice that operates within a dominant culture (cf. Rodowick, 1997; Naficy, 1999).

When we turn to the specific practice of a 'minor cinema' the problem of representation is made explicit. For Deleuze, the basis of 'minor cinema' is when 'the people no longer exist, or not yet ... *the people are missing'* (cited in Rodowick, 1997, p. 153). This cryptic remark relates to how a 'minority' is conceived in Deleuzo-Guattarian terms. It is not ascribed as a numerical or demographic aggregate of the majority. Rather, the minority is what deviates from the 'standard model' (norm or 'constant') which defines the majority. As Deleuze and Guattari maintain: 'The problem is never to acquire the majority, even in order to install a new constant. There is no becoming-majoritarian; majority is never becoming. All becoming is minoritarian' (1987, p. 106). In this respect, the minority is a state of 'becoming', an operative active relation which has the potential to deterritorialize the norm. The standard model that defines the majority does not pre-exist for the minority. Deleuze elaborates:

> One might say the majority is nobody. Everybody's caught ... in a minority becoming that would lead them to unknown paths if they opted to follow it through. When a minority creates models for itself, it's because it wants to become a majority, and probably has to, to survive ... But its power comes from what it's managed to create, which to some extent goes into the model, but doesn't depend on it. A people is always a creative minority, and remains one even when it acquires a majority: it can be both at once because the two things aren't lived out on the same plane. (1995, pp. 173–4)

He recognizes the definable state of a minority in relation to the majority model, that is, what is regulated by the discourse of a representational identity politics. But a minoritarian politics differs from the majoritarian standard in terms of a qualitative difference in the exercise of power: the creative deterritorializing power of a *collective* becoming as opposed to that of stratification and domination. The assertion of a minor cinematic practice in relation to a 'missing people' refers to the failure of representation (and representational identity politics) – the unrepresentability of the 'excess' or alterity of the other (see Chapter 2). It is 'a people' that exists or are actualized by a collective minoritarian-becoming. As Rodowick suggests, a minor cinema is not based on a unified or unifying minority discourse or identity politics, rather it 'must produce collective utterances ... whose paradoxical property is to address a people who do not yet exist and, in doing so, urge them toward becoming' (Rodowick, 1997, p. 154).

A minor cinema is not necessarily constituted in terms of an avant-garde or formalist practice,[15] though it is useful to identify a specific kind of minor film practice as 'fabulation' (Rodowick, 1997), a quality which popular British-Asian film under analysis here shares. Rodowick points out that the Deleuzian notion of 'fabulation' is essentially 'a storytelling function' which is related to a minoritarian collective enunciation. However, it is not a form of narration that is determined by a regime of truth and representation – what Deleuze refers to as 'truthful narration'. Conventional documentary, ethnographic or fictional cinema embodies a truthful narration in its transcendental perspective and objectifying gaze of others by relying on the 'truth-producing power of representation' (Kawash, 1998, p. 133). We have seen that contemporary multicultural representations have heightened an 'Occidental' desire to tell the truth about ethnic otherness vis-à-vis the trope of authenticity. In contrast, the performative function of fabulation seizes the 'power of the false' which does not seek to represent the truth of others or of 'the people', but 'wants to free fiction from the model of the true ... of the colonizer' (Rodowick, 1997, p. 160). Fabulation displaces a realist/non-realist problematic of representation framed by a traditional truth/falsity ideological distinction, because the 'power of false' refers to the discursive production of truth. Moreover, as Deleuze asserts: 'the production of truth involves a series of operations that amount to working on a material – strictly speaking, a series of falsifications' (1995, p. 126).[16]

The political function of fabulation offers the possibility of actualizing or 'inventing a people' (other than that of an ethnicized Other) – a people that are 'missing' which cannot be represented by dominant culture (Kawash, 1998). As a fragile and speculative creative process, fabulation requires an active mobilization in order for it to evade a hegemonic power which attempts to limit and co-opt its forces of becoming. The practice of minority artists therefore is significant in their role as 'intercessors', as Rodowick indicates:

> The task of a minority artist ... is to serve as an intercessor: to create or invent a minority discourse as the basis of a collective enunciation. The postcolonial filmmaker must not only disarm the harmful fictions of colonization ... but also contribute to the invention of a people by creating new forms of subjectivity and collective enunciation apposite for a postcolonial ... idea of nationhood. (1997, p. 160)

The minority practitioner as intercessor is significant for exploring the alterity of the other in new multicultural post-national spaces. However, collective enunciation only occurs if it is able to break down and initiate a transformation in the identity relations of self/other, majority/minority or dominator/dominated. The performative function of fabulation therefore is not governed by a singular narration (of the film-maker or the intellectual), as this is liable to produce a truthful narration of the other or be contained by the dominant discourse. Instead,

> the filmmaker must establish a free indirect relation with a minority intercessor. This means constructing a narration between two points of enunciation where author and subject continually exchange roles so that their relative positions become indistinct or undecideable. In this way the narration passes between them as 'a reflected series with two terms' each of which falsifies the other. In this encounter, the intellectual's discourse is deterritorialized in one direction, and the minority subject's in another. Both become-other in the creation of a new minority relation. (Rodowick, 1997, p. 162)

The function of fabulation in its potential to activate a collective becoming-minoritarian has been used to analyse minor cinema which is considered distinct due to its creative experimental form (though not necessarily avant-garde or formalist), for example, in political African cinema; and it could equally be applied to the British work of *Sankofa* and *Black Audio Film Collective*. But it will be argued in the next chapter that the more popular independent British-Asian films such as *Bend It Like Beckham* and *East is East* also do not possess a single point of narration, though this is more to do with their politically ambivalent dialogic mode of articulation, rather than an experimental strategy of multiple narration. If we read Black film (including popular British-Asian productions) in terms of a minor cinema, its critical practice does not merely seek to challenge racialized representations by positing the complexities and multiply identity-differences of minority groups. Rather, Black film's expressive cultural politics may also activate and intensify a becoming-other (for example, a 'becoming-Black' or '-Asian', as well as a becoming-white), in its transformative potential to disrupt hegemonic national culture in which whiteness is naturalized and ex-nominated (Chapter 3). However, we should guard against conceiving Black film as essentially a deterritorializing practice, because its performative effects are always site-specific and respond to existing norms. Although it still may be considered as a 'privileged' site to explore minoritarian-becomings, because it 'names a singularity of deterritorializing sites and movements' (Nealon, 1998, p. 134).[17]

Nevertheless, we have found that the theoretical work on both Black British film and minor cinema appears to suffer from implicitly valorizing artistic practices which embody a modernist aesthetic. The aesthetic value of these productions is conceived in terms of their ability to break with the normalizing representations of dominant culture in order to introduce 'newness'. It is notable that in the accounts of Black film by both Mercer and Willeman, while maintaining that these films are grounded in everyday culture, a tendency persists in presupposing these films do *pedagogical* work in the production of new alternative knowledges to effect social change. The problem is, that the postulated radical cultural praxis of 'experimental' Black film remains couched in a modernist framework of understanding (the aesthetics of the text). This understanding has been exacerbated by the limited critical analysis of films using more popular representational strategies.

One of the motives for selecting British-Asian films for exploring an alterity pedagogy is because they uniquely work in a contemporary multicultural representational arena of the 'popular'. In Chapter 3, it was maintained that the affective investments of students inhabit the spaces of popular media culture, and a pedagogic practice can begin from these sites if we are to try and articulate students towards new forms of ethical agency. These British-Asian films are popular cultural productions through their consumption by 'mass' audiences, though more specifically, because of the everyday cultural 'content', significations and vernacular filmic languages they employ. Moreover, it becomes apparent that films like *Bend It Like Beckham* and *East is East* are politically ambiguous (risky) texts precisely because they operate in the contested arena of popular culture.

Popular culture has been considered a subordinate space for the articulation of the experiences, pleasures, memories and traditions of a variety of marginalized groups in society (Hall, 1992b). But as Hall points out, popular culture has become

> the dominant form of global culture, so it is at the same time the scene par excellence, of commodification, of the industries where culture enters directly into the circuits of a dominant technology – the circuits of power and capital. It is the space of homogenization where stereotyping and the formulaic mercilessly process the mater-

ial and experiences it draws into its web, where control over narratives and representations passes into the hands of established cultural bureaucracies ... It is rooted in popular experience and available for expropriation at one and the same time. (p. 26)

From a Bakhtinian perspective, Hall does not consider popular culture in terms of binary oppositions such as 'authentic versus inauthentic' or 'resistance versus incorporation'. Once such a move is made, it liberates us from thinking about popular culture in terms of the degree of oppositionality or incorporation into the (capitalist) mainstream and hegemonic culture. Rather, popular culture dialogically operates in a complex contradictory terrain that is an on-going site of (and for) struggle – a multiply inscribed, unstable domain in which different meanings, values and affects combine, confront and repel each other. Moreover, this is not an abstract site of struggle, but takes place in particular arenas of daily life. It means that popular culture can mobilize resistances and oppositions to hegemonic representations and oppressive structures, or be complicit with them, depending on how it is *articulated* with other formations and practices in a specific historical situation, and by particular social groupings (Grossberg, 1993). The embattled arena of popular culture does not lead to a political indeterminacy, but forces us to consider it in terms of a minor politics: how it is able to negotiate and make available new polyvocal spaces, and whether existing configurations of power are contested and disrupted.

The distinctiveness of popular British-Asian film is that its 'minor' status is precariously imbricated with the contradictory arena of the *popular*. Conceived now in terms of *minor-popular* film, these diasporic texts can offer a deconstructive practice of hegemonic culture in their potential to open up radical polyvocal multicultural spaces. Hall has highlighted that the diasporic conditions of production of Black popular culture means that it is always impurely constituted,

the product of partial synchronization, of engagement across cultural boundaries, of the confluence of more than one cultural tradition, of the negotiations of dominant and subordinate positions, of the subterranean strategies of recoding and transcoding, of critical signification. (Hall, 1992b, p. 28)

As a minor-popular practice, these British-Asian films should not be conceived as a critical project only in terms of their 'hybrid' aesthetic practices or modalities of production. While it allows us to delineate the specificities and singularizing qualities of these films as *diasporic minor texts*, it does not reveal anything concrete about how they actually function politically (say in, a teaching situation). Nealon rightly argues against considering any Black cultural productions as (modernist) aestheticized projects in their deterritorializing *effects* because it neglects their social specificities. He writes:

> There is no liberatory deterritorializing – no freedom or transforma-
> tion – per se; only site-specific, more or less forceful imbrications of
> form and content that can respond to – disrupt and reinscribe –
> existing norms. Deterritorialization, if it happens, always happens in
> a specific context, in response to a specific content. (Nealon, 1998,
> p. 136)

By moving beyond textual appreciation and aestheticized interpretations of Black cultural productions, we are left with the 'interven-
tionary force of specific transformations ... the production of concrete
effects' (p. 137). But what makes performative texts such as *Bend It Like
Beckham* and *East is East* pedagogically significant is how they come to
utilize, and what they do with already existing, stereotyped and
Orientalized representations of Asian culture and identity. In other
words, the deterritorializing potential of these films is located in
their ability to 'institute difference' (Buchanan, 2000) in and against
dominant culture. Given that these films work with over-determined
racialized signifiers of Asian ethnicity circulating within popular
culture, how they institute difference – their singularizing force – is
what can make them politically meaningful.[18] This difference would
not necessarily be a creation of the 'new' in a modernist sense, but is
constituted by a multiplicity in terms of the minoritarian-becomings
these films are able to activate. Their status as popular texts however,
means that the expressive cultural politics of these films are likely to be
ambiguous and contested. It suggests that the ways in which they are
deployed and 'struggled with' in a specific teaching situation becomes
a critical site for an alterity pedagogy.

6
Diaspora Pedagogy: Working with British-Asian Film

In the previous chapter, a pedagogic distinction was stressed between Black film as embodying a deconstructive critical practice, and the actual site-specific performative effects of these texts. It is not just a matter of utilizing these films in a teaching situation with the assumption that they will successfully move students to new sites of non-appropriative ethical agency. Given the ambiguous status of films such as *Bend It Like Beckham* and particularly *East is East*, even when they are deployed as minor-popular texts, there are no guarantees that they are capable of producing 'positive' ethico-political outcomes. These 'semi-commercial' films are significant because unlike experimentalist Black/Intercultural cinema, they make visible and solicit representations of Asianess through ostensibly popular film forms and languages. Their contestable politics of representation result in interpretations and judgements crossing ideological fault-lines, and invariably leading to disagreements over textual meanings. The expressive cultural politics of these films makes them distinctive for an alterity pedagogy – the ethical potential to intensify forces of a minoritarian-becoming. These texts remain politically ambivalent however, as they may produce reactive affects which close down the creation of ethical alliances. The condition of ambivalence should not be confused with *a priori* textual judgements over the ambiguity of (polysemic) textual meanings. As argued in Chapter 4, what gives rise to contestable meanings for racialized texts in the age of neo-liberal multicultural globalization needs to be reckoned with from a 'materialist' standpoint.

The first part of this chapter elaborates the earlier claims made about British-Asian film as minor-popular texts by examining *Bend It Like Beckham* as a notable example of this 'genre'. It offers a reading of the film's representational and expressive politics in order to explore the contention that this type of cinema is ambiguous because it operates in the contradictory racialized terrain of popular multiculture. The goal is not to dwell on a particular ideological interpretation of *Bend It Like Beckham*, but rather to establish that conceived as a minor-popular text, it is capable of constituting a site of investigation that articulates the multiplicities of a diasporic Asian expressive culture. The reading of *Bend It Like Beckham* is not figured on merely advancing a critique, but more in terms of how the film could be put to use in a teaching situation. While the performative effects of the film are not knowable in advance, how the text attempts to institute a politics of Asian alterity remains a key concern.

East is East is also examined in-depth, and a key motive for its selection is because of a significant populist appeal as a so-called 'culture clash' comedy. In comparison to *Bend It*, an anti-racist ideological reading of *East is East* is likely to condemn the film for circulating neo-Orientalizing stereotypes of South Asian (Muslim) culture (see Nobil 1999/2000). While the expressive cultural politics of *East is East* are ambiguous, it will be maintained that the film can be deployed as a *minor-popular* text – as a contested site of collective enunciation that has the potential to disrupt and make redundant essentialist representations of both 'Asian' and 'British' culture, or at least raise these issues for scrutiny. Moreover, as part of the project of *Multicultural Encounters*, *East is East* was used in my own university teaching practice. It enabled an analysis of the film's performative effects, (even though difficult to map in practice). *East is East*'s deployment explored realizing a tactical rhizomatic reading praxis (Chapter 3), which attempts to take up and activate the connections and affects the film engenders, rather than instructing students to focus only on interpreting the text for its (suspect) ideological meanings.

The presentation of the analysis of *East is East* in an actual teaching situation interrogates how a pedagogy for alterity may, or may *not*, work in practice. I offer it as a site-specific example for grappling with the difficulties of undertaking an alterity pedagogy. The intention is not to try and naively verify the operations of an affective rhizomatic pedagogy, or somehow faithfully demonstrate that students have been successfully rearticulated to new sites of ethical agency through a process of becoming-minoritarian. It is unlikely, if not impossible, that such site-specific multifarious processes can be empirically represented or authenticated; and this issue goes beyond the question of devising an appropriate research methodology (cf. Scheurich, 1997). Nevertheless, it is possible to momentarily grasp selective elements and fragments of these complex processes of affective knowledge-production by analysing student interactions (dialogue) and written responses. Thus, claims made about the film's site-specific performative effects need to be situated contingently in terms of the un/representability and un/knowability of a classroom pedagogy.

Bend It Like Beckham

Anyone can cook aloo gobi, but who can bend a ball like Beckham? (Jess)

The director of *Bend It Like Beckham* (2002), Gurinder Chadha, is one of few successful British-Asian film-makers. Her varied work, such as *I'm British But ...* (1990), *Bhaji on the Beach* (1993), *What's Cooking* (2000) and *Bride and Prejudice* (2004) have attracted international critical acclaim.[1] In comparison to other 'low-budget' films such as *La Haine* and *Menace II Society* (Chapter 3), Chadha's films are significantly more populist and arguably, cinematically 'inferior'.[2] Her output has increasingly shifted towards gaining commercial appeal, especially with the offering of *Bride and Prejudice*. It was *Bend It Like Beckham* however, which gained Chadha international recognition and commercial success. The film received a nomination for a Golden Globe Award (Best Musical or Comedy), as well as winning 17 other awards.

The plot of *Bend It Like Beckham* revolves around the female character, Jess Bhamra (Parminder Nagra), a 17-year-old British-Asian West Londoner obsessed with playing football. Her parents are oblivious to such sporting interests, and expect Jess to attend university and pursue a 'respectable' profession which is valued amongst South Asian communities (such as a medical doctor or a solicitor). While maintaining her studies, Jess regularly plays football with a group of males in her local park. She is befriended by Jules (Keira Knightley), and a subplot of the film plays on a supposed lesbian relationship between them. Jules belongs to the Harrington Harriers, an amateur female football team, and Jess quickly establishes herself as one of its star players. The male coach, Joe (Jonathan Rhys-Meyers) considers both Jess and Jules to be exceptionally talented, and encourages them to purse a professional career in the USA female soccer leagues.

Jess acts as the dutiful daughter and has to keep her football playing hidden from her parents. The central tension of the narrative, as well as the film's source of humour is centred on Jess surreptitiously pursuing her dream to become a professional player against the ostensibly 'traditional' demands of her parents.[3] Jess's mother (Shaheen Khan) is deeply troubled by her lack of interest in acquiring home-making skills such as cooking, in order for Jess to one day make a 'good Indian wife'. In comparison to Jess, her sister, Pinky (Archie Panjabi), displays conventional, stereotyped feminine behaviour and desires, such as shopping for clothes, marriage and domesticity. She has no comprehension as to why Jess is so interested in playing the masculine sport of football. Somewhat in contrast to the rest of the family, the father (Anupam Kher) is more sympathetic to Jess's enthusiasm for football. Although he does not approve of Jess pursuing any kind of footballing career, especially because of his own experience of racism and exclusion in British sport (as a once talented cricketer before migrating from Kenya). He also disapproves of Jess establishing a romantic involvement with her white coach, Joe. But after watching Jess play in a qualifying match, he comes to realize how serious Jess is, as well her extraordinary sporting talent. The film ends by her father reconciling with Joe, and making the rest of the family understand that they need to grant Jess the opportunity to study in the USA while pursuing a professional soccer career.

If it was not for the populist appeal of *Bend It*, the film could have easily come across as over-burdened with a variety of social issues: arranged/love marriages; generational conflict; acceptable femininities; the transgressions of an inter-racial relationship; lesbian/gay sexuality; maintaining 'traditions' of Asian culture vis-à-vis the preservation of female family 'honour' (*Izzat*), coupled with the fear of the 'Westernization' of Asian female youth; and in addition, the spectre of racism limiting life-choices. Chadha has indicated that she purposefully picks what she perceives as 'taboo subjects' in exploring Asian female subjectivity in Britain (Stuart, 1994). Some of these social issues are considered as 'taboo' because they can remain unspoken within Asian 'communities' due to a double-bind of certain patriarchal values operating within the context of a dominant racist white culture. The problem is that public discourses available to explore these issues exist in racialized social spaces. The actual repressive socio-cultural practices which attempt to prescribe fixed roles and modes of behaviour for Asian females are de-historicized in Western discourses of the other, which has lead to Asian women being represented as the helpless passive victims of an oppressive Asian patriarchy (Parmar, 1982; Puwar, 2000). Complex and contested issues such as arranged marriages, generational conflict and female honour are liable to be ethnicized and reduced to the preserves of an authentic Asian culture. Such issues form a significant part of potent popular representations in the neo-

Orientalist construction of contemporary Asianess. The danger is, as Bhattacharyya and Gabriel have pointed out, that Chadha's films may replicate 'common-sense assumptions about "diasporic" Asian culture' (1994, p. 59). Given the still relatively limited repertoire of Asian imagery in the mainstream media, it is a risky venture for any film-maker to focus on issues that may reinforce and further promulgate neo-Orientalist tropes of an Asian culture supposedly founded upon backward and unchanging patriarchal values.

Chadha avoids (rather than opposes) depicting a patriarchal South Asian family environment or a despotic father, which have been common stereotypes of such families (as present in *East is East*). In some respects, the generational tensions between Jess and her parents are those experienced by many young people, irrespective of ethnicity. The director tries to offer a nuanced representation of the family, which is sympathetic to the parents as well as celebrating Jess's autonomy and self-determination. Chadha's authorial intent depicts a young British-Asian female who is neither alienated from her South Asian 'roots', nor British culture. The familiar 'clash between cultures' thesis of young South Asians unable to negotiate their traditional home environment with the modern British (white) ways of life, is contested from a multi-layered perspective which seeks to de-essentialize both such reductive racialized ideologies.

Bend It's story is outwardly told through an accessible film language and populist modes of address (particularly through the use of music and comedy). Its social issues are tempered throughout with comedy ranging from acute irony to farce. As in the case with Chadha's other films such as *Bhaji on the Beach*, *Bend It* comes across as easily recognizable to varied audiences by being 'part soap opera ... part romantic comedy, while also borrowing from the British realist tradition and Bombay popular cinema' (Malik, 1997, p. 212). Chadha has insisted that her work operates in the 'mainstream', along with it being especially accessible to, and resonating with, diasporic Asian communities (Bhattacharyya and Gabriel, 1994). However, while the film centres on an Asian family, a materialist reading locates the site of 'freedom' for Jess as structured by an in/visible whiteness, expressed most readily through the two main white characters, Jules and Joe. Chadha may be merely reflecting contemporary multi-racial mixing and friendships found in a cosmopolitan London, though the pressure to pander to a mainstream market by including significant roles for white actors is not unique for 'minority' films explicitly marked by their ethnicity. Nevertheless, the site of racial and sexual freedom for Jess ultimately lies in USA, which is symptomatic of a globalized multicultural capital-ism (Chapter 3). Jasbir Puar and Amit Rai argue the USA is constructed as the site of salvation for racial others:

> unlike Britain, the United States promises for Jess an acceptance for her browness along with an escape from her conservative familial home and extended neighbourhood community ... In short, the United States symbolizes opportunity, escape and reconciliation of the clash of cultures. It purports to be a safety valve for the unyield-ing racism, sexism and homophobia of other places. (Puar and Rai, 2004, pp. 75–6)

This points to *Bend It* being an ambiguous text. On one hand its ide-ological leanings legitimately wants to explore the multiple differences, contestations and resistances of Asian female subjectivity in a racist Britain, yet its popular filmic language of expression appears to operate on a terrain which can readily Orientalize Asianess. The film does not work from an avant-garde practice that actively seeks to create new lan-guages of representation outside of existing hegemonic cultural know-ledges. Neither does *Bend It* follow the highly aestheticized strategies and complex narrative structures of experimentalist Black/Intercultural cinema which formally deconstruct racialized binaries and stereotypes that essentialize minority cultural representations (Chapter 5). Rather, the 'minor politics' of *Bend It* more or less works inside the contradic-tory and ambivalent terrain of the popular in attempting to articulate an Asian alterity in dominant culture. According to Malik, the style and genre of Chadha's films 'render redundant those critical discourses which depend on rigid dichotomies of Black versus White, negative versus positive, representative versus non-representative, realism versus fantasy and so on' (1997, pp. 210–11). Her films eschew positing one-dimensional positive images of Asian women or culture. On the con-trary, they avoid idealizing Asian female subjects, and try to offer a critique of Asian patriarchy outside of the Orientalist dichotomies of tradition versus modernity. As Chow has remarked, such a critical prac-tice is an 'arduous task, implying as it does the need to work negatively on those who are already bearers of various types of negation' (1998, p. xxi).

Chadha's films explore Asianess by interrogating the politics of gender in the contested spaces occupied by South Asian communi-ties. The question of 'belonging' and 'home' for these diaspora communities has been central to negotiating their post-colonial displacement and marginalization (Brah, 1996; Bhatia, 1998). Although, as Bhatia maintains, the narratives of 'home' and 'community' – often articulated as 'tradition' – are riven with contradictions, and often deleterious to femininity and womanhood:

> even as it contests the dominant discourses of nationhood and borders, the grounds on which communities defend the homeland and assert their cultural identities assume patriarchal cultural traditions as the norm ... They perpetuate women's systematic subjugation and are detrimental to their position in a racist society where stereotypes of 'Asian' women abound and affect their subjectivities. From a gendered position, therefore, the homogenized discourse about the 'homeland' becomes a contested terrain and assumes a fractured identity that questions these narratives, as they are, out of particular conditions of displacement. (1998, p. 512)

'Asian' fabulation

There is no easy way of exploring female subjugation in an Orientalizing context, and on a few occasions, *Bend It* attempts to raise these complex issues which results in a rather 'heavy-handed' approach. Some of the scenes mirror the laden dialogue and character behaviour found in the 'realist fiction' of television soap operas. For example, in an important qualifying match Jess is sent off for retaliating against a player calling her a 'paki'. Joe later consoles her by declaring 'I'm Irish, I know how you feel.' It is not simply the case that the scene is 'unrealistic'; rather its dramatic qualities lack subtlety. Nevertheless, this is not always a limiting aesthetic to the expressive cultural politics of the film, because its multiple modes of address can complicate and problematize the Orientalist drive to tell the 'truth' about Asian culture. Moreover, there is a reflexive quality present in *Bend It* that is aware of the difficulty in a popular filmic exploration and representation of the intersectional post-colonial politics of race, gender, sexuality, class and religion.

In a scene in the Harrier's changing room, Jess is asked by another player, whether her parents are aware of her playing for the team:

Jess: Nah, my mum and dad ain't got a clue
Mel: Where do they think you are?
Jess: That I've got a job at HMV
Mel: Blimey, that's not on
Jess: Indian girls aren't supposed to play football

Mel: That's a bit backward, ain't it?

Jules: Yeah, but it ain't just a Indian thing is it? I mean, how many people come out and support us?

Mel [to Jess]: So are you promised to someone then?

Jess: Nah, no way. My sister's getting married soon – it's a love match

Mel: What does that mean?

Jess: It's not arranged

Other player: So, if you can choose, does that mean you can marry a white boy?

Jess: White – no. Black – definitely not. A Muslim – eeh euh! (gestures a finger cutting across her throat)

The scene seemingly invokes a set of common assumptions about 'Asian' culture, though does not offer idealized counter-representations. The question of the lack of acceptance of 'Indian girls' playing football is 'universalized' by Jules, when she points out that such prejudices are not limited to Asian communities. (This is particularly evident from Jules's experience of her own mother, who is aghast by her own daughter's lack of heterosexual feminine virtues.) The changing room scene also touches on the thorny question of 'inter-racial' marriage and differential acceptance of other ethnic groups amongst certain Asian families. Chadha highlights such dubious practices through 'everyday banter', rather than raising it as an issue to be resolved.

While *Bend It* employs a popular and familiar filmic language of representation, its register of address questions the exigency of a unitary 'truthful' narration about Asian culture. The film's performative function of fabulation (Chapter 5) can articulate a dialogic point of enunciation for the viewer. We find that this mode of storytelling is set up right from the opening scenes of the film. *Bend It* begins by the display of the film credits being accompanied by the commentary of a football match. To British audiences, the voice of John Motson's commentary would be immediately familiar. The match is between the real-life teams of Manchester United and Anderlecht, and Motson's commentary focuses on the skills of the world-class player, David Beckham (Jess's hero). The credits disappear and we see the actual game in play. We first encounter the film's protagonist, Jess Bhamra, by her startling presence in the Manchester team – a diminutive-looking Asian female in comparison to the other male players. But Jess scores a superb goal with a header from a ball crossed by Beckham. The

United supporters are in a state of frenzied cheering and Motson celebrates Jess's footballing prowess. The scene cuts to the studio of Match of The Day (the premier BBC television football programme). The panel, made up of the real team of the show, lavish praise on to Jess and conclude she will be a star of the future. The main host (ex-England player, Gary Lineker) then unexpectedly turns to Jess's mother on the panel (who has been out of sight to the viewer). He assumes she is proud of Jess's achievements, but instead, the mother is disgusted by her antics and publicly admonishes Jess (in mixture of English and Punjabi), much to the bemusement of the host and the rest of the panel. The scene seamlessly shifts to the bedroom of Jess, conjoined by the continuity of the mother's scolding, now aimed at Jess for inanely viewing football videos of Manchester United. The bedroom is strewn with football paraphernalia, especially posters of (the shaven-headed) David Beckham. Jess's mother can only respond with anguish: 'Your sister's getting engaged, and you're sitting here watching this skin-head boy!'

We need to acknowledge that *Bend It* cannot escape being involved in the production of the contemporary hypervisibility of Asianess. In its efforts to resist telling the truth about Asian culture, or at least complicating it, the film's plot, social issues and characters are still ethnically marked by a racialized dominant culture. The endeavour to explore Asian alterity without being regulated by a neo-Orientalist discourse – the dichotomy of a 'primordial-traditional' or 'postmodern hybrid' authentic ethnicity – is an immanently difficult project. *Bend It* struggles not be contained by the binarism of hegemonic Orientalist discourse, as the film explores other possibilities of Asianess to be articulated. When Jess meets her friend Tony in the park, she is in tears after her parents have effectively prohibited her from playing for the Harriers team:

> Jess: It's out of order! Anything I want is just not Indian enough for them. I mean, I never bunked-off school to go daytimers [disco's] like Pinky or Bubbly. I don't wear make up, or tight clothes like them! They [parents] don't see all those things.

Even in this condensed dialogue, the contestations of Asian tradition and acceptable forms of femininity are both raised and problematized in a manner which resists positing an external critique of seemingly contradictory 'Asian values'. The performative ambiguity of the character of Jess interrupts, though does not necessarily deny, possible normative conclusions about Asian culture: that young Asian women are simply 'caught between two cultures'; or at best, actively negotiate between them as hybrid diasporic subjects. (To conclude that cultural negotiation is the condition of hybrid Asian subjects can too easily reduce it to one of choice, rather than grasp the complexities of racialized agency and the multiplicities of Asian culture.)

What counts as 'Asian culture' and 'tradition' in *Bend It* is not critically deconstructed (as often found in experimental Black/Intercultural Cinema). Rather, it is literally played with in the film, often through a comedic mode. For example, Jules's mother, is comically exposed for her exoticization of Jess and stereotyping of Asian culture – 'I made a lovely curry the other day' – much to the embarrassment of Jules who appears to be more at ease with Jess's marked ethnicity. The dichotomy of tradition versus modernity is also humorously challenged during the engagement ceremony of Pinky and Teetu (Kulwinder Ghir) at the Bhamra home. The living room is filled with attentive guests, and during the ritual, a mobile phone ring-tone disturbs the austere occasion. A line of elderly Asian women sitting on an adjacent sofa clad in their South Asian party attire, simultaneously reach for their phones buried in their handbags. To their dismay, the ringing phone is Teetu's (who proceeds to answer the trivial call while in the middle of his engagement ceremony).

An 'English' film

Chadha reflecting on her films has provocatively maintained that they are: 'very English ... Britain isn't one thing or another ... There are endless possibilities about what it can be – and is – already (cited in Stuart, 1994, pp. 26–7). Labelling *Bend It* as an English film open ups the interstitial spaces of Britishness and Asianess to other possibilities of a multicultural post-national formation. While the film's assimilation into a commodified 'Bollywood' global culture is difficult to ignore (Puar and Rai, 2004), to claim an 'Englishness' for *Bend It* invites audiences to question the cultural construction of national and diasporic identities.

The film is set in Hounslow, a suburb of West London near Heathrow airport. It is an area which is symbolically associated with South Asian (especially Sikh-Punjabi) settlement. The Bhamra's live in an idyllic suburban street, lined with semi-detached housing and green spaces. But they appear to live in a residential area which is predominantly white rather than Asian. During the wedding ceremonies of Pinky, bright lights adorn the outside of the house and it becomes a site of conspicuous Asian celebrations with numerous social gatherings. Their household is frequently displayed from an aerial point of view in the film, and stands out against the relatively quiet homes and gardens of the surrounding white neighbours. The quintessential 'English' suburb exists as a white space in the national popular imagination, and the presence of the Bhamra household lays a claim to this space from a de-territorializing minoritarian standpoint which is constructed from 'within' the majoritarian culture.

The affirmation of a diasporic South Asian presence and an opening up of the possibilities of reconfiguring national specificity is evident by *Bend It*'s everyday affective aesthetics. These are most expressive in the film's self-conscious deployment of music and comedy. Chadha's filmmaking is recognizable for uniquely mixing both 'hybrid' British-Asian pop and music from South Asia, alongside contemporary urban sounds. The shifting sounds of both 'Asian' and 'non-Asian' instrumentation, rhythms and vocals over familiar scenes of urban high streets, parks and football fields seek to invoke an alternative post-national imaginary. At the heart of the *Bend It*'s musical score is a syncretic soundtrack, involving artists ranging from Bally Sagoo, Malkit Singh, Nusrut Fateh Ali Khan, Melanie C and Victoria Beckham. British-Bhangra music features significantly in the film, which itself has recently evolved from North Indian folk music styles and its form has mutated through being influenced by black dance music genres – making it a uniquely diasporic expressive culture. The music has been a significant site for Asian youth's contested positionality in relation to a culturally hostile and exclusionary British nation. This does not necessarily prevent Bhangra from being 'othered' by neo-Orientalist discourses, though its development as an urban soundtrack of a contemporary multi-racial Britain makes it increasingly difficult to assign it to the margins of British culture (Sharma, 2006). One of the principal means by which *Bend It* shifts its registers of address is through the use of music. During many of the sites explicitly marked by an Asianess (the home, wedding and high street) in comparison to rest of the outside world (especially the football field), the soundtrack incessantly alters between 'Asian' music and contemporary urban sounds. Although, the sonic marking of music as 'Asian' and 'non-Asian' becomes increasingly difficult to sustain, for example Bhangra becoming British urban music. The film's narrative embodies the multiplicities of cultural hybridization through its musical aesthetics, making possible a range of affective (minoritarian) responses, some of which may mobilize Britishness and Asianess to be experienced differently.

ians

ve success of *Bend It* amongst mainstream audiences, along with other films such as *Bhaji on the Beach, East is East* and *My Beautiful Laundrette*, does not lie much beyond the supposition that they are principally considered as 'British-Asian' *comedies*. Notably, these films integrate comedy in their narratives, 'a mode of address not generally associated with cinematic representations of race' (Malik, 1997, p. 212). Moreover, for these texts to work successfully as comedies in the 'mainstream', they must be able to speak to and resonate with a (British and trans-) national popular imagination. This however, immediately faces the difficulty that historically Asians have been figures of intense ridicule in Euro-American popular culture. In particular, British Television comedies like *Ain't Half Hot Mum* and *Mind Your Language* attained both popularity and notoriety by propagating derogatory racial stereotypes (Cohen and Gardiner, 1982).[4] The perceived ethnicized differences of Asians (strange foods, exotic rituals, feeble physicality and absurd accents), have been subject to particular representational strategies – a derisory racialized humour emerges from the fixing of these differences as being absolutely 'other'.

The recent celebration of the hit television comedies such as *Goodness Gracious Me* and *The Kumars at No. 42*, along with the other popular British-South Asian films, indicates not only a visibility but also a place for Asian representation in the national imaginary from an ostensibly minoritarian 'perspective'. Chadha has claimed that her 'films have comedy in them to wrong foot people, to disrupt their expectations and make them think differently' (cited in Stuart, 1994, p. 26). We should not underestimate the significance of members from subordinated groups having the means to control the production of their comedy (Littlewood and Pickering, 1998). Nevertheless, it can not be known in advance whether white audiences are now laughing along *with* 'minorities' or still *at* them. The social function of minority-based comedy is invariably double-edged: as a mechanism of social control and further subordination of marginalized groups; or, as a way of negotiating, resisting and subverting racialized discourses of power. The risk remains that *funny* Asians are prescribed to an ethnicized othered status, rather than empowered to refashion spaces in the public sphere by creatively exploring everyday social relations from a perspective of difference. While acknowledging that the strategy of comedy is ambiguous, Chadha's films have been noted for using 'English' (working-class) humour. She has acknowledged the influence of English comedy, particularly from the genre of *Carry On* films (Stuart, 1994; Bhattacharyya and Gabriel, 1994). If *Bend It* offers a potential to reconfigure the grounds of national specificity, its deployment of 'English' comedy appears to be pivotal for a deterritorializing practice. While it is difficult to characterize exactly what makes English comedy *'English'*, it is still possible to demonstrate how *Bend It* is able to draw upon this cultural form and deploy it otherwise in claiming the legitimacy of a *British-Asian* post-national multiculturalism.

Anthony Easthope (1999) makes a useful attempt to identify some of the key constituents of English comedy. English humour both relies on, and figures in, the 'negative' of classic oppositions of 'serious/silly', 'truth/pleasure' and 'fact/fiction'. While *Bend It* deals with social issues, its comedy potentially averts a mode of storytelling as the 'truthful narration' of the other, because the film operates also in the realms of 'silliness', popular pleasures and fantasy. However, the risk and political ambiguity of comedy is that these oppositions can also be overlaid with other racialized binaries such as white/ black, mind/body and intelligent/stupid etc. Easthope maintains that, amongst other things, English humour involves 'the use of irony' and 'a tendency towards fantasy and excess' (p. 163). He acknowledges that these features appear in other national cultures, though are more condensed in English humour. We can note that humour in Asian popular culture, such as in Bollywood film, heavily relies on fantasy and excess, and particularly the inordinate visuality of comedy.[5] Moreover, in the British case, the humour of fantasy and excess is most apparent in 'working-class' forms of comedy. It makes fun of the pretentiousness of middle-class life or aspirations, and attempts to acknowledge the 'fact of the body (sexual, excreting, eating)' (p. 176).[6]

It is unsurprising that Chadha cites the influence of *'Carry On'* films, as this genre has been celebrated for expressing this kind of lascivious class-based comedy (Gray, 1998). *Bend It* is littered with sexual humour, especially via femininity and the female body. Comedy of this kind is not the preserve of working-class Englishness, the film also indulges in risqué Punjabi (female) humour, replete with sexual innuendo. During the engagement celebrations of her older sister, Pinky at the Bhamra home, Jess performs the dutiful daughter-hostess role, serving 'Indian sweets' to the guests, many of whom are relatives. On these occasions it is likely that the younger sibling will be publicly cross-examined for her non-marital status. Jess is ridiculed for still being single by her 'aunties':

> Auntie: It will be your turn soon, aay? Do you want a clean shaven boy like your sister, or a proper Sikh with a full beard and turban? [Laughs mockingly as Jess attempts to turn away] ... Aay! It's only our men who have a big engine and a full MOT! [Raucous laughter amongst the women]

Bend It also uses humour to question (heterosexual) hegemonic femininity, particularly in relation its idealization. The film purposefully celebrates the sporting female body, with many scenes lingering over the physique and skills of the players of the Harriers football team.[7] The viewer's first encounter with Jules is with her mother in a shop selling women's underwear. While Jules heads towards the sports section, her mother fails to convince Jules of the virtues of a 'push-up' bra with inflatable inserts: 'all the girls have bought one ... oh no not the sports' bras dear, they don't enhance.'

The clothes Jess wears most of the time, loose baggy sports wear, contrasts sharply to those worn by the feminized Pinky (and her female friends). In a dressing scene involving both sisters, their mother and a seamstress, Pinky insists that her wedding outfit tightly fits around her chest, in order to accentuate her curves – much to the approval of her mother. Jess, on the other hand, wants no such kind of apparel.

> Seamstress (measuring Jess): ... bust 31 ...
> Jess: No, it's too tight. I want it looser
> Mother: Dressed in a sack – who's going to notice you? Tori toh shape hone che diya?
> Seamstress (to Mother): Don't worry Suki-ji, [pointing at Jess's breasts] in one of our designs, even these mosquito bites will look like juicy, juicy mangoes!

Bend It's sexual politics seek to contest the confines of an 'appropriate' femininity for both Jess and Jules through humour. Nevertheless, its ideology of sexual difference is open to further contestation in terms of how lesbian sexuality is utilized as a central narrative device, but ultimately remains marginalized. After prying relatives mistakenly spot Jess being overtly affectionate with Jules in the street, Jess's parents conclude that their daughter is a lesbian, which would bring disrepute upon the family.[8] Similarly, Jules's mother who considers soccer as wholly unfeminine, also believes her daughter is a lesbian after eaves-dropping upon a heated conversation between the young women (who are actually arguing about being romantically involved with their coach, Joe).

The film's humour explores how Jess and Jules are subjected to the force of a heterosexual matrix (Butler, 1990; 1993a). The strictures of femininity are not just confined to an Asian family in the film, as Jules is also forced to negotiate her femininity against her mother's hetero-sexual values. However, from a critical ideological standpoint, the film sidesteps an exploration of the representation of lesbian (South Asian) sexuality, and the tacit lesbianism between Jess and Jules remains unspoken. According to Gayatri Gopinath 'the film ... renders its brand of liberal feminism palatable through a strategic containment of queer female sexuality' (2005, p. 128). As reported in subsequent interviews with cast members, a lesbian story-line between the two main protagonists was originally planned, but in the final narrative it is reduced to a source of innuendo and humour. The repressed les-bianism of the text may lend itself to reinforcing it as a deviant sub-jectivity in the face of the continuing hegemony of heterosexuality in popular South Asian/British culture. Although, the film's heightened polyvocality – through its ambiguous use of difference and humour – does not mean that such a reading is the only one available, or it is a matter of advancing a de-facto counter-hegemonic reading of the film's sexual politics. *Bend It Like Beckham* was one of two films selected for the 'Outstanding Film' category in the 15th Annual Gay & Lesbian Alliance Against Defamation (GLAAD) Media awards in Los Angeles. Nonetheless, it still would be naïve to ignore the film's suspect heterosexual racial politics, even though such a nomination does highlight its contestable representations and polyvocality.

The point of offering a deconstructive reading of *Bend It* is not to admonish the film's sexual or racial politics. Rather, it is to valorize the grounds upon which a critical pedagogy could be performed. One of the intentions of the film's representational strategies was to promote a diversified set of identities which pluralize Asian subjectivity, outside of a discourse of positive/negative images. A pedagogy exploring the film's politics of identity, nevertheless may legitimately conclude that the repressed lesbianism of the film was more than a missed opportunity for opening up the identity-differences of minority South Asians. The film failed to productively explore lesbian sexuality at a discursive level, and perhaps even buttress a heterosexual matrix. Moreover, by offering such a critique, a critical pedagogy could further deconstruct South Asian subjectivities by opening up the question of non-normative racialized sexualities. The utility of the text, is not only dependent upon its own ideological ambivalences and 'shortcomings', but also how a pedagogic critique of the film can further intensify interrogations of identity and difference.

A purely deconstructive reading practice is unable to grasp that the hegemony of identity and representation continues to govern and displace an encounter with the film's alterity politics. The pedagogic critique of *Bend It*'s repressed lesbianism is thus symptomatic of the problematic of the logic of identity and representation, which is unable to account for the excess of difference (see Chapters 2 and 5). It is not the case that a deconstructive pedagogy of identity will be ideologically flawed in the reading of *Bend It* in some way or another. Rather, such a practice will find it difficult to animate a pedagogic encounter with South Asian *alterity*. The cultural studies' pursuit of highlighting the multiple identity-differences of South Asian subjects or deconstructing their identities by pluralizing or complicating differences, such as accreting hybridities or valorizing a lesbian subject-positions, does not necessarily undermine the structure of Orientalism which continues to govern how the Asian subject is encountered as an ethnicized object of knowledge. In other words, to declare that South Asians possess complex, multi-layered hybrid identities, crossed by differences of class, gender, sexuality, religion etc. remains tied to a neo-Orientalist discourse: the demand for the *truth* about Asianess. It is from this kind of understanding and limit, that I explore an alternative practice of an alterity pedagogy with the film *East is East*.

Teaching with *'East is East'*

Sanjay: Why do you think most of the reviews label *East is East* as a 'British' comedy?
Student (white male): Well … it's a *funny* film, ain't it?

In comparison to *Bend It Like Beckham*, comedy is the defining feature of the film *East is East* (1999). This film received prolonged standing ovations at the Cannes film festival, and was critically acclaimed at the Edinburgh film festival before its cinematic release. It was directed by Damien O'Donnell (first feature for this new Irish director) and the screenplay written by Ayub Khan-Din. *East is East* was adapted from Khan-Din's own successful play which appeared in London's Royal

Court – a semi-autobiographical account of his 'racially-mixed' family growing up in 1970s Britain. The film was hailed as the best British comedy in recent years. It was a surprise box-office hit, and has been compared favourably with other recent successful low-budget British productions such as *Trainspotting, The Full Monty, Lock, Stock and Two Smoking Barrels,* and *Billy Elliot (The Guardian,* 6/01/2001).

East is East is set during the early 1970s in North Manchester, a largely white 'working-class' area in the north-west of England. It centres on the conflicts between a father, 'George' Khan and the rest of his family. George, migrated to Britain in the 1930s from Pakistan and has been married to Ella for 25 years, a white English woman from Yorkshire. They run a chip shop together and have seven children. The story revolves around the disharmony and hostilities arising from George attempting to arrange marriages for his sons against their wishes. Nazir, the eldest on his wedding ceremony flees the scene in front of a full congregation of relatives and guests. Consequently, Nazir is disowned by George who has to bear the shame of an errant son publicly rejecting 'Pakistani-Muslim' cultural traditions. The second son, Abdul is far more accommodating than his older brother, and acquiesces to his father's authority. Tariq, the third eldest son, is rather rebellious and secretly has a white girlfriend (Stella). He detests the idea of having an arranged marriage, and regularly sneaks off to the local disco where he is known as 'Tony'. In contrast, Maneer is shown to be a practising Muslim, the only member of the family who has embraced his father's faith. Tariq especially dislikes Maneer's fearful conformity, and frequently calls him 'Gandhi' in a derogatory manner. Saleem, the fifth son, is a 'hippie' foundation art student, though appeases his father by pretending to be studying the more acceptable vocational subject of engineering. Meenah, the only daughter, is a loud and strong-willed young girl who favours playing football than demurely wearing 'Asian' dress on special family occasions. She shares, alongside her brothers, a fear and loathing of their father's rampant authoritarianism, reflected by all of them privately referring to him as 'Ghengis'. Sajid, the youngest member of the household appears amusingly as permanently cocooned in an unwashed 'Parka' jacket, and is often tormented by his elder siblings.

East is East's central story-line unfolds in a relatively straightforward manner. George Khan's gay son, Nazir after rejecting his arranged marriage ends up working in a fashion boutique with his male lover. The public humiliation causes George to be even more determined that his next two eldest sons should follow their father's 'cultural tradition'.

156 Multicultural Encounters

Unknown to Abdul and Tariq, George arranges their marriages with the daughters of a Bradford butcher, Mr Shah. Much of the narrative of the film is structured by the antagonism building up between George and his increasingly estranged family, which explodes eventually in scenes of brutal domestic violence. He becomes frustrated at his wife's lack of enthusiasm for their two other sons being married, as Ella believes they too like Nazir, will become alienated and leave home. The resistance to George's demands results in Ella receiving a horrendous beating. We see the father gradually lose control of his family and threaten them with violence to conform to his will. It is only near the end of the film, after a disastrous meeting with the prospective in-laws (the Shah's), that the rest of the family finally unite and stand up to his patriarchal authority and violence. Ella orders George to leave the house, and he breaks down pleading that he wanted only 'to help', but it is to no avail. The film ends on a reconciliatory note however, with Ella finding a tearful George alone in the chip shop the following morning. It seems that the vanquished George has realized that he cannot control the destinies of his children. Ella offers him a cup of tea, which the remorseful George gladly accepts.

The plot of *East is East* engages with a complex set of social issues, primarily through a dramatic comedic mode. It offers a particular story of how a family of 'mixed-race' working-class children grew up in a northern British town in the early 1970s under the tyranny of an authoritarian father who attempts to impose so-called Pakistani-Muslim 'cultural' values and traditions. George is not just portrayed as a 'chip shop despot' (Spencer, 1999) – on occasions he comes across as a deeply flawed and troubled character replete with pathos. The father desperately desires that his brood be raised as 'good Muslim Pakistani's', but the irony or rather hypocrisy of the situation is – as Tariq highlights in a furious confrontation – that George himself has hardly followed the diktat of 'tradition' by marrying a white English woman.

The commercial success of *East is East* can be attributed to its filmic 'authenticity' in recreating a 1970s Manchester which deftly paints a portrait of the gritty lives of northern working-class communities. The younger Khan children play blithely outside on the grey cobbled streets, the back-to-back housing is cramped with only outside toilets, and everyone has to bathe in tin baths, which 'don't 'arf scratch yer arse' as Meenah wryly comments. The mode of story-telling of *East is East* has much in common with the British social-realist tradition of 'kitchen-sink' dramas. The site of the chip shop, endless cups of tea and the need to urinate into pots at night are familiar motifs that effortlessly draw upon the conventions of a working-class realist tradition in British cinema. The film also resonates knowingly with the current nostalgia of 70s life-style in popular culture. The iconography of parka jackets, bell-bottomed trousers, space-hopper toys and Formica aesthetics appeals to the 'retro' sensibilities of contemporary audiences. Moreover, its gritty narrative realism is eclipsed by its central comedic form, leading to several film critics celebrating it as a 'tragi-comedy'.[9]

'Culture-clash'

It is *East is East*'s comedy that drives the film and has led to its 'mainstream' success. The majority of the reviews of the film identify its popular pleasures emphatically as an English/British comedy. For example:

> but make no mistake, this very English comedy is rooted in snobbery, hypocrisy, dogma, poverty and racism ... when it's hurting, you can only laugh. (*Timeout*, nd)

> [*East is East*] thrives on the easy laffs [sic], ripe vulgarity, hectic pace and cacophonous din familiar in end-of-pier sketches and breezy seaside postcards. Fresh, frank, impudent and self-mocking, it marks a giant leap over the threshold of multicultural casting and ethnic British cinema ... The attitude and humour are as fresh as a smack in the face ... Shot with huge affection, this is one of the sharpest British films of the year. (*Evening Standard*, nd)

To draw comparisons with *Bend It Like Beckham* is relatively easy, as *East is East* also explores the complex issues of arranged marriages, generational conflict and Asianess/Britishness through unconstrained, self-mocking working-class styles of humour. Both films also work notably in the contested and ambiguous terrain of the popular in their deployment of representations of 'Asian' culture and identity. The iconoclasm of *East is East* is however, far more immediate and deliberate in comparison to *Bend It*. Much of the comedy of *East is East* is predicated upon the juxtaposition of stereotyped cultural differences between 'Asian-Muslim' and 'English' (working-class) culture.

The opening scenes of the film quickly establish its mode of comedy. To the up-lifting sounds and beating drums of the song 'The Bannerman', we see a tuneful Roman Catholic parade taking place around the narrow streets of Manchester. The local community lines the path of the parade, and we find the Khan children at the heart of it. Meenah holds a large cross with the figure of Christ, and Maneer, Tariq and Saleem carry on their shoulders a figure of the Virgin Mary adorned with flowers. Abdul clutches a Catholic banner behind them, and Sajid is sprinkling flower petals as they all merrily march along to the music. Walking along side them is Tariq's girlfriend Stella, and her best friend Peggy. An anxious Ella runs toward them and informs that their father has returned early from the Mosque and is now watching the parade. The tempo of the film's score quickens as the Khan clan start to panic. The motley gang rush comically towards an alleyway while still carrying the papist statues. An aerial camera view shows them frantically running down the alley in parallel with the parade. They manage to pass behind George (who looks impressed with the festivities), and grin victoriously when they successfully rejoin the parade.

The theme of religion (conflated into fixed cultural differences) is a key source of humour in *East is East*. In another scene, George staring out from his chip shop spots his children scattering as they try to elude the Mullah who has come to take them to the Mosque in his van. George storms over to the family house, catches the guilty-looking Saleem and hurls him towards the van. He eventually finds a whimpering Sajid hiding under the bed. Pulling him out, feet first, George drags the helpless Sajid unceremoniously down the hallway and yells 'you bastard' in a mixed Pakistani-Mancunian accent. There are several scenes of slapstick humour in the film which involve the Khan children evading the imposition of their father's cultural authority. One scene in particular stands out. Tariq, Saleem and Meenah are secretly gorging on pork sausages and bacon while their father (and mother with Sajid) are out of the house.[10] Through this transgressive act of consumption, they appear to savour the taste of the food even more in the knowledge of defying the religious expectations of their father. Maneer's objections are ignored as he fears that their father will smell the distinctive aroma of the meat upon his imminent return. He rushes around in a state of desperation spraying the house with sickly smelling air-freshener. A knock on the door causes all of them to freeze in a moment of panic. Meenah finally opens the door only to find Ernest (Sajid's best friend). She rudely dismisses him, but then spots her father returning to the house. Meenah darts back screaming and a frenzied mini-stampede ensues as they try to get rid of all the evidence. Sausages are stuffed hastily into mouths as they charge about the house clutching greasy frying pans, while Maneer continues choking everyone with the air-freshener.

It is not simply the case of pointing out that the film's humour works on the basis of cultural difference, as many forms of comedy operate through such stereotyped forms. The mode of address of Asian comedy being doubled-edged often leads to an ambiguous representational politics. In a review of *East is East* in the specialist magazine-journal *Sight and Sound*, Spencer praises the film for shattering the shibboleths of 'tradition' while not reproducing racist sentiments, or being confined to the demands of 'political correctness':

> Eschewing the racist gags of the 70s and the politically correct stand-up of the 80s ... [Khan-Din's] kitchen-sink comedy is stamped with the same self-mocking confidence as such recent sketch series as *Goodness Gracious Me*. Like the characters in *East is East*, English culture-clash comedy look like it's come of age. (Spencer, 1999, p. 37)

The description of the film as an 'English culture-clash' comedy signals that this specific mode of humour has found a favourable expression in contemporary British popular culture. The problem is that the articulation of 'culture-clash' tends to demand or at least presuppose fixed cultural elements. The extant danger that these cultural differences are governed by racialized discourses of the other is likely to render *East is East*'s representational strategies problematic.[11]

An ideological reading of *East is East* in relation to its politics of representation leaves it more than suspect. Nobil (1999/2000) scrutinizes the film's racial and gender politics. He not only objects to its pervasive stereotyping of 'Eastern' culture, but also that of white working-class people. Moreover, he deems Khan-Din's film as bearing a 'deep-seated misogyny'. Nobil questions the mother figure of Ella, who even after receiving a severe beating from George, admonishes the children for speaking against the brutality of their father. Similarly, he believes that the crude 'fat slag' jokes made against white working-class women, and the 'comically repugnant physical appearance of Pakistani brides, to whom George seeks to wed his sons ... are meant to appeal to the most base sexist and racist instincts of a white audience' (Nobil, 1999/2000, p. 106). It is the film's stereotypical portrayal of Asian-Muslim culture which Nobil takes most issue with, insisting that *East is East* is gravely flawed because it ridicules Muslim culture, rather than representing its complexities.

> *East is East* invites us to enjoy a film about Asians in Britain in terms of what it likes best: arranged marriages, domestic violence and oppression ... It seems that the archetypal image of the eastern male [George Khan], brutish and oppressive, retains a powerful hold over the English imagination. His broken English and bizarre accent provides a constant source of amusement by which Muslims are frequently constructed and understood ... Pakistani culture provides all the biggest laughs in the film, which ends stereotypically in an 'arranged marriage sequence' – a prerequisite in any mainstream movie about Asians. (pp. 105–6)

Nobil advances a forceful interpretative reading of *East is East* for propagating Orientalist representations of Asianess. He goes as far as asserting that mainstream white audiences would consume the film in a wholly negative manner.

Nobil could also consider that it is the spectre of an *assimilatory* hybridity which is the most compelling articulation of identity formation in the film. Arguably, this form of hybridity is the representational strategy which encodes the cultural condition of the 'miscegenated' Khan children. When Tariq discovers he and his brother, Abdul, are to have an arranged marriage, Tariq responds with rage, shouting to the rest of his siblings: 'I'm not marrying a fucking paki!' It is doubtful that the signifier 'Paki' has been emptied of its racialized connotations in contemporary culture. Its invocation distantiates Tariq from a 'traditional' Asian culture and people. The film appears dangerously to posit a stance of individual liberty versus cultural tradition which may map too readily onto the Orientalist dichotomy of 'Western freedom' against 'Eastern repression'. At the end of the film, family life appears to have returned to some kind of normality. It seems that for the viewer, there is no longer any room for George's Muslim cultural background to be articulated.

In the final analysis, his children's disavowal of what is marked as 'Muslim culture' is not necessarily problematic, though the cultural premise of *East is East* embodies a form of hybridity which fails to address the grounds on which the *racialized* dissonances of multicultural difference are played out (Chapter 5). Through the patriarchal figure of George Khan, the film sets up a dichotomy which represents and situates his Asian-Muslim culture as something traditional, ossified and pre-modern in comparison to progressive 'white' culture (of individual freedom) available through the mother. 'Asian culture' does not appear to be able to enter into the modern world, unable to negotiate the spaces of a liberatory multiculture. The Asianess of the *father* has no grounds to be hybrid in itself (as it seems to come ready formed by the 'traditions' of primitivism and religious dogma in the film). Is the hybridity of *East is East* ultimately one of cultural assimilation for the Khan children which leaves whiteness intact? Are they 'caught between two cultures' in which there is little space for negotiating elements of their Asian culture, or exploring how this 'culture' historically emerges and changes? Or in other words, the only acceptable Asian is a modern 'hybrid Asian', in comparison to the implied impossibility of a traditional '*hybrid Paki*'?

This kind of reading of *East is East* seeks to highlight the film's suspect representational politics. At this point, it is tempting to conclude that *East is East* is more of a 'popular' text than it is 'minor'. However, its deployment in a teaching situation through a specific reading praxis can offer other deterritorializing pedagogic possibilities. Furthermore, the limits of an ideologically driven interpretative reading neglects exploring the expressive cultural politics of the film which has the potential to mobilize other ways of knowing.

Instituting difference?

East is East avoids confronting issues of racism directly. On the contrary, such concerns are raised, but through a contentious comedic mode that is always in danger of trivializing the significance of the racial antagonisms in 1970s Britain. In the scene with Tariq, Saleem and Meenah slumped on the sofa eating sausages, they watch a television news programme of the infamous Enoch Powell addressing the nation. His speech urging for the repatriation of immigrants provokes Tariq to respond facetiously, 'Let's 'ave a whip 'round and send dad back home!' However, Tariq's sarcasm ambivalently highlights the spectre of racism in an everyday situation by effectively debunking the racist discourse of Powell at the same time. The seemingly anachronistic figure of Powell is used as a motif for expressing the exclusionary nationalism during the period the film is set in.

It is also through the inane character of Mr Moorhouse (Earnest's grandfather and Stella's father) that Powell's racism is both raised and contested in the film. Powell's sentiments are echoed by Mr Moorhouse when we frequently hear him calling the Khan family a 'bunch of picanninies'. Mr Moorhouse's brand of racism is however deftly ridiculed on a number of occasions. During a regular football game outside on the street, Meenah lines up to take a penalty kick, only to see the ball smash Mr Moorhouse's window and tear through his Enoch Powell poster. As the children scramble away speedily, we see the enraged red face of Mr Moorhouse squarely framed by what is left of the Powell poster – a laughable sight as he pointlessly shouts obscenities at his grandson, Earnest, who has long since disappeared. It is Earnest, who does the most to comically undermine his Grand-father's racism. Earnest wants to be part of the Khan gang, and he spends most of his time hanging outside their house with Sajid, much to the disgust of his grandfather. Mr Moorhouse is an active supporter of Powell, and in one scene on a high street, he and a friend along with Earnest are distributing leaflets for a local Powell meeting. While Mr Moorhouse shouts for a petition to be signed for repatriation, he spots George Khan across the road returning from a visit to Bradford carrying a large bag. The grandfather turns to his friend while pointing at George and remarks scornfully 'Ey look, there's one of 'em now. Got 'is bags packed – already on 'is way home!' Earnest however, with an endearing smile, excitedly shouts out the Islamic salutation: 'Salaam Wale Kum, Mr Khan!' The grandfather is horrified, and left looking rather humiliated as he smacks Earnest, screaming, 'Shut up, ya little bastard!'

East is East exhibits a performative fabulation in a similar manner to *Bend It*. Its mode of storytelling also offers a dialogic point of enuncia-tion through its (comedic) affective registers of address. *East is East* as a minor-popular text rests on its ability to credibly recreate an 'authen-tic' British working-class culture by including the interruptive presence of Asianess. The nostalgic representation of 1970s Manchester which centrally figures the Khan family attempts to offer an alternative multi-cultural historical narration of working-class experiences in Britain. On the way to a trip to Bradford, as the van carrying the Khan family negotiates the twisting contours of the hilly road, the song '*Chalo dildar chalo*' from the classic South Asian film, *Pakeezah* (1972, Kamal Amrohi) plays in the background to the view of England's 'green and pleasant land'. The van passes a signpost for the City of Bradford, but it is partly scrawled out and literally put under erasure: the graffitied sign of 'Bradfordistan' instead greets the family.[12]

A working-class 'authenticity' is established throughout film by the astutely observed dialogue of the characters – an expressive Mancunian vernacular which acutely captures the acerbic wit and humour of their daily social interactions. For example, again during the scene when the

Khan children are secretly eating sausages, when the knock on the door panics them, it is Meenah who nervously peers through the letter box only to discover the small scrawny figure of a blotchy faced, bespectacled Earnest standing there.[13] The following ribald exchange takes place:

> Meenah [through the letter-box]: Wha' d'ya want, pongo?
> Earnest: Is yer Sajid back yet?
> Meenah [opening the door]: He's havin' 'is knob cut off – d'ya think he's gonna go 'round spazing with you when 'e gets back?
> Earnest: D'ya wanna a toffee Meenah?
> Meenah [knocking them away]: Fuck off! Do ya think I want fuckin' ringworm like you, ya whiffer!

The supposed incongruity of the Khan children speaking in a broad Mancunian drawl (Spencer, 1999) proffers to disrupt both absolutist notions of Britishness and Asianess. Moreover, the 'mixed-race' identity status of the Khan children complicates existing 'black' versus 'white' racial dichotomies which govern dominant racialized representations (Piper, 1998; Ifekwunigwe, 1999). The threat of miscegenation to the racial status-quo means that the positive articulation of an assimilatory hybridity is not necessarily an ideological given in the film; at times the children's condition of cultural hybridity appears to be rather more ambivalent (and we shall find this was implied by some student responses). The privileges of whiteness (Dyer, 1997) are not simply available to the miscegenated Khan's, even as they aspire to reject their father's Pakistani-Muslim cultural background.

There are a few affective scenes in *East is East* which capture something of the nuances and negotiations of being working-class British-Asians. During their visit to Bradford, they go to George Khan's cousin's cinema. In a blatant act of nepotism, his cousin fulfils Ella's request to watch *Chaundvin Ka Chand* (1960, Guru Dutt) by changing the current film playing, mid-way. The Khan family comfortably settle in the cinema seats with popcorn in-hand, awe struck as the radiant female star begins to sing the film's title track – a rare moment of shared bliss for all the family.[14] In another scene, Tariq, Saleem, Maneer and Meenah are in the backyard, grimacing at their daily task of preparing the fish for their parent's shop. It is Maneer's role to gut the fish while Meenah sweeps up the offending bones. The sounds of another song from *Pakeezah* begins to play on the film score. Wearing over-sized Wellington boots, the tough football playing Meenah begins to dance to '*Inhee logo ne*'. She improvises expertly with the broom as Maneer too, starts moving to the music. Tariq and Saleem, illicitly sharing a cigarette, look on enjoying the spectacle.

The most memorable scene in the film – one which Nobil has referred to as the expected 'stereotypical ... arranged marriage sequence' – expresses most intensely the political ambiguity of *East is East*. The scene serves to mock the social and status-ridden pretensions surrounding the practice of arranged marriages, and its sheer comic excess can leave the audience doubting the 'reality' of the situation. It is worthwhile to recount this scene for its blend of both subtle and extreme comic elements, in addition to its ambivalence towards 'Asian culture'. The sequence begins with the Shah's car heading towards the Khan's house. The parka-hooded Sajid is returning home oblivious to road traffic and Mr Shah nearly knocks him over. Sajid instinctively makes an obscene gesture with two fingers, but is alarmed to discover that it is the Shah's in the car. Sajid scurries off, shouting 'Mam ... the paki's are here!' as he runs in to his house. George, is upstairs and upon overhearing Sajid, returns a distraught (almost comically bemused) look directly at the camera. Abdul and Tariq are seated anxiously in the living room, tormented by the prospect of meeting their intended brides. Ella wearing conspicuous Asian gold earrings, welcomes the Shah's by directing them to the room she euphemistically describes as 'the parlour' in a feigned upper-class accent. As Mr Shah greets the two Khan brothers, he amusingly confuses their names and disregards Abdul's feeble attempt to correct him. The first Shah daughter enters the room and looks up at Abdul in reverence. She is clad heavily in cheap jewellery and tawdry Asian engagement dress – her visual appearance is comically grotesque. Abdul's face quivers on seeing her, and Tariq smirks believing he has been spared. But his look abruptly changes as the second daughter enters. She shares her sister's gormless looks and tacky spectacles, though lacks the protruding teeth, and instead fashions thickset eyebrows. Much of the humour of the scene is not only based on the 'ugliness' – absolute ethnic otherness? – of the intended brides, but both Tariq's and Abdul's impotence towards the situation. Moreover, as both families settle down in the living room, it is the awkward silences which characterize much of the comic tension of the whole sequence.

The laboured efforts to make 'small talk' between the families only exacerbates the tension of the situation. When Ella inquires if they found the house without any trouble, Mrs Shah replies 'All these *little* houses, they all look the same, to me'. Ella is highly conscious of the fact that the Shah's consider themselves to be of superior class than the miscegenated Khan's. (Perhaps owning a butcher's shop in Bradford carries more social status than a fish and chip shop in Manchester.) Meenah is aware of her mother's anxiety, and accordingly responds to Ella's strained elocuted request for tea with the words, 'right-tee ho'. Mrs Shah tries to make meagre amends by maternally asking young Sajid his age. He retorts rudely, 'Not old enough to get married, so don't ask me'. George is embarrassed at his son's insolence, but Mr Shah bursts out laughing. He affectionately rubs Sajid's (unwashed) parka clad head, but his laughter ceases upon discovering a sticky residue left on his fingers. Ella attempts to exonerate Sajid's irascibility by naively informing the Shah's that he has been recently circumcised, which only further fuels their unease as well as George's. Throughout the scene George attempts to ingratiate the Shah's, irrespective of their disparaging comments against his family. Mrs Shah objects to Meenah wearing a sari (an original demand made by George) because it not considered to be 'traditional' dress. However, George contradicts Ella's rejoinder that it was sent by his own relative from Pakistan. Similarly, he accedes all too easily to the request that Abdul and Tariq should live with the Shah's because his own house is considered too cramped. Even though, as Ella protests, sending the sons away would not follow *tradition*. It is clear that George's deference and embarrassment is rooted in the view that his family are not 'proper' Asian-Muslims – a belief ultimately shared by the Shah's.

The antagonisms of class and status are revealed in the final part of the scene. Ella becomes increasingly frustrated with her husband's appalling deferential behaviour. She leaves the room to find some cigarettes and is pleased to see Saleem, who has finally returned from college with a completed art project that he has been working on. Ella has been covertly supporting Saleem financially, and is eager to see his artistic efforts. Maneer, Meenah and Sajid along with their mother look on as Saleem carefully opens his presentation box: they are confronted by a life-size latex vagina. Ella is utterly disgusted, exclaiming 'You dirty little sod!' Saleem's protestations that it is 'art ... about female exploitation' falls on deaf ears as Ella tries to snatch the offending object while shouting, 'I'll burn the bleedin' thing!' A scene of pandemonium ensues. The noisy fracas is heard from the living room as the bewildered guests wonder what is occurring. Suddenly the living room door bursts open, and Saleem is thrown towards Mrs Shah and lands almost between her legs; the pudenda he was clutching flies across the room and falls squarely on her lap! There is a moment of stunned silence before both Mrs Shah and Saleem scream in horror. The shocked Mrs Shah can no longer repress her extreme antipathy towards the Khan's, which also releases Ella's own pent up animosity:

> Mrs Shah: This is an insult to me and my family! I will never allow my daughters to marry into this *junglee*[15] family of half-breeds!
> Ella: They may be 'alf-bred, but least they're not frigin' in-bred like those two monstrosities [referring to the Shah daughters].
> George: Ella...
> Ella: Never mind 'Ella'! Who the frig do you think *you* are, comin' in and telling me my house isn't good enough for your daughters? Well ... your daughters ain't good enough for my sons, or my house. If I hear another word against my family, I'll stick that fanny over your bastard head!
> Mr Shah [turning to George]: Your wife's a disgrace.

It is notable that both Mrs Shah and Ella make reference to 'breeding' and 'progeny' in trading insults and maintaining their social status. It is a hazardous racialized terrain to traverse for *East is East*, even through a comedic mode of farce and excess. Similarly, the presence of the comically grotesque Asian brides bluntly mocks the edicts of normative female 'beauty' in arranged marriage practices, but the question of a misogynist racism follows perhaps too closely. Nevertheless, contrary to Nobil's seemingly realist representational reading, *East is East* knowingly uses a series of highly stereotypical and excessive comical representations of both Asian and white working-class culture and people in establishing itself as a British film.[16] The ambivalence of *East is East* arises from its affective capacities producing both active and reactive affects – its institution of difference appears to be remarkably ambiguous. The truthful narration of Asianess may be undermined by the deterritorializing function of English comedy (as claimed for *Bend It*), but the pitfall exists that the comedic idiom – silliness, banality, and witlessness – is the dominant representational and affective mode through which Asianess is made knowable. It is this reason which makes *East is East* such a culturally loaded text to work with.

Situated pedagogy

The final part of this Chapter elaborates an alterity pedagogy vis-à-vis a specific classroom teaching example. It reports on a small-scale exploratory intervention of an 'imperfect' pedagogy. While the intention is not to empirically verify the theoretical contentions advanced in this book, by examining the specific example of a 'situated pedagogy' (Lather, 1991), a modest and admittedly limited opportunity to 'close the gap' between theoretical work and the everyday practices of teaching is presented (Williamson, 1981/2). A situated pedagogy for Lather provides the possibility of putting to work the resources of theory through particular concrete instances of practice. Furthermore, such a pedagogic praxis is contingent upon the broader institutional and specific learning context within which it operates.

The situated pedagogy for this study arises from an example of my own teaching practice, as a lecturer within a British university. It was based on a taught module entitled *Youth Cultures* offered as part of a undergraduate teaching programme in a cultural and media studies department. The module was a second level (year 2) option available to students studying degree programmes such as cultural, media and communication studies. The university attracts a significant number of students from its surrounding region, largely from lower socio-economic groups and many students work part-time during their studies. The university's overall student body is ethnically diverse, being almost 50 percent 'non-white'. The make-up of the students attending the *Youth Cultures* module reflected this diversity, in this case 'white' students constituted approximately 60 percent of the class. The most significant group of visible 'minorities' were from African-Caribbean backgrounds, followed by South Asians and additionally, a significant minority of 'mixed-race' students as well as some from other non-European countries. There were also several students of Irish descent, and a few from mainland Europe, including Eastern Europe. A total of 42 students were registered for the module with a comparable balance between males and females. Their ages ranged from approximately 18–35, though the majority were between 19–25 years old.[17]

Attempts to innovate a radical pedagogy cannot escape the institutional (and increasingly regulated) context of university teaching. All taught modules are governed by the wider university degree scheme regulations, which defines the validation and assessment practices of the teaching programme. The *Youth Cultures* module as part of named degree programmes carries an accreditation which students are required to formally pass for it to count towards their final qualification. Nevertheless, there is a degree of flexibility for implementing the specific learning programme of a particular module. *Youth Cultures* was taught by using a mixture of whole class lectures and workshops, and smaller group seminars on a weekly basis. The seminars were both tutor and student-led, that is, every other week one small student group led the seminar class without the presence of the tutor. While there was a framework for learning with guidance from the tutor, the independent student-led seminars provided an opportunity for students to take greater responsibility for defining their own learning. They were assessed on the module by both written and oral work. Students were required to submit an essay (which could be a title of their own choice), a shorter critical review essay of a selected article used in the seminars and a reflective report based on an oral group presentation. The presentation component encouraged small groups of students to work collaboratively and use different media and methods of communication to reflexively explore issues raised by the module. Furthermore, the group presentations were peer-assessed which allowed students to gain an understanding, and make more transparent, the criteria used in assessments. The pedagogic design of the module does not claim to be exceptional, as many university modules employ a range of teaching formats and assessment procedures. Moreover, the module was relatively new and has been undergoing a constant process of re-fashioning (much of which based on student feedback and discussion).[18]

The broad aims of the module were to explore the formation and representations of youth identities and (sub)cultures, and how young people 'resist', negotiate, and appropriate mediated images and values associated with youth. A key area addressed the discursive politics of youth culture in relation to mass and alternative media, processes of commodification and questions of multiculturalism. The module did not seek to explicate particular meanings and forms of youth identities and cultures, but offered multiple frameworks and perspectives for interrogating their social and ethico-political significance.

Given the field of study of popular youth culture, the intimate and experiential knowledge of particular youth cultural forms by some students far exceeded mine as the course tutor. While this does not erase tutor authority or the institutionalized relations of power between the tutor and students, it nevertheless could enable interruptions of the dynamic of power in the actual teaching situation. The multiple modes of learning (and assessment) attempted to invite students to draw on, and critically reflect, appraise and deterritorialize their own experiences, knowledges and popular pleasures of youth culture from the position of being participants, producers as well as consumers. A significant theme of the module was to explore the 'multicultural' formation of youth cultures and identities. For example, ideas of cultural diversity and hybridity were considered, in addition to the contentions that youth cultures can be sites for transgressing the boundaries of fixed cultural difference (cf. Gilroy, 1987; Back, 1996). A discursive approach to understanding youth cultures eschewed positing a singular mode and determinate framework of understanding. Students were encouraged to critically question established academic orthodoxies, as well as their own modes of understanding.

The situated pedagogy outlined above has briefly indicated aspects of the institutional and local learning context. In developing a pedagogy for alterity, it is naïve to maintain that an ideal rhizomatic pedagogic practice is possible under these conditions. The multiple points of closure such as teacher authority, curriculum content and assessment modes cannot be disavowed. Neither should we believe that the unruly knowledge-productions and (minoritarian) 'becomings' that occur in a teaching situation are simply contained by the immediate context of learning or broader institutionalized practices. A central goal for the pedagogy being advanced is to foster and *accelerate* the forces of becoming for activating deterritorializing affects and ethical alliances (see Chapter 2). Furthermore, the teaching of the module was predicated on an 'anti-method' which attempted to work from a 'tactical' perspective. In practice though, it meant that using particular approaches such as student-led seminars, peer assessment and even critical reflection can become sedimented and neutralized into a formulaic teaching technique. It may be the case that students quickly learnt to reproduce the expected protocols of academic inquiry (especially as some of these techniques are becoming standardized across degree programmes). A particular mode of teaching does not of course inherently embody a 'radical' deterritorializing practice. Nevertheless, for the *Youth Cultures* module, transformations as well as connections were sought constantly between the modes of teaching and the subject matter under study. The module utilized the everyday experiences of the students, but at the same time tried to move them towards other ways of knowing.

It was from within this situated pedagogy, that the question of alterity was speculated. The film, *East is East* was deployed in *Youth Cultures* to animate some of the key themes of the module. It was introduced as a popular British film that provided opportunities to explore the formation of youth identities. While its 'multicultural' character was highlighted as a site of interrogation, the film was not marked explicitly as an 'Asian' text. The tactical deployment of *East is East* was figured on at least two other fronts. Firstly, in relation to the film's popularity and resonance with the mixed student body studying the module. *East is East*'s cinematic release was well-received and the majority of class were at least knowledgeable of its existence, and a significant number of students had already seen the film. Its main-stream success indicated its popular currency in contemporary media culture, with favourable reviews and commentary. Furthermore, the recent entry of 'Asian' cultural forms and productions into the popular/public sphere also influenced the reception of *East is East* – making it a significant text of interest to many of the students.

Secondly, the tactical deployment of *East is East* attempted to effect a reading praxis for an alterity pedagogy. This type of a praxis considers the text in machinic terms and asks what a film 'can do', rather than simply requiring students to interpret the text's ideological meanings. However, in practice, a film's *affects* and mobilizations cannot be untangled from its *meanings* (cf. Gilbert, 2004). Many students studying the module were relatively conversant with methods of semiotic textual analysis, and the exposure of ideological meanings or conflictual readings of a film was familiar territory. Such an approach was not shunned, but the emphasis was on mobilizing students' affective investments through their interrogations and engagements with *East is East*.[19]

The task of realizing a rhizomatic reading praxis is laden with difficulties. There is no pedagogical blueprint for this activity (and if there were, this kind of universalist practice would be profoundly limited). The approach taken was open-ended. The pedagogy did not aim to discover a definitive method, but through its own performative articulation, a contingent practice was developed. Inciting students' affective investments implicated them engaging with *East is East* on multiple fronts. The research method for generating student responses used three specific types of engagements. The most simple engagement involved them responding to an individual anonymous questionnaire immediately after the screening of the film. (This questionnaire was primarily used as research instrument to gain a general indication of the reception of the film.) Clearly a limited device, the questionnaire nevertheless functioned to stimulate students and enable them to initially reflect upon *East is East*. The questionnaire focussed upon their own views and required qualitative responses. These responses indicated crudely the type and degree of engagement with the film, and to some extent, what understanding and knowledge students were bringing to the film.

The second mode of engagement took place in the seminar sessions and was centred on student discussions. This initially involved a 'free-format' whole class seminar discussion which enabled students to raise issues and comment on the film. It took place in both the tutor and student-led seminars. Such open-ended modes of discussion may produce multitudinous rhizomatic connections, though often remain 'unknowable' – usually experienced as what often appears to be nebulous or meandering seminar discussions! Conversely, these connections can be rapidly contained or shut down by tutor intervention, or equally circumscribed by a handful of the most vocal students in the seminar space.

The open-ended discussions were followed by a series of questions which were supplied to the smaller student working groups within the seminars. (There were approximately three small groups for each seminar class, consisting of three to five students each.) The students were given the opportunity to discuss these questions in their small groups, and also to present their responses to the rest of the seminar class for further deliberation. The questions were arranged thematically, in order for the student groups to explore different aspects of the film. The themes were not intended to delimit students' thinking and responses, but aimed to provide an array of 'sites of mobilization' through which their affective engagements and investments could be 'refracted' or 'unfolded' (see Chapter 3). The grouped themes contained a number of questions that allowed students to select those considered to be most appealing or appropriate. There were four discursive themes which encouraged students to make and multiply connections arising from the film. They engaged with the following sites of reflexive exploration: the idea of Britishness and British identity; youthful identities and cultural specificity; rewriting alternative endings; and interrogating reviews of *East is East*. While these sites attempted to deploy the film in order to create and accelerate multiple linkages, at the same time, they addressed 'how the mobilization of meaning and affective investments within the film's form and content functioned as part of a broader cultural and pedagogical practice that was neither innocent or politically neutral' (Giroux, 1993, p. 42). Here, the emphasis lay on exploring what made the text intelligible and why for students, which involved them interrogating their own popular pleasures and interpretative frameworks. For example, some student groups were asked to rewrite alternative endings for the film (cf. Britzman *et al.*, 1993). This activity endeavoured to mobilize students to narrate their affective investments in imagining different possibilities. Also it offered a tracing of the grounds of their own meanings, desires and pleasures. Another set of student groups were asked to explore the basis of the

favourable reviews of the film in relation to opening up and questioning their own viewpoints and sites of investment. Furthermore, as a
counterpoint to these reviews, my own more critical reading of *East is
East* was supplied to these students. There was a danger that the students could be compelled to follow the tutor's position, though they
were encouraged to critique my review.

The dynamic of power between the students and me as both their
tutor and as a researcher cannot by ignored. My dual role as a tutor
and researcher seems at first to be a 'double-bind'. Students are already
governed by an institutionalized tutor authority, and in the last
instance an educational disciplinary power (Gore, 1993). Moreover,
undertaking a research project, even one in which students are 'consenting participants', still positions them as subjects of a research
gaze.[20] There is no simple solution for un-doing the hierarchy of power
operating in a teaching/research encounter, though the dynamics of
power may nevertheless be disrupted. This begins from a 'student-
centred' pedagogy which attempts to conceive teaching as an open-
ended dialogic process, rather than a monologic transmissionist
activity (Freire, 1972; Giroux, 1992). Furthermore, the alterity pedagogy being explored rests on instituting an ethical standpoint which
would permeate the student-tutor relationship. The ethics of classroom
research need not deny existing relations of power, but can acknowledge that the production of both research and pedagogic knowledge is
a collaborative enterprise. To bifurcate the teaching/research encounter
is neither possible nor useful. Rather than conceived in terms of a
'double-bind' which potentially subjugates students, this encounter
can be reconsidered as an ethical situated knowledge-production for a
transformative pedagogical praxis.

From a tactical perspective, the teaching practice had to take account
of hegemonic identity discourses, multiple differences and antagonisms in the classroom situation as well as tutor authority. The ethnic
diversity of the students offered a unique learning environment, but
the differences and struggles of power *within* the student body needed
to be acknowledged too. It is an understatement to say that the fissures
of 'race', class, gender and sexuality were in constant play in such a
fraught space. Furthermore, the question of tutor authority and my
own subject-position – perceived as 'Asian' male (and maybe a middle-
class, heterosexual) lecturer – instituted a particular dynamic of power.
While an 'open-ended' style of teaching was being innovated in a perpetual effort to evade a hegemonic perspective from establishing itself,
it is difficult to deny that student responses could escape the spectre of

a 'political correctness' discourse which can pervade cultural studies classrooms (Cohen, 1992; Jay, 1995). In particular, my 'Asian' identity could curb specific racialized standpoints from being expressed, especially among the white students (although the co-presence of other 'minority' students could have produced a similar effect as well). Nevertheless, it is also possible that my embodied status as a 'non-white' lecturer was perceived by some students as illegitimately occupying a location historically reserved for white (male) figures. Consequentially, my racialized 'Asian' subject-position could actually serve to undermine my authority in the classroom (cf. Simmonds, 1997; Puwar, 2004).

The possible assumed contradictory location of my subject-position was further marked out by the selection of *East is East* in the teaching programme, which was considered as a British-Asian text by the majority of the students. The classroom knowledge-productions of the students cannot be disengaged from my own presence. Rather than attempt to erase my cultural specificity and 'influence' (an impossibility), by offering a review of the film, my own position was made relatively explicit. The review was written in a polemical style and offered a provocative reading in terms of the film's politics of cultural hybridity, though from a position beyond demanding positive representations of Asian culture. It refrained advancing a definitive ideological position, and tried to mobilize students to engage with the film from an alternative perspective. Students were given the opportunity to critique the review in the form of an assessed assignment (in addition to the seminar discussion).[21] Part of the remit of the assignment was to analyse the grounds on which the review was made and offer their own critical perspectives. Interestingly, some students (positively) identified my review as being written from a minority 'Asian' perspective, as opposed to the position of mainstream 'white' reviewers.[22] Simon (1995) has highlighted that the cultural specificity of the tutor cannot be ignored in classroom encounters and pedagogical relationships. In terms of his own identity conceived as a performative accomplishment, he writes: 'I am arguing that "teaching as a Jew" denotes a pedagogical condition, initiated by my specificity as an embodied Jew, which enhances the achievement of knowledge through the interactive return of difference in the dynamics of teaching and learning' (Simon 1995, p. 92). While my pedagogical practice did not wholly embrace the idea of say 'teaching as an Asian', neither did it disavow my embodied subject-position.

It was the site of mobilization exploring youthful identities and 'Asian' cultural specificity that was the most problematic to deploy. The immediate problem of representational thinking over-determines the appellation of identity. The act of naming an 'Asian' identity or culture runs the risk of it invoking a fixed ethno-racial identity-difference. The key goal would be to summon identity as a performative subjectivity and ask what a specific identity 'can do' instead of what it 'is' or 'represents'. While this perspective underpins an affective pedagogy of 'becoming', in a concrete teaching situation it does not necessarily escape the problem of the naming of an Asian identity. One tactic was to initially refuse its explicit naming in relation to *East is East*, and examine how it was situationally invoked by students themselves. This approach was taken in relation to only certain questions being used for selected student discussion groups, though it was anticipated that the distinction between a 'pedagogic' and student naming of identity (Asianess) is obfuscated in practice. In fact, the determining reason for tactically deploying *East is East* was to explore the possibility of actively invoking Asianess and mobilizing students to non-appropriative ethical relationships – a fraught practice which could readily fail. This charged arena of cultural difference alongside the 'impossibility' of escaping the vestiges of representational identities proved to be most pedagogically challenging.

The complexities of the teaching situation outlined above, in conjunction with the multifarious un/knowable connections taking place, meant that it was not possible to adequately capture the performative effects of the deployment of *East is East*, or produce a coherent or comprehensive research account. This is not an evasive assertion in order to obscure the inadequacies of the research methodology or, for that matter, an alterity pedagogy itself. The problem of representation governs all research accounts in their production of knowledge. Poststructuralist critiques of the stability of the meaning of the sign have profoundly questioned the 'truth' status of research accounts (Clifford and Marcus, 1986). Over the last two decades ethnographic fieldwork has suffered a crisis over its representational strategies. It has been argued that research accounts are governed by regimes of power-knowledge, and can no longer be considered as merely mimetically re-presenting the world (Scheurich, 1997). The epistemological implications for ethnographic research have been far reaching. It has given rise to a range of innovative research strategies and textual experimentation which attempt to address the problem of representation (see Clifford and Marcus, 1986; Lather, 1991; Atkinson, 1992; Garber *et al.*, 1996; Denzin, 1997). The methodology of the classroom-based research presented in this chapter is influenced by these 'postmodern ethnographies', and in particular in terms of the 'messy text'.

> ... that are aware of their own narrative apparatuses, that are sensitive to how reality is socially constructed, and that understanding that writing is way of 'framing' reality. Messy texts are many sited, intertextual, always open-ended, and resistant to theoretical wholism, but always committed to cultural criticism. (Denzin, 1997, p. 224)

The research findings in the form of a 'messy text' do not however escape the problem of representation. The textual (re)presentation of the multiplicity of student voices is governed by a narrative apparatus in the framing of their responses. A reflexive stance cannot secure a transcendental position of an all-knowing subject (researcher) who is able to capture or simply represent the unruly knowledge-productions in a teaching situation. Nevertheless, the following presentation of student responses consists of three 'crafted narratives' which seek to bring some kind of understanding – though not a rigid ordering or arborescent organization – to the chaotic data base of student responses. It follows that the performative effects of *East is East* and the mobilizations of students to other (possibly) ethical sites of investment are rendered 'knowable' vis-à-vis such a 'messy text': an attempt to fleetingly 'capture' the possible rhizomatic connections and *un*representable knowledges that transgress existing cultural hegemonies in an actual pedagogic situation.[23]

Identity markers

To claim that an alterity pedagogy was able to elude the ideological markers of identity would be at best naïve, and at worst, in danger of erasing the groundings and material forces of difference and power. While it will be argued that the deployment of *East is East* may have mobilized students to other ethical sites of belonging, it equally unleashed the problems and contradictions of teaching difference. Britzman *et al.* capture the antinomies of this fraught arena when they write:

> The very language we borrow to pin down identity, to situate an experience, to recognize an event, and to render intelligible the meanings of others is ... both a linguistic right and a site of ideological

struggle. Antagonizing these discursive boundaries ... are the contra-dictory and conflicting ways people embody, conceptualize, and perform the politics of identity. The familiar litany of race, class, gender, sex, and so on, is not the originary explanation. Rather these social markers are emblematic of the treacheries of representation: the unruly and contentious relations among the imagined conditions of knowledge, identity, lived experience, and social conduct. (Britzman *et al.*, 1993, p. 188)

There is always a risk that *East is East* exhibits the social marker of cul-tural identity (ethnicity) as manifest in its story-line. The 'treacheries of representation' can be played out intensely by some students main-taining 'identity' and 'culture' as a property of social groupings in their discussions of the film. Here is an excerpt from a student-led seminar exploring the cultural complexity of the Khan children.

Vernon (black male): I don't think ... that these youth identities [of Khan children] are culturally hybrid. Because, like, as the film showed, these kids were half Asian and half white, but they never like created a culture of their own that could be distinct from native white British culture and the traditional culture of their father.

Sarah (white female): What about the cultural things like when the family sat down and had dinner, a meal ...?

Lisa (black female): Well the only meal they had was pork ... which they weren't allowed [...]

Sarah: Yeh, but cooking in Asian families, it's a big thing ... I knew an Asian family where the British mother cooked curry ...

Malcolm (black male): What? The mother was white in the film! ...

Lisa: It was a stereotypical English women's culture ...

Sarah: No, they [the film] didn't really show where the culture lies ...

Vernon: But you ain't listening – I'm focussing on the kids ... Even though they were made of two different cultures ... they weren't hybrid ...

Lisa: They cleaved to their British side of culture ... the sausages, the banners ... (Seminar Group A)[24]

This type of exchange is fairly typical of the kinds of assertions, inter-ruptions and dissonances that occurred. While it is legitimately argued that the Khan children identified with a 'British culture', the language of identity, in particular that of 'hybridity' – conceived as a cultural condition of the fusion of two prior cultural elements – can at times pervade student discourses. Most evident is the notion that 'culture' is a thing composed of identifiable attributes and an essential marker of identity. Perhaps the teaching of difference and multiculture through invoking over-determined terms such as 'culture' and 'hybridity' runs the risk of further reifying identity. The representational practices of *East is East* can also be accused of contributing to this type of thinking: identity is itself the origin or source of problems, rather than as an effect of power (Britzman *et al.*, 1993). A few students consider the miscegenated condition of the Khan children as 'being portrayed negatively' in the film, which 'all seemed to be about problems caused from this' (questionnaire 28). Furthermore, a significant number of students dislike the popular description of the film as a 'culture-clash comedy' found in the reviews because they felt it meant that the 'two cultures do not mix', or that they 'cannot blend – they are separate' (questionnaire 15).

Some responses imply that when the problem of identity surfaced, it can be made 'safe' through a process of erasing (Asian) cultural specificity. For example, in the case of the task of rewriting an ending for *East is East*, one student group concluded that the film should have flashed forward and showed Sajid (the youngest son) marrying a white English woman with full support from his father. When the group was further probed as to why they would have liked to see such an ending, they replied, 'It shows the father has accepted that he lives in a multicultural society'. Students championing a 'miscegenated' relationship appear to positively celebrate cultural/racial mixing, but simultaneously relies on demanding the transformation of George Khan. His Asian-Muslim cultural specificity as a source of problems needing to be discarded for a progressive multicultural future to unfold.

It was not always the case that the ideological straight-jacket of identity prevails in the classroom. There were a number of enactive moments when students appear to want to move beyond its confines. In comparison to the previous seminar group, a student group in another session offer an alternative reading of the cultural condition of the Khan children.

Kath (white female): The kids ... they're just part of a youth culture, its just global. Even if they have a heritage from British and Pakistani culture, it's like a dual identity: when they're on their own, they just act like other kids. [...]
Sanjay (tutor): Do you think their youth identities are something different from that of their parents or of 'dominant' British culture?

Kath: Well a lot of what they do – it's the same all over the place, for teenagers. I mean, even when they're eating those sausages ... okay, they change when their father's arriving ...
Jason ('mixed-race' male): Yep ... they're just larking about.
(Seminar Group B)

While a few other students in the group object to their viewpoint, in this instance, the students want to understand the Khan children from a more 'universalist' perspective which does not explicitly rely on the marker of ethnicity as determining the children's way of life. It does not seem to be case that these students hope to simply move beyond or dismiss identity, but rather understand the Khan children as exhibiting the everyday youthful identities found in 1970s Britain.

The preoccupation with identity in the seminar discussions at the outset was judged by me to be a limiting factor and 'stumbling block' (Butler, 1993a) for an ethical pedagogy. However, during a seminar discussion (involving my participation), questions of identity proved to be an affective site where some students appear to be initiating 'rhizomatic connections' that bring in other ways of embodied thinking. For example:

Sanjay: ... One of the difficulties of this kind of film is how it chooses to represent a 'culture', whether there's something we call 'Asian' culture, or working-class culture ...
Jane (white female): We've been talking and saying that the whole film's supposed to be just about that: nobody wants to lose their sense of what their identity is. That's why the father fights so hard, the children fight so hard, even like the Grandad [Mr Moorhouse] in it, the one who supports Powell, he's trying to keep his sense of identity. [...]
Kenan (Asian Male): Well, Muslim culture is portrayed in a negative way in the film, like it's seen through a Western perspective – I think the audiences should be aware of this bias [...] But British culture is also seen to be tyrannical. Both cultures are shown to be trying to hold on to the traditions and values of their own history – that's the main theme of the film.
Sam (white female): Yes, it is about fearing losing your identity. The Asian father, he fears if his kids do not conform, their identity will be lost ... [K]ids feel if they give in ... they will never get to develop their own identity. The mother takes the kids on a church parade to hold onto their identity. And that Grandad fears immigrants, they pose a threat to his culture and identity.
(Seminar Group B)

While the students' discussion occupy the terrain of cultural identity, they figure that what is at stake in the film is the 'loss' of identity. Students seemingly do not bemoan such a loss or threat to identity, but appreciate its ideological significance and 'hold' over all the characters in the film. This kind of interrogation of identity produces some responses which desire to violate the boundaries of identity formation further, and instead embody what can be considered as a specific deterritorialization of 'culture' and 'identity':

Hegemony is clearly at work in this very political film ... Remove all traces of Asian Culture from *East is East* and replace it with, African, Irish, Punk, Mod, or Rave culture and the result is unlikely to change. (Student essay 5)

Kelly (white female): Well, the film is really about struggles of youth culture – the struggle to find out who you are; and that goes on in everyone's lives doesn't it? ... Yeh, it looks at Asian and British culture, but it could do it with any two cultures. It's just trying to find out where you belong ... Actually, I think it becomes kinda irrelevant that it's about Asians. (Small group A2)

Bad fiction: telling the 'truth' about Asians?

The presence of negative stereotyping of 'Asian culture' in *East is East* troubled a significant number of students, many of whom were not black or Asian members of the class.

The use of stereotypes demonstrates an ignorance and lack of knowledge of other cultures. It does not present any information or present any new insights into Asian and Muslim culture. (Student essay 2)

I felt that stereotypes are still important to contest[,] as much as the existing power relations that are so prevalent in the social reality. (Student essay 12).

Jordan ('mixed race' male): [...] It is a stereotype of Muslim families ... that they have a kind of maniac, a tyrant as a dad. It ended up reinforcing those ideas.
Sarah: ... That girl I know, Robin, her father was very much like that ... But it's a dangerous one [stereotype] ... I mean we're students, we've got a different insight into these type of films ...

Laura (white female): ...that's why we watch them ...

Sarah: ... But say we're two twenty-five year olds off the street who're going to watch the film because we think it's funny and we're laughing at these Indians ... going *'ha ha ha'*; but all we've gotta do is just turn 'round and say *'who the fuckin' hell does he think he is* [George Khan]. *He's in this country, he should ...'* Really, it breeds racism doesn't it, *'how can he say that, he's a Paki, he's married a white woman'* ... an' all that – it's dangerous ... (Small group A1)

A number of students consider *East is East* to made from a 'Western perspective' (see the point made by Kenan earlier), and again, this opinion is also advanced by some of the white students during seminar discussions. They argue that the film is 'biased' against Asian culture, though this is specifically discussed in relation to the depiction of the father, rather than the Khan children. Similarly, there is a demand by some for a more 'balanced' representation of Asian culture. While many of the students consider the negative stereotyping of marginal cultures problematic and potentially racist, they distance themselves from the more susceptible 'mass' audience of the film. The group discussion above reveals these students as thinking themselves as 'critically' informed readers of texts. This position is expressed most emphatically by a reflexive response from a student in their review essay:

I found it a pleasant way to spend a lecture, however, many scenes made me feel uncomfortable, maybe even ashamed. Not uncomfortable with myself as I was confident that I knew where the film was coming from, but rather uncomfortable with the many negative images the film creates and how easily many of them can be either misinterpreted or taken too seriously. (Student essay 4)

In this respect, the pedagogic encounter of *East is East* means that it can nevertheless function in terms of a contradictory minor-popular text (rather than as a text simply propagating racial stereotypes).

There is an almost unanimous agreement amongst the students that the father, George Khan, is a brutal figure in the lives of his children. What concerns many of them however, is the need to account for his actions. For a few students, this is explained reductively in terms of the father's behaviour being attributed to the brutality of a 'traditional Muslim culture'.[25] This position however, is vehemently opposed particularly by some of the 'minority' students.

For example, the following heated exchange took place in a group discussion:

> Michelle (black female): ... All these plans for his kids, he gives them up. He has no choice, everyone's against him.
> Rajinder (Asian female): In the end, he's just a father. The kids have a right to choose ... When the son says 'it's over', he realises he can't go an controlling them ...
> Laurent [white male]: But he's not trying to control them, it's his culture. That's the way he is, what he is.
> Michelle: C'mon, it's not his culture ... to go an' beat your wife! Wha'cha on about! (Small group B1)

Some students appear to display a high degree of sympathy (and even empathy) towards the character of George Khan. They see him as an isolated figure living in Manchester in the early 1970s and berated the film for failing to convey properly the difficulty of his predicament. As one student comments, 'the film didn't show the real pain of the situation' (Seminar Group A). Another student insists that while the father was negatively portrayed: 'a lot of what he did was because he was under attack, from everything. Every single culture does that ... He's not an odd creature, he did what most people would do. It was about social pressure – it wasn't a *race* thing.' (Small group A3)

There is an acknowledgement of the prevalent racism during the setting of the film by many of the students, although a few consider that the film fails to show these harsh conditions and instead focussed too much on 'entertainment' and 'humour'. Moreover, some students feel that the negative portrayal of 'Asian culture' offers the Khan children little opportunity to embody it positively. While the following group discussion tends to assume culture as a property, it nevertheless suggests a desire for the Khan children to be able to legitimately express their 'Asianess'.

> Carla (white female): Do you think the kids know where they're coming from? It's mainly from their mum's side
> Rajinder: There's so much abuse from the father, they don't care about his culture. [...]
> Carla: But I think it's a sad ending
> Rajinder: What do you mean?
> Carla: Well, the Pakistani, Asian culture, it's never properly taken up by the children. They're supposed to be mixed ...

Rajinder: That's because they were brought up in a white neighbour-
hood, taught British customs ... It wasn't easy for them to adapt.
Anyway, it did show bits, like when that girl was dancing in the
yard ...
Carla: It still doesn't mean that they had to reject their culture.
(Small Group B1)

The limited and negative stereotypical representations of Asian culture
and identity prove to be a major area of concern for many students.
This is not particularly surprising given the high proportion of 'minority' students studying the module demonstrated a (political) awareness
of racial stereotyping in the media. Nevertheless, for many of the
students in general, it also emanates from a 'critical' perspective which
has been nurtured through the tools of semiotic and ideological
analysis during the course of their studies.
   The limits of the approach of ideological analysis becomes apparent
however, when students consider the film as a British comedy and its
claims to 'authenticity'. Moreover, the troublesome question of the
film's 'realist' status in relation to the type of truth being advanced
about 'Asian culture' emerges as a potential site of deterritorialization,
as well as a difficult issue to resolve for some students. One of the small
discussion groups (A1) examining the reviews of the film thought the
film was successful because it 'portrayed a gritty northern working class
way of life' and had 'a strong female lead ... typical of working class
British films'.[26] A few of the students directly label the film in terms of
following a 'social-realist tradition' and compare it to other recent
successes such as *The Full Monty*. The group contend that the film
're-packaged complex issues for a British market' and while it has 'elements of truth', it is a comedy which just shows 'extremes of the situation'. Although, for some of the more mature students, the film
resonates favourably with their own youthful experiences.

The real life representation of a street community. (I can see some of
my relatives fitting in, in places!) ... It's like the way I was brought
up as a Catholic. (Questionnaire 14)

I felt a relation to the 70's setting of the film as this was a time that
I grew up in and brought back some nostalgic memories of those
times. In particular I related to the Muslim families' discipline
which was a very important aspect of my upbringing coming from a
Caribbean family. I spent a lot of time laughing at the chastising of

the father which was very similar to the way I received discipline in my family. (Student essay 2).

The issue of *East is East*'s 'authentic' portrayal of working-class (Asian) British life in the 1970s appears to be the key representational strategy for securing its 'realist' mode of address for the students. However, it is the use of highly stereotypical characters and 'extreme' comedy which seemingly disrupt the truthful narration of the film for some students. When the issue of comedy is considered, the group who initially felt that the film's negative stereotypical representations of Asian culture were problematic appear to shift their position during the course of their discussion.

> Sarah: ... It's a British comedy, it's known by audiences, they know the stereotypes. A lot of them are from those other films from the seventies, you know, those gritty northern working-class people and the down-to-earth language they use. [...]
> Laura: It's a stereotype of the Asian father, but they're all stereotypes aren't they? ... It used comedy, okay it could be so true, but it's really funny ...
> Jordan: You always get that comedy element when you get two cultures together ... And loads of British films have comedy, it's part of their commerciality – it's what's expected ... (Small Group A1)

There are some other instances of student responses indicating that the comedic elements of *East is East* does not coincide with what they consider to be the actual workings of Asian culture. What these responses reveal is that while students unsurprisingly possess certain beliefs and knowledge about 'Asian culture' (which may include a position of 'ignorance'), there is a degree of refusal to accept a simplistic or reductive representation of this 'culture'.

> The stereotyping of Asians, the working-class, youth, etc. are far too obvious. In *East is East* those stereotypes may upset (which I somewhat doubt) with the way they are being represented, as comedies are more often than not, guilty of such representations. (Student essay 12)

> Sanjay: Do you think the film tries to tell you something about what it might mean to be 'Asian' in Britain?
> Lana (white female, German): Well, I don't have any real experiences of Asian culture ... but I think it does represent Asian culture in a bad way.

Sanjay: In what ways do you feel ...
Lana: Like that their religion's so strict...but it's not really the case, it's because it's [*East is East*] made for Western eyes ...
Kath: Yes, it's a comedy – just shows extremes – it's not really like that.
(Seminar Group B)

In the film multiculturalism is ignored as the children try to move away from their father's background to become part of the British white working-class. That is in contrast to today's society where if you don't embrace multiculturalism then you will be left behind and also left out. If the film had been set in this new century with the same story then it would have had a gritty realistic feel to it would which have made people film uncomfortable that society was like that. Instead it allows the audience to feel that it is not like that anymore. So it therefore gives the feeling of that was then and as a comedy film it has to, otherwise the audience would be faced with a gritty and realistic storyline that is not so easy to comprehend while you're eating your popcorn. (Student essay 4)

The thoughtful response by the student above in their essay raises the question of realism in relation to the issue of temporality and historical location. It appears to implicitly contend that the element of comedy proscribes any simple truth about Asian culture, even though its nostalgic setting allows the issue of cultural difference and assimilation to be explored from a distance. What is of most concern is the idea that one has to embrace 'multiculturalism' to be part of contemporary society. We shall see that this issue was a vital site of contestation for some white students, especially in relation to their own subjectivities.

Becoming-white?

The power of whiteness as an 'absent present' or as Richard Dyer (1997) notes, to be 'everywhere and nowhere' results in an evasion of it being named in (everyday) social discourses. Furthermore, Charles Mills maintains that it those groups which are racially unmarked who are likely to be oblivious to the privileges of whiteness.

In a racially structured polity, the only people who can find it psychologically possible to deny the centrality of race are those who are racially privileged, for whom race is invisible precisely because the world is structured around them, whiteness is the ground against which figures of other races – those who, unlike us, are raced – appear. The fish do not see the water and whites do not see the racial nature of a white polity because it is natural to them, the element in which they move. (1997, p. 76)

During discussions about the representations of British identity and Britishness/Englishness in *East is East*, particular components of white identities rather than whiteness were raised by students.[27] That is, the particularities of class or regional identities were highlighted in seminar and group discussions, while whiteness remains ostensibly exnominated (cf. Williams, 1997). In hindsight, it appears that white students are unwilling or unable to openly express aspects of their own racialized subjectivities during class discussions. This situation is presumably unremarkable given the politics of whiteness, even if it does mark one of the limits of the classroom pedagogy (see Chapter 4). Though the complex dynamics of power between white students, an 'Asian' tutor and other 'minority' students makes it difficult to reach any easy conclusions. Nevertheless, while the class discussion did not seem to engender 'knowable' student responses to whiteness, a number of white students did reflect upon their subjectivities in their written work. Much of this was in direct response to my provocative review article of *East is East*.

The two extracts below were typical of the written responses by some white students:[28]

My initial reaction to reading Sanjay Sharma's review of *East is East* was one of disappointment. The film has the classic elements of a good film such as strong characters, comedy, drama and good storyline. The first time I watched it, I was engrossed in it even though when it had finished I felt sad rather than 'all laughed out' which was how I expected to feel as it had been described as being a comedy. After reading Sharma's article it enforced the reasons why I found the story sad. It made me aware that maybe I was one of the 'white folks slapping their thighs and falling out of their seats in fits of laughter.' I was disappointed that I did not have such an eye and failed to look at the underlying topics behind it. (Student essay 8)

When I watched *East is East* for the first time I had no idea of the sheer amount of political representations that the film portrayed. Like those 'white folk' along with many Asian folks, I watched this film in titters of laughter, oblivious to the politics of representation working through the text. (Student essay 11)

These responses seem to indicate that the review article raised a level of awareness about the representational cultural politics of *East is East*. However, it is not only the case that their engagement with the article was confined to one of politico-ideological exposure of representations of cultural difference. The modes of expression in the students' writing – highlighting the potency of the humour and in the use of terms such as 'disappointment' – also indicate affective responses towards their pedagogic encounter of *East is East* as well as my review article. It is notable that many students identify and repeat the phrase of 'white folks ... laughing' used in my original article in relation to discussing their own identification with the film. Moreover, there is evidence that students are attempting to grapple with the difficulty of interrogating whiteness in relation to not only the necessity of the political transformation of white culture, but also in relation to probing their own affective responses towards the film:

> Although there were points in the film that I was not sure whether to laugh or cry. I feel a little guilty of falling into the trap of laughing at little Sajid shouting, 'Mam, quick the Paki's are here' ... As a white person myself I think I laughed at the irony of the situation, knowing that there are a lot of raciest [sic] white people who would consider Sajid a 'paki'. (Student essay 4)

> But I do feel that although it doesn't rip whiteness apart, it does leave the question of what is whiteness. Is whiteness the colour of your skin? A state of mind? Or a mixed race Asian family growing up in the North? These questions can't be answered just like that, but I'm sure whiteness is not a little ginger haired boy [Earnest] who is fascinated with Sajid and his family's culture. Although he was a perfect example of a little English boy who was adapting to multicultural surrounding [sic] better than some of his elder family members. (Student essay 8)

It could be that the student above interrogating whiteness is articulating a moment of deterritorialization (and reterritorialization). Her/his account shifts to questioning the identity-status of the miscegenated Khan family growing up in a Northern town in England, and then highlights Earnest's disruptive 'multicultural' presence. The movements in this passage do not institute a rhizomatic multiplicity which escapes the vestiges of identity (see Chapter 4). Nonetheless, the act of questioning whiteness points towards an ethical anti-racist agency without *guilt* (cf. Sivanandan, 1982), opening up the possibility of momentarily breaking out of the representational logic of identity.

One of the contentions forwarded in my review article was that in the final analysis, the majority ('white') culture is left more or less intact in relation to the assimilatory demands made upon Asianess. This assertion incited the following kinds of responses from some white students:

> This article's biggest flaw is its failure to properly address the issue that majority culture (whiteness) also loses out in a multicultural society. Minority cultures do lose out to a far greater extent than the majority culture, but one cannot say that majority culture is left intact. (Student essay 12)

> I feel that all cultures are having to adapt to Britain's multicultural society, and that also the only acceptable white person is a hybrid one. If you're not hybrid as a white person it is easy to be assumed a racist ... I really don't feel that *East is East* sets out to discard Asian culture nor do I feel that it deliberately selects only certain parts of Asian culture to represent. I certainly don't believe it is a new form of racism. What I do feel is that the film tried to show how a lot of Asian youth want to do their own thing and make their own decisions, and if this meant making George Khan look like the villain then so be it. (Student essay 4)

There is an urgency in many of the students' responses in asserting the exigency of majority culture/white people to transform towards contemporary 'multicultural' conditions. Most of all, to deny such a movement would result in 'cultural loss' and even lead to occupying an anachronistic 'racist' subject-position. While some white students may have failed to address adequately the relations of power between majority and minority cultures, their affective investments towards 'multiculture' articulates a desire to eschew a culturally dominant white subjectivity. Perhaps such investments activated a deterritorializing movement of 'becoming-white'?

Conclusion

This chapter has attempted to substantiate and elaborate an example of a pedagogy for alterity. The first part offered 'readings' of the films *Bend It Like Beckham* and *East is East* in order to highlight how they could work as minor-popular British-Asian films. It became apparent that their ambivalent status – particularly through a comedic mode of address in representing Asianess – meant they were politically and culturally ambiguous texts, which could engender both active and reactive effects. Nevertheless it was maintained that in a site-specific pedagogic encounter, films such as these could institute the possibilities of mobilizing students to new non-appropriative sites of ethical agency.

The latter part of the Chapter presented a concrete example of teaching practice in which the film *East is East* was deployed. It is important to stress that the situated pedagogic practice was an open-ended tactical enterprise, contingent upon the institutional context of its operation as well as the specific teaching situation. The culturally diverse student body alongside an 'Asian' tutor attested a complex dynamic of power circulating both within and beyond the classroom pedagogy. It was in terms of this situated, tactical and 'imperfect' pedagogy, that the multifarious student responses were analysed. An epistemologically naïve notion endeavouring to produce a totalizing picture of the student's multiple engagements with the film was avoided, as fleeting fragments of students' discourses could be momentarily grasped. As a corollary, the student responses to *East is East* were rendered in terms of a 'messy text' composed of three 'narratives', and it was maintained that only the 'knowable' elements of the pedagogic encounter could be represented. The presentation of a situated example of teaching was offered as a site-specific pedagogic praxis for alterity.

The deployment of *East is East* unleashed many of the difficulties and antinomies of teaching about difference and 'multiculture' in a university setting. It became evident that the vestiges of 'identity' and 'culture' plagued students' discourses, although there were interruptive instances which appeared to affirm students' desires to move beyond identity and be mobilized otherwise. There were identifiable moments of reflexive responses and affective engagements with *East is East* that had the potential to deterritorialize students, in particular, the disruption of normative white subject-positions. However, the political ambiguity of *East is East* may have instituted a series of reactive affects which remained repressed or silenced in the classroom.

Epilogue: The Problem with Pedagogy

> I feel strongly that, until and unless we grant non-Western authors and texts – be these texts fiction, theory, film, popular music, or criticism – the same kind of verbal, psychical, theoretical density and complexity that we have copiously endowed upon Western authors and texts, we will never be able to extricate our readings from the kind of idealism in which the East-West divide ... is currently mired. Granting such density and complexity would mean refusing to idealize the non-West – be it in the forms of a culture, class, gender, group; a text, author, character – and instead reading the non-West in such a manner as to draw out its unconscious, irrational, and violent nuances, so that as an 'other', it can no longer simply be left in a blank, frozen, and mythologized condition known perfunctorily as an 'alternative' to the West. (Chow, 1998, p. xxi)

The provocation by Chow marks the contested pedagogical, political, and ethical terrain that this book has struggled against. The reified and idealized 'other' continues to be at the centre of neo-liberal multicultural education whereby difference is proscribed in the management of cultural diversity. Chow urges the recognition of the alterity of the other, which can lead to de-centring the cultural hegemony of the West. This risky, ethical challenge to pedagogically engage the other beyond racialized frameworks of knowledge has been the principal concern of *Multicultural Encounters*.

The argument of the book has moved from theoretical critique to situated practice, though it has been a manifold movement for realizing a site-specific pedagogic praxis for alterity. It has involved a careful

189

examination of the foundations and investments in forms of identity politics that continue to give 'recognition' and 'voice' to racially subordinated groups in neo-liberal democracies. Nonetheless, if we are to question existing political closures of liberal and radical educational approaches, the logic of identity and representation need no longer be at the heart of multicultural pedagogy.

The three educational standpoints of 'identity, 'border difference' and the 'other' were presented in terms of their pedagogic articulations of agency. Critical multicultural pedagogy conceived as a tactical intervention (rather than a universalized method), means that each of these standpoints have a utility for particular teaching situations. There still appears to be an underlying tension in this claim, however. Throughout the book, it has been maintained that the educational standpoints of *essentialist* identity and *specific* border difference are unable to activate an ethical alliance, unlike the standpoint of the *singular* other. To assert that either essentialist or inter-subjective theorizations of specificity are inadequate in comparison to a vitalist ontology of singularity, belies the question of praxis. It may be the case that all three standpoints can be legitimately deployed for a critical multicultural teaching practice (and at times are, in spite of our knowledge or intentions!)

I highlighted how different conceptions of identity can engender particular kinds of pedagogies. Educational theorizations of identity and difference need to grasp the limits of these pedagogies – what they may or may not be able to accomplish, which multicultural pedagogies of cultural/media studies have ostensibly failed to address. Thus, interrogating the limits of a critical multicultural pedagogic praxis is not only about striving to close the gap between 'theory' and 'practice' (Williamson, 1981/2), and nor can an alterity pedagogy claim a universal practice. The use of popular British-Asian films were intended to address a specific set of representations of, and encounters with, Asianess circulating in an age of multicultural globalization. While an analysis of alterity provides a general understanding of the possibilities of an ethical agency, the production of such subjectivities occur in site-specific encounters. It is worth reiterating that just as there is no general 'other' (only concrete social agents), there is no pedagogy in general for addressing questions of alterity.

The example of my own teaching practice was a limited effort, both in terms of the actual pedagogy as well as the research methodology. In hindsight, the pedagogy lacked a creative edge as well as being still over-determined by representational practices. Although, the intention

was to modestly innovate a practice that could work in everyday teaching situations and modes of assessment (rather than being identified as
a 'specialist' anti-racist pedagogy, or one that is dependent upon new
media learning technologies for instance). It was a pedagogy operating
within the institutional constraints and pressures found today in many
universities. This should not thwart attempts to innovate more creative
and intensive activities that engage students in different ways, particularly in relation to the multitude of affects unleashed in teaching
encounters which I have been unable to adequately address (see
Gallop, 1995; hooks, 2003; Probyn, 2004). At a more practical level,
teaching with the film *East is East* provided a reflexive example of what
one may actually do with an ethnically marked text. The turn to
multicultural texts for cultural/media studies programmes has been
remarkable for highlighting questions of racialized representation and
power, but they are habitually used by students for 'rehearsing our
lessons of denunciation' (Probyn, 2004, p. 29). The approach offered
not only interrogated such student responses, but attempted to
activate alternative ways of encountering difference which did not
insist on truth of the 'other' or its capacity for escape as figures of
'teleological deliverance' (Keith, 1999; Puwar, 2006).

The 'rhizome' emerged as a concept for innovating a practice which
could deterritorialize students towards ways of knowing outside
of extant racialized knowledges. While a proper explication of the
rhizome is both theoretically and practically challenging – and often
sloppily invoked in contemporary cultural studies – there is a more
immediate problem with the impossibility of realizing any kind of
'rhizomatic pedagogy'. Education is a deeply institutionalized disciplinary practice governed by forms of teacher authority and modes
of assessment, which is increasingly being determined by neo-liberal
agendas (Giroux, 2004). Disrupting the dynamics of institutional
power, at least at a micro-political level, is nevertheless an activity
worth pursuing. The continuing effects of racialized forces of domination should not foreclose thinking about other ways of living with difference. An alterity pedagogy can not offer any political guarantees or
multicultural resolutions in the classroom. Nor does it force students
to '... conform to some image of political liberation nor even they
resist, but simply that they gain some understanding of their own
involvement in the world' (Grossberg, 1994, p. 18).

Admittedly, the task of developing an ethical multicultural pedagogy
is a troubling, if not flawed, undertaking. To develop a pedagogy which
seeks to resist (but neither deny) teacher authority and engages with an

already racialized other is a difficult, if not impossible, task. It remains haunted by the danger of re-invoking the imperial, and now 'postmodern', demand to 'know the other', particularly at a time when ethnicity and otherness have acquired a hypervisibility in global popular multiculture. The interrogating gaze of a 'multicultural ethnicity apparatus' (Chow, 1998) demands that the other reveal its authentic self, through which somehow the 'truth' about Western culture will surface. It is a relation which continues to valorize and domesticate the other – a parasitic, appropriating and violent relation to otherness at the heart of the formation of Western culture. The possibility of encountering alterity is always present though, as manifested in the fleeting, everyday demotic forms of multiculturalism which evade capture. Consequently, it entails activating a de-centring of the cultural hegemony of the West, and instituting the possibility of becoming otherwise. *Multicultural Encounters* has attempted to take up this im/possible challenge for pedagogy.

Notes

Preface

1. The meaning of the term 'multicultural education' shifts in relation to the context of its usage in this book. In general, it also includes anti-racist forms of education. When necessary, a distinction is made between 'neo-liberal' multicultural education and the supposedly more 'radical' anti-racist approaches.
2. When referring to the joint work and concepts of Deleuze and Guattari, the term 'Deleuzo-Guattarian' will be employed as it highlights the significance of both theorists.

Chapter 1 Introduction: What's Wrong with Multiculturalism?

1. I would caution a reading of 'Black' as simply essentialist as it denies the discursive nature of its production. See Hall (1991b), Mercer (1994) and Housee and Sharma (1999) for an account of Black as a politicized identity.
2. Fuss (1990) does make a similar point early in her book, but she concludes that the 'risk of essence' is too great. We need to ask however, to great for whom?
3. Theorists such as Hall (1988) and Spivak (1993) tacitly maintained that the value of a strategic 'essentialist' identity politics may be apposite for racialized or subaltern groups under specific conditions of racial oppression. Again, it is worth stressing the significance of politico-educational context for the mobilization of this type of identity politics. However, an anti-essentialist critique against a politics based on an absolutist identity (or the 'innocent notion of the essentialist Black subject') prevails in the more recent post-structuralist accounts of identity formation – see especially Mercer (1994).
4. See also Kincheloe and Steinberg (1997) who have elaborated upon McLaren's codifications of multiculturalism. The work of Giroux (1992; 1994) is related closely to McLaren's work on critical multiculturalism, especially in terms of border pedagogy and identity which will explored in the next Chapter.
5. We need to be aware that McLaren largely works from a North American perspective in his conceptualization of multiculturalisms.
6. The problem of the representation of national identity for an alterity pedagogy will be taken up in Part II – see especially Chapter 5.
7. Elsewhere Hall has written: 'Identity is ... a structured representation which only achieves its positive through the narrow eye of the negative. It has to go through the eye of the needle of the other before it can construct itself. It produces a very manichean set of opposites' (1991a, p. 21).

8. For example, when Spivak (1988a) writes of 'the subaltern who cannot speak', she refers to the marginal status of a wholly disenfranchized female South Asian subject. It would not be the same as say, a diasporic female Asian-other located in the West. (In this respect, as she argues, that a distinction needs to made between imperialism and racism.)

9. Falzon's account of ethics is derived from Foucault rather than Levinas. While Foucault and Levinas differ in their account of the ethical, they share a general concern of the autonomy of the other. Falzon's reading of Foucault appears to offer a more socially and historically grounded notion of ethics in comparison to Levinas. The latter thinker seemingly borders on a finalist appeal to a religious piety in positing the 'infinity' of the other. See Howard Caygill (2001) for an insightful political assessment of ethics in the work of Levinas. For an entertaining account that ostensibly demolishes the Levinasian project, see Alain Badiou (2001).

Chapter 2   Borders, Agency and Otherness

1. The 'white angry man' is largely a North American phenomenon, although it is considered symptomatic of the problem of modalities of identity politics. This figure attempts to articulate a victimized status on the grounds of being marginalized from contemporary economic and political power (the norm which he supposedly occupies).

2. For example see Gillborn (1990; 1995), Giroux (1992; 2000), Kincheloe and Steinberg (1997), McLaren (1995; 1997) and Rattansi (1992; 1999).

3. For the British case, see for example Back (1996), Bhabha (1994), Gilroy (1987; 1993), Hall (1988; 1991b), Hebdige (1987), Mercer (1994) Sharma *et al.* (1996) and Rattansi (1992; 1999).

4. Anti-essentialist driven critiques of hybridity tend to homogenize manifold notions and operations of difference. For example, May (1999c) has edited an important and timely volume, especially for connecting debates of critical multiculturalism between USA and European educationalists. Nevertheless, in his own article, May (1999a) presents an overly-generalized anti-essentialist critique of hybridity, and does not distinguish between alternative accounts of hybridity which have a bearing upon a range of different possible educational and pedagogic strategies.

5. I am using a combination of the schema presented by Grossberg (1993; 1994) and Young (1995). In particular, Young draws upon Bakhtin in noting that both (i) syncretic cultural fusion ('organic hybridity') and (ii) radical cultural difference (liminal or 'intentional hybridity'), can be identified as two specific deployments of hybridity. Bakhtin's (1981) nuanced understanding of hybridity has been influential in contemporary accounts of identity and inter-subjectivity, especially in the work of Bhabha (1994).

6. See Araeen (1989), Gilroy (1987; 1993), Hall (1988) and Mercer (1988; 1994).

7. This issue will be studied further in Chapters 5 and 6, especially in relation to representations of British-Asian 'culture' and 'identity', and the possibility of their pedagogic engagement.

8. See especially Giroux (1992; 1994), Giroux and McLaren (1994), Kanpol and McLaren (1995), Sleeter and McLaren (1995) and McLaren (1995; 1997).
9. It is worth reminding the reader that educationalists such as Giroux, McLaren and Rattansi do not cohere to a single educational standpoint, and nor do they deploy only a one notion of identity production. For example, McLaren (1997) also promotes the standpoint of the other in his turn to exploring questions of ethics.
10. According to Deleuze and Guattari (1984), the agency of the modern subject structured by a 'lack' is contingent upon a capitalist social order, and is not just an ahistorical ontology of subjectivity.
11. Within Bhabha's account the cultural specificity of a particular 'minority' identity can be understood outside of an anti/essentialism problematic, see Housee and Sharma (1999).
12. It will be argued that even in this account of difference, it is founded on a 'politics of lack'. For a critique of 'lack' in Fuss's psychoanalytical stance, see Fernández (1993).
13. For a somewhat flawed 'marxist' critique of Bhabha, see Shohat and Stam (1994) and Parry (1994).
14. The critique of the universalization of hybridity can be made from the charge that Bhabha appears to conflate 'syncretic hybridity' with 'liminal hybridity'. In spite of his intentions, it is not always clear whether Bhabha describes the third space as a site of the production of subjectivity, or it is actually occupied by the 'subaltern'; and/or more problematically, by the post-colonial 'migrant' as found in the elite cosmopolitan figure of Salman Rushdie.
15. George Yudice (1988) also argued against locating minority agency in these terms. Nealon reads Bhabha as theorizing individuation in terms of inter-subjectivity – the specific (see Chapter 1). Peter Hallward (2001) offers an alternative account, which constructs Bhabha as advancing a singular conception of individuation.
16. As Patton (2000) notes, the concept of 'desire' has affinities with Foucault's notion of 'power' as being productive. In Grossberg's account, the term 'power' is employed rather than 'desire'.
17. This understanding of subjectivity as agency is comparable to that found in Nealon (1998), which will be used to elaborate upon Grossberg's work.
18. 'Deterritorialization' in the context of identity formation implies the possible creative openings, transformations and movements – 'lines of flight' – in the production of new ways of living. It is it related to the Deleuzo-Guattarian concept of 'becoming'.
19. Conceiving the agency of a minority as a 'statement of power' requires further elaboration. It is best understood in terms of a Deleuzo-Guattarian notion of 'minoritarian' politics which will be addressed later in this chapter.
20. See especially Moraes (1996) and McLaren (1997) for a pedagogy inspired by Bakhtin. For a more philosophically orientated account, see also Peters (1996).
21. Butler is attentive to the 'material specificity of the restrictions' which allow the maintenance of particular normative identities as Nealon (1998) points out. We would therefore need to account for 'marginalized' or racialized

identities in their specific historical contexts and in relation to the foreclosures or multiple exclusions which make particular identities im/possible or un/liveable.

22. The pedagogic practice of engaging with the 'outside' (difference) will be developed in the Chapter 3 in relation to the concept of the 'rhizome'.

23. The development of a coherent concept of 'affect' is elusive in the work of Deleuze and Guattari, although Brian Massumi (1996; 2002) has significantly elaborated upon this concept. In particular, he argues for a distinction between 'affect' and 'emotion': the autonomy of affect lies outside of its narrativization into an emotional (meaningful) response. Elspeth Probyn (2004) offers a timely account of how 'affect' has been taken up in critical and feminist pedagogy. In my study, while an 'affective' pedagogy is pursued, in practice it remains rather underdeveloped. It is worth stressing that the focus on what texts can do rather than what they mean should not be simplistically conceived as a pedagogic rejection of meaning over the valorization of affect. See Jeremy Gilbert (2004) for a useful discussion of the inter-relation and 'inseparability' of meaning and affect.

24. 'Minorities' should not be considered in numerical terms, or necessarily in terms of how they wish to be included in a broadened societal 'standard' such as a liberal multicultural norm which recognizes the identities of black people, women or homosexuals (Patton, 2000).

Chapter 3   Teaching Difference: Representations and Rhizomes

1. In Britain, these have especially developed in the fields of media and cultural studies, for example Alvarado and Boyd-Barrett (1992), BFI (1990), Buckingham and Sefton-Green (1994), Buckingham *et al.* (1995) and Masterman (1985). In the USA these have mainly been identified as critical pedagogy and media literacy, see Giroux and McLaren (1994), Giroux *et al.* (1996), Giroux and Shannon (1997), Scholle and Denski (1994), Simon (1992) and Sleeter and McLaren (1995). There are also a range of feminist pedagogies such as Gore (1993), Holland *et al.* (1995), Lather (1991; 1994) and Luke and Gore (1992), Mayberry and Rose (1999) and Weiler (2001).

2. Luke (1992) took issue with the androcentric limits of the critical pedagogy work of Giroux and McLaren. However, it was Ellsworth (1992) who attacked critical pedagogy for failing to recognize its own authoritarian practices. While some of her criticisms are overstated, nevertheless, she did raise the important question of politico-pedagogic status of 'emancipatory knowledges' in the classroom. This issue will be explored later on in this chapter.

3. See Simons (1994) for an alternative characterization of progressive pedagogies operating in higher education.

4. In relation to multicultural schooling in Britain, see for example Brandt (1986), Carrington and Short (1989), Epstein (1993), Jeffcoate (1979), Lynch *et al.* (1992), Troyna and Carrington (1990) and Dadzie (1999). For British higher education teaching, it has been rather limited in comparison to

schooling. For example, the edited collection, *Race and Ethnic Studies Today* (Bulmer and Solomos, 1999) and the Institutional Racism in Higher Education Toolkit Project (Turney *et al.*, 2002) raise the complexities of theorizing 'race' and cultural difference in university teaching, though there is relatively little discussion of innovating pedagogic practice.

5. The limitations of radical pedagogies based on encouraging students to 'expose' existing oppressions will be discussed later.

6. For example, see Dadzie (1999), Cohen and Gardiner (1982), Foster (1990), NUT (1996) and Stephan (1999).

7. Hall (1988) is careful to emphasize the political legitimacy of the struggle for (positive) black representation (the 'relations of representation'), as the type of racialized conditions which have engendered such an anti-racist response is still present today. Although, the problem of the im/possibility of the representation of 'other cultures' outside of a racialized discourse will be explored in the next section.

8. What came to be known as 'Screen Theory' worked from a structuralist-psychoanalytical perspective. This differed from the work of the CCCS which was more influenced by discourse theory and trying to theorize an active agent. For an account of their differing perspectives, see for example Davies (1995) and Willeman (1994).

9. In Britain, the most influential work has been by Hall (1980; 1988; 1991b; 1992a; 1992b; 1996; 1997a). For other important work, see Cohen (1991; 1992; 1998), Donald and Rattansi (1992), Ferguson (1998), Mercer (1988; 1994) and Willeman (1994).

10. Judith Williamson has argued that there is 'a huge gap between theoretical work and teaching', and the perpetual developments in theory do not readily translate into the everyday practices of teaching. '[T]eaching is ... anchored in a concrete situation ... so it involves not so much saying new things but saying the same basic things again and again, and finding different ways of saying them' (1981/2, p. 81). The lack of congruence between theory and educational practice could also be because complex poststructuralist theoretical developments during this period were not readily accessible and only had a limited academic audience.

11. This type of 'knowing' student who expresses forms of 'cynical knowledge' will be highlighted later.

12. Buckingham's emphasis on classroom-based research replays the tensions found in media/cultural studies between the theoretically driven work about subject formation and empirical audience studies research. See also Morley (1992).

13. For example, see Belsey (1980), Grossberg (1992), Kellner (1995), Morley (1992) and Willeman (1994).

14. See especially the work of Richards (1986; 1992; 1998) and Buckingham and Sefton-Green (1994).

15. Cohen highlights that the Anansi stories were rejected from the school curriculum where his research took place because they failed to conform to the multicultural demands of positive black representation! Buckingham and Sefton-Green (1994) have previously done work along similar lines, especially in their example of the contradictory masculine 'action hero' character of 'Plaz'.

16. In terms of theorizing racism in relation to questions of 'desire' and phantasy, a psychoanalytic perspective is present in the work of Cohen (1991; 1992; 1998), Rattansi (1992) and in Hall (1997a). Theorizing the complex intersectionality of racism and sexuality has made psychoanalysis attractive in this respect; see for example Gilman (1985) and Kaplan (1997). There has been significant work in pedagogy from this perspective, such as Appel (1999), Kelly (1997), Todd (1997) and Walkerdine (1990). Nevertheless, as argued previously, theorists do not always coherently deploy one specific understanding of the subject/identity. For example, Cohen, Rattansi and Hall advance the need for a psychoanalytical understanding of 'race' and sexuality while also employing a Foucauldian notion of subject formation. This is not the place to launch a critique of a psychoanalytical understanding of 'race' and alterity, although the notion of a subject founded upon a 'lack' has been examined in the previous chapter; also see Fernández (1993). Furthermore, psychoanalysis primarily has theorized sexual difference and desire, which is not necessarily produced on the same grounds, nor should be conflated with, the ontology of racial difference. Nevertheless, see Kalpana Seshadri-Crooks (2000) for an interesting study which conjoins racial and sexual difference from a Lacanian perspective.

17. The point is that Cohen does supply an 'affective' reading of the 'cowgirl warrior', even though it is not explicitly sanctioned by his psychoanalytical framework. Note that my own reading of this pedagogic intervention is obviously limited by the discourse of Cohen's original account.

18. Buckingham (1993; 1996) has claimed that critical pedagogy's focus on media literacy has significantly lacked an adequate basis of 'classroom practice' for developing its pedagogy. His contention to some extent is correct, although it does not necessarily wholly negate the importance of the theoretical work on media literacy.

19. For example, see Alvarado and Boyd-Barrett (1992), Buckingham and Sefton-Green (1994), Flemming (2000), Masterman (1985), Lister *et al.* (2003) and Lusted (1991).

20. While this chapter outlines a way of thinking about a pedagogy for alterity, we shall see its actual realization and practice is a site-specific activity.

21. For instance, both Hall (1997a) and Ferguson (1998) attempt to use both neo-Gramscian and Foucauldian perspectives in their analysis of racialized representations.

22. Hall's article appears in the edited collection *Representation: cultural representations and signifying practices* (Hall, 1997b). This collection is part of the Open University (OU) textbook series, *Culture, Media and Identities*. These textbooks are not only central to the OU teaching programme, but have been influential in defining the teaching of cultural and media studies.

23. We have found that a performative ethical agency (subjectivity) is structured by the irreducibility of the other. While a totalizing knowledge about the other is not possible, it does not proscribe the continuous 'social dialogue' that produces our dialogical existence (Falzon 1998).

24. Deleuze and Guattari (1987) offer the example that the generalized and diverse use of a particular language has a rhizomatic structure, as it has no ideal-speaker/listener and nor is there a homogeneous linguistic community.

25. Multiplicity expresses the principle of heterogeneity: 'relations are external to their terms ... [I]t is a question of the middle: something happens "between" two terms, which leaves two terms intact in their singularity' (Marks, 1998, p. 34). Deleuze develops the concept of immanence from Spinoza – see Todd May (2004) for a useful account of immanence.
26. Deleuze (1995) describes himself as an 'empiricist' in the sense that he considers there to be nothing 'outside' of the real, and neither is the real mediated by the act of representation. The concepts of the 'virtual' and 'actual' are deployed to argue that the real does not have an outside.
27. This issue becomes significant in the next chapter when I try and think through a pedagogic practice which explores filmic representations of 'Asian culture and identity' outside of existing racialized regimes of knowledge.

Chapter 4   Reading Racial Crisis

1. The concept of 'mass movement' for Deleuze and Guattari (1987) refers not to its size, but to its quality or nature. We need to think of it in machinic terms and how it is actualized, rather than its dimensions or magnitude.
2. These representations of otherness habitually stand for something else, such as a primordial connection to nature, irrationality, authenticity, passivity or conversely aggression, or exotic sensuality (Root, 1995; Shohat and Stam, 1994).
3. The three films in the series are: *The Matrix* (1999); *The Matrix Revolutions* (2003); and, *The Matrix Reloaded* (2003). Much of my analysis of *The Matrix* trilogy will focus on the first of the film series. For the sake of brevity, I usually refer to the trilogy as a singular text, and simply write '*The Matrix*'.
4. Other films associated with the 'New Black Realism' have included: *Boyz N the 'Hood* (1991), *New Jack City* (1991), *Straight out of Brooklyn* (1991) *Juice* (1992). In interviews, Kassovitz denies that he has directly drawn upon these 'hood films, as he considers many of them as commercially exploitative. Though clearly, much of the urban aesthetic of *La Haine* has been influenced by the 'New Black Realism'.
5. The verlan (vernacular) language of Hubert, Vinz and Said was not fully discernible for middle-class French speaking audiences; and elements were lost in the English translation (Schroader, 2001).
6. Although much of the following argument is applicable to *La Haine* too.
7. There have been an increasing numbers of 'art-house', martial-arts Chinese films aimed at the Western market such as *Crouching Tiger, Hidden Dragon* (2000, Ang Lee), *Hero* (2002, Zhang Yimou) and *House of Flying Daggers* (2004, Zhang Yimou). Their reception has ostensibly been framed by an Orientalist aesthetic of the exotic (Xu, 2004).
8. For those readers who missed it, '*The One*' is based on the transposition of the moniker, *Neo*.
9. For an alternative reading, see Hallward's (2001) account of the singularizing force of post-colonial theory.
10. The fear, of course, is that there are Others that are unknowable, untranslatable, uncontrollable – they must be either domesticated or destroyed.

Chapter 5   Critical Practice: 'Minor-Popular' Film

1. The distinction between the Black workshop and independent sectors has further blurred from the 1990s, particularly in terms of multiple sources of funding for both these sectors. The workshop movement has now effectively ceased due to lack of public funding.
2. The next chapter will provide a more in-depth reading of the expressive cultural politics of two popular films, *Bend It Like Beckham* and *East is East*. The latter film will also be explored via its deployment in an actual teaching situation.
3. The dissolution of the political 'anti-racist' identity category of 'Black' and the shift towards more 'ethnicized' identities makes it somewhat problematic now to situate a British-Asian Film within the discourse of Black Film. However, it can be argued that 'Black' was never simply an essentialist identity-category (Housee and Sharma, 1999).
4. These questions have animated the debates about the limits of 'realist' anti-racist educational strategies, see Rattansi (1992).
5. Supposedly the 'postmodern' collapse of the representational practices of 'high' and 'low' cultural forms makes it more difficult to identify specific innovative aesthetic practices as belonging to the realm of the so-called avant-garde. Nevertheless, 'experimental film' still appears to retain a distinctiveness based on its formal aesthetic qualities.
6. In Chapter 2, it has been maintained that the process of hybridity (as cultural syncretism and liminality) does not guarantee an anti-racist political project. Moreover, its ontology may deny the alterity of the other. Both Mercer and Willeman draw on a Bakhtinian perspective which highlights the transformative potential of the 'minority', but does not adequately attend to the question of alterity. Nevertheless, it is productive to stress the perspective of Mercer and Willeman more in terms of a 'minor' politics.
7. We should however be careful not to homogenize or make assumptions about cinema audiences. For example, during the presentation of a 'Black Film' or a short season of these films, art-house cinemas may attract different (and more culturally diverse) audiences. Moreover, independent productions have often been funded by Channel 4 or BBC television, meaning that they are usually transmitted on terrestrial television not long after their cinematic release.
8. Hall (1988) and Mercer (1994) pointed to the need to develop a 'politics of critique' for emergent Black cultural productions. My concern however, is in relation to how popular British-Asian films can be used for a pedagogic classroom practice.
9. See also a critique by Dhillon-Kashyup (1988) on similar (limited) grounds.
10. An Orientalist discourse may include 'Arab' and 'Chinese' groupings within a definition of Asian, making the division of humanity more complex and shifting than it appears in Goulbourne's account.
11. My use of the term 'Orientalizing' indicates the modality of knowledge production of the South Asian other and the specificity of its racialized discourse. It is not necessarily the same as the discourse of the 'Orient' examined by Said, although similar characteristics are present.

12. *Goodness Gracious Me* attracted an 80 percent 'white' television audience in Britain, and won a 'Best New Comedy Award' in 1998.
13. The 'first lady', Cheri Blair, wife of the current British Prime Minister, Tony Blair, has been famously pictured on more that one occasion wearing expensive, designer *shalwar kameez* South Asian dress. The question of which 'Asian cultures' are acceptable is always open to contestation. The recent alarm over 'extremist' elements of so-called 'Muslim communities' has raised serious doubt over liberal toleration of multicultural difference.
14. The Channel 4 television documentary, *Brimful of Asia* (1999, Pratibha Parmar) highlights the entry of a new Asianess into the popular and public spheres of British culture. While it notes the Orientalizing reception of these cultural practices, the film itself suffers from celebrating the hybridity of 'second-generation' Asians.
15. There appears to be a kind of modernist, avant-garde 'formalism' that is present in Deleuze's (1986; 1989) analysis of a post-war cinema of affect. His framework has nevertheless been increasingly influential. For example, Marks's (2000) study of intercultural cinema only focuses on experimental film and thus heavily relies on highly aestheticized representational film practices. Shaviro (1993) and Gormley's (2005) study of cinema explores popular film genres, though both still tend to rely on the formalistic qualities of these texts in their analysis.
16. This should not be confused with a dialectical operation of negation. Rather, the production of a 'truth' is through the movement of serialization, see Rodowick (1997).
17. Comparing Nealon's (1998) example of Jazz and Blues, Black film can be thought in terms of singularizing 'forces of becoming' which are in a constant interplay of deterritorialization and reterritorialization, and connecting to other sites. Black Film in a pedagogic deployment therefore could constitute a 'block of becoming': a student could in a sense 'become-Black Film'; Black-Film could become-black, -Asian, or -white; white could become-other, and so on.
18. It is the particular or singularizing kind of difference instituted in the repetition of difference (the production of meanings, affects, subjectivities etc.) is what would make the expressive politics of these films significant. See the earlier account of multiplicity and the rhizome in Chapter 3.

Chapter 6   Diaspora Pedagogy: Working with British-Asian Film

1. *Bhaji on the Beach* was the first full-feature length UK film directed by a British-Asian woman, and also the first independent 'Asian' film since Kureishi's *My Beautiful Laundrette* (1985) to cross over to wider audiences outside of the comparatively small-scale art-house cinema sector.
2. In comparison to directors such as the Hughes (*Menace II Society*) or Kassovitz (*La Haine*) who possess a reflexive awareness of classic film genres and display an acute sense of cinematic aesthetics, Chadha has established herself as a populist film-maker whose style is influenced by television melodrama and 'Bollywood' film.

3. It is interesting to note that in spite of the intentions of the director, Chadha, some reviews of the film characterize Jess's family as traditional, particularly in terms of curtailing her freedom and expecting Jess to marry. The utilization of 'tradition' in these cases ignores that the family also want their daughter to excel in higher education and become a doctor. While such career aspirations are fairly 'conservative', educating a daughter may not be considered 'traditional' for particular modes of South Asian patriarchy. The deployment of tradition for both media discourses about South Asians, as well as South Asians themselves, is contestable and historically contingent, to say the least.

4. While these texts propagated racist stereotypes, they were nevertheless actively watched and 'enjoyed' by minority communities (Sharma, 1990). Much of the realist anti-racist critiques against negative racial stereotypes have failed to take account of the ambivalence of comedic texts.

5. 'Bollywood' cinema appeals to a huge number of speakers of diverse languages, both inside and outside the sub-continent. This partially accounts for why it is an intensely visual cinema.

6. Easthope points out that in dominant English culture, the body occupies a distanciated and 'othered' status. He argues that working-class humour attempts to recuperate the body by bringing it into an 'active relationship with social life' (1999, p. 176).

7. The focus on an active 'sporting femininity' by Chadha is clearly meant to be contrasted with the prolific contemporary media representations of overtly sexualized female bodies. A sporting femininity appears not be simply defined against hegemonic modes of femininity (or masculinity). Moreover, it also differs from the emergence of what McRobbie (1999) has identified as assertive or ironic 'new-sexualities' which reflexively question conventional gendered stereotypes.

8. The humour of the scene revolves around the obnoxious relatives immediately turning up at Jess's house and informing her parents that their daughter was seen kissing a 'white boy'. The cropped-hair Jules is mistaken for being male. When Jess returns and is confronted with the revelation that she was seen with a 'boy', Jess defends herself by declaring that Jules is in fact female, which only makes matters worse.

9. *East is East* has a dedicated website which lists numerous praizeworthy reviews. Available at: www.eastiseast.co.uk.

10. George and Ella are bringing back Sajid from hospital. In an earlier scene at the Mosque, Sajid is discovered to be still uncircumcised. For George it proves further embarrassment and he insists upon Sajid's 'tickle-tackle' being sorted out. Throughout the operation Sajid remains clad in his Parka jacket, although it fails to offer him any protection against the act of circumcision. As a source of humour, circumcision appears to be rather dubious, particularly for audiences who have little understanding of this religious practice.

11. We shall find that some students found the idea of 'culture-clash' highly dubious and limiting.

12. The suffix of '-*istan*' now connotes the spectre of an invading Islamic terrorist threat, since the dubbing of England's capital as 'Londonistan' (Kepel, 2005).

13. The pre-pubescent Earnest is infatuated with Meenah, much to the embarrassment of Sajid.
14. There is a forgotten history of the South Asian diaspora in relation to the development of self-run cinemas as unique social spaces, which facilitated in the construction of a sense of multiple belongings (Puwar and Powar, 2005).
15. The deeply offensive Hindustani expression 'junglee' connotes being uncouth, uncivilized and 'animal-like'.
16. The obvious problem is that Asian and white (working-class) stereotypes do not function in the same manner, and nor do they necessarily have the same political effects. Stereotypes of Asianess are subject to specific types of fixing within racialized discourses.
17. The description of the student body is based on my personal knowledge and is therefore impressionistic. It is offered only to crudely indicate the diversity of the students attending the course.
18. Many universities are in a chronic state of under-funding in Britain (*The Guardian*, 23/02/2001), which has led to high student-staff ratios, lack of proper resourcing and has made innovations in curriculum and pedagogy less appealing. The emphasis on establishing research-driven academic cultures is leading to the marginalization of teaching activities.
19. It is worth repeating that classroom pedagogy utilizing methods of ideology critique (inadvertently) engages with student's affective investments. The pedagogy being explored here seeks to harness this latter practice.
20. The question of 'consenting participants' is especially problematic. Students may feel obliged to be included in a research endeavour in their submission to the authority of the tutor. It can lead to a research relationship which exploits students.
21. The review of the film was only given out to two student groups. They were allowed to choose whether they wanted to undertake the assignment; or alternatively, review another article used in the seminars during the programme. My provocative review of *East is East* proved to be a significant site of engagement for a number of students.
22. The danger exists that my review could be read as an authentic marginalized voice (cf. Simmonds, 1997; Nicoll, 2004). Although, as we shall see, some students questioned my reading of the film.
23. Nevertheless, as a multi-voiced text, the possibility of the reader to interrogate and re-write it is encouraged.
24. The various student responses were generated from the following four sites of engagement: (i) *Seminar Group A* and *Seminar Group B* (whole class); (ii) *Small Groups A1-3* and *B1-3* (belonging to each of these larger Seminar Groups A and B. Thus, there were six small groups in total); (iii) *Questionnaires*; (iv) *Student Essays*. Student responses labelled as Seminar Group A, for example, indicates the response was generated in the whole seminar class discussion. In comparison, Small Group A2 indicates the response was generated within that smaller student group's discussion (and not in a whole Seminar Group A class discussion). Both (i) Seminar Group and (ii) Small Group responses, were recorded and transcribed. Student names have been altered to ensure anonymity.

25. It could have been the case that other students held this point of view, though resisted expressing such a position.
26. The figure of the mother, Ella, played by Linda Bassett has been singled out for her 'authentic' working-class performance by several film reviewers. Many students also shared this view.
27. It is important to make a distinction between the relationship of 'white' identities to whiteness. Whiteness as a marker of racial privilege means that white people negotiate their relationship to whiteness, and not all white people necessarily take up its privileges (Dyer, 1997).
28. The assessed written work does not bear the names of students because of the practice of anonymous marking. Although, during the course of their essays, several students declared themselves as 'white', and in those instances it was possible to register this in my analysis of their responses.

Bibliography

Ahmed, S. (2000), *Strange Encounters: embodied others in post-coloniality* (London: Routledge).

Althusser, L. and E. Balibar (1997), *Reading Capital* (London: Verso).

Alvarado, M. and O. Boyd-Barrett (1992), *Media Education: an introduction* (London: BFI/Open University).

Anthias, F. and N. Yuval-Davis (1992), *Racialized Boundaries: race, nation, gender, colour and class and the anti-racist struggle* (London: Routledge).

Anzaldúa, G. (1987), *Borderlands/La Frontera: the new mestiza* (San Francisco: Spinsters/Aunt Lute).

Appel, S. (1999), *Psychoanalysis and Pedagogy* (London: Bergin & Garvey).

Araeen, R. (1989), *The Other Story: Asian, African and Caribbean Artists in post-war Britain* (London: Hayward Gallery).

Aronowitz, S. and H. Giroux (1991), *Postmodern Education: politics, culture, and social criticism* (London: University of Minnesota Press).

Atkinson, P. (1992), *Understanding Ethnographic Texts* (London: Sage).

Back, L. (1996), *New Ethnicities and Urban Culture: racisms and multiculture in young lives* (London: UCL Press).

Badiou, A. (2001), *Ethics: an essay on the understanding of evil* (London: Verso).

Bakhtin, M. (1981), *The Dialogic Imagination: four essays* (Austin: University of Texas Press).

Banerjea, K. (2000), 'Sounds of whose underground? The fine tuning of diaspora in an age of mechanical reproduction', *Theory, Culture and Society* 17(3), pp. 64–79.

Banerjea, K. and J. Barn (1996), Versioning terror: Jallianwala Bagh and the Jungle, in *Dis-Orienting Rhythms: the politics of the new asian dance music* (eds) S. Sharma, J. Hutnyk and A. Sharma (London: Zed Books).

Belsey, C. (1980), *Critical Practice* (London: Methuen).

Bennett, D. (1998), Introduction, in *Multicultural States: rethinking identity and difference* (ed.) D. Bennett (London: Routledge).

Bennett, D. and H. Bhabha (1998), Liberalism and minority culture: reflections on 'culture's in between', in *Multicultural States: rethinking identity and difference* (ed.) D. Bennett (London: Routledge).

BFI (1990), *Media Education in Primary Schools* (London: British Film Institute).

Bhabha, H. (1990), The Third Space: interview with Homi Bhabha, in *Identity* (ed.) J. Rutherford (London: Lawrence and Wishart).

Bhabha, H. (1994), *The Location of Culture* (London: Routledge).

Bhatia, N. (1998), 'Women, homelands and the Indian diaspora', *The Centennial Review* XLII(3), pp. 511–26.

Bhattacharyya, G. and J. Gabriel (1994), 'Gurinder Chadha and the *Apna* Generation: Black British film in the 1990s', *Third Text* 27, pp. 55–63.

Biesta, G. and D. Egéa-Kuehne (eds) (2001) *Derrida and Education* (London: Routledge).

Bonnett, A. (2000), *White Identities: Historical and International Perspectives* (Harlow: Prentice Hall).

Bourne, J. (1987), 'Homelands of the Mind: Jewish feminism and identity politics', *Race and Class* 29(1), pp. 1–24.

Boyd, T. (1997), *Am I Black Enough For You?* (Bloomington & Indianapolis: Indiana University Press).

Brah, A. (1996), *Cartographies of Diaspora: contesting identities* (London: Routledge).

Brandt, G. (1986), *The Realization of Anti-racist Teaching* (London: Falmer).

Britzman, D., K. Santiago-Válles, G. Jiménez-Múñoz, *et al.* (1993), Slips that show and tell: fashioning multiculture as a problem of representation, in *Race, Identity and Representation in Education* (eds) C. McCarthy and W. Crichlow (London: Routledge).

Brown, W. (1995), *States of Injury: power and freedom in late modernity* (New Jersey: Princeton University Press).

Buchanan, I. (2000), *Deleuzism: a metacommentary* (Edinburgh: Edinburgh University Press).

Buckingham, D. (1986), 'Against demystification', *Screen* 27(5), pp. 80–95.

Buckingham, D. (1993), 'Going Critical: the limits of media literacy', *Australian Journal of Education* 37(2), pp. 142–52.

Buckingham, D. (1996), 'Critical Pedagogy and Media Education: a theory in search of a practice', *Journal of Curriculum Studies* 28(6), pp. 627–50.

Buckingham, D. (ed.) (1998) *Teaching Popular Culture: beyond radical pedagogy* (London: UCL Press).

Buckingham, D., J. Grahame and J. Sefton-Green (1995), *Making Media: practical production in media education* (London: English and Media Centre).

Buckingham, D. and J. Sefton-Green (1994), *Cultural Studies Goes to School: reading and teaching popular media* (London: Taylor and Francis).

Bulmer, M. and J. Solomos (eds) (1999) *Ethnic and Racial Studies Today* (London: Routledge).

Butler, J. (1990), *Gender Trouble: feminism and the subversion of identity* (London: Routledge).

Butler, J. (1993a), *Bodies that Matter: on the discursive limits of 'sex'* (London: Routledge).

Butler, J. (1993b), Endangered/Endangering: Schematic Racism and White Paranoia, in *Reading Rodney King/Reading Urban Uprisings* (ed.) R. Gooding-Williams (London: Routledge).

Butler, J. (2000), Ethical Ambivalence, in *The Turn To Ethics* (eds) M. Garber, B. Hanssen and R. Walkowitz (London: Routledge).

Carby, H. (1992), The multicultural wars, in *Black Popular Culture* (ed.) G. Dent (Seattle: Bay Press).

Carrington, B. and G. Short (1989), *'Race' and the Primary School: theory into practice* (Berkshire: NFER-Nelson).

Caygill, H. (2001), *Levinas and the Political* (London: Routledge).

Chow, R. (1993), *Writing Diaspora: tactics of intervention in contemporary cultural studies* (Bloomington and Indianapolis: Indiana University Press).

Chow, R. (1998), *Ethics after Idealism* (Bloomington and Indianapolis: Indiana University Press).

Clarke, S. (1991), 'Fear of a Black Planet: race, identity politics, common sense', *Socialist Review* 21(3–4), pp. 37–59.

Clifford, J. and G. Marcus (eds) (1986) *Writing Culture: the poetics and politics of ethnography* (London: University of California Press).

Cohen, P. (1991), *Monstrous images, perverse reasons: cultural studies in anti-racist education* (London: Centre for Multicultural Education University of London Institute of Education).

Cohen, P. (1992), 'It's racism what dunnit': hidden narratives in theories of racism, in *'Race', culture and difference* (eds) J. Donald and A. Rattansi (London: Sage/Open University).

Cohen, P. (1998) Tricks of the trade: on teaching arts and 'race' in the classroom, in *Teaching popular culture: beyond radical pedagogy* (ed.) D. Buckingham (London: UCL Press).

Cohen, P. and C. Gardiner (eds) (1982) *'It ain't half racist mum': fighting racism in the media* (London: Comedia/CARM).

Colebrook, C. (2000), Introduction, in *Deleuze and Feminist Theory* (eds) I. Buchanan and C. Colebrook (Edinburgh: Edinburgh University Press).

Cunningham, D. (2003), 'Stalling Zion: Hegemony through Racial Conflict in The Matrix', *Rhizomes*, 7, accessed 10/06/2005, http://www.rhizomes.net/issue7/cunning.htm

Dadzie, S. (1999), *Toolkit for Tackling Racism in Schools* (Stoke-on-Trent: Trentham).

Davies, I. (1995), *Cultural Studies and Beyond* (London: Routledge).

Deleuze, G. (1983), *Nietzsche and Philosophy* (London: Athlone Press).

Deleuze, G. (1986), *Cinema 1: the movement-image* (London: Athlone Press).

Deleuze, G. (1989), *Cinema 2: the time image* (London: Athlone Press).

Deleuze, G. (1994), *Difference and Repetition* (London: Athlone Press).

Deleuze, G. (1995), *Dialogues* (New York: Columbia).

Deleuze, G. and F. Guattari (1984), *Anti-Oedipus: capitalism and schizophrenia* (London: Athlone Press).

Deleuze, G. and F. Guattari (1986), *Kafka: toward a minor literature* (London: Minnesota).

Deleuze, G. and F. Guattari (1987), *A Thousand Plateaus: capitalism and schizophrenia* (London: Athlone Press).

Deleuze, G. and F. Guattari (1994), *What is philosophy?* (New York: Columbia University Press).

Denzin, N. (1997), *Interpretative Ethnography* (London: Sage).

Denzin, N. (2003), 'Screening Race', *Cultural Studies-Critical Methodologies* 3(1), pp. 22–43.

Deussing, R. (1996), 'Interview: Mathieu Kassovitz', accessed 12/05/2005, http://old.thing.net/ttreview/febrev.04.html

Dhillon-Kashyap, P. (1988), 'Locating the Asian experience', *Screen* 29(4), pp. 120–7.

Diawara, M. (1991), 'The nature of mother dreaming', *Third Text* 13, pp. 43–58.

Diawara, M. (1993), Black American Cinema: The New Realism, in *Black American Cinema* (ed.) M. Diawara (London: American Film Institute/Routledge).

Donald, J. and A. Rattansi (eds) (1992) *'Race', culture and difference* (London: Sage/Open University).

Dyer, R. (1997), *Whiteness* (London: Routledge).

Easthope, A. (1999), *Englishness and National Culture* (London: Routledge).

Edwards, V. (1996), *The Other Languages: a guide to multilingual classrooms* (Berkshire: University of Reading).

Ellsworth, E. (1992), Why doesn't this feel empowering? Working through the repressive myths of critical pedagogy, in *Feminisms and Critical Pedagogy* (eds) C. Luke and J. Gore (London: Routledge).

Elstob, K. (1997/8), 'La Haine (Hate)', *Film Quarterly* 51(2), pp. 44–9.

Epstein, D. (1993), *Changing Classroom Cultures: anti-racism, politics and schools* (Stoke-on-Trent: Trentham Books).

Evening Standard (nd), accessed 10/10/2003, http://www.eastiseast.co.uk

Falzon, C. (1998), *Foucault and Social Dialogue* (London: Routledge).

Fanon, F. (1986), *Black Skins, White Masks* (London: Pluto).

Ferguson, R. (1998), *Representing 'Race': ideology, identity and media* (London: Arnold).

Fernández, J. A. (1993), 'Félix Guattari: towards a queer chaosmosis', *Angelaki* 1(1), pp. 99–112.

Flemming, D. (ed.) (2000) *Formations: 21st Century Media Studies Textbook* (Manchester: Manchester University Press).

Foster, P. (1990), *Policy and Practice in Multicultural and Anti-racist Education: a case study of a multi-ethnic comprehensive school* (London: Routledge).

Foucault, M. (2000), *The Essential Works of Michel Foucault, 1954–1984. Vol. 1, Ethics: subjectivity and truth* (London: Penguin).

Foucault, M. (2003), *Society Must Be Defended: lectures at the College de France 1975–76* (London: Allen Lane).

Freire, P. (1972), *Pedagogy of the Oppressed* (London: Penguin).

Fuss, D. (1990), *Essentially Speaking: feminism, nature and difference* (London: Routledge).

Gabriel, T. (1989), Towards a critical theory of Third World films, in *Questions of Third Cinema* (eds) J. Pines and P. Willeman (London: BFI).

Gallop, J. (1995), *Pedagogy: a question of impersonation* (Bloomington and Indianapolis: Indiana University Press).

Garber, M., B. Hanssen and R. Walkowitz (2000), Introduction: The Turn to Ethics, in *The Turn To Ethics* (eds) M. Garber, B. Hanssen and R. Walkowitz (London: Routledge).

Garber, M., R. Walkowitz and P. Franklin (eds) (1996) *Fieldwork: sites in literary and cultural studies* (London: Routledge).

Gilbert, J. (2004), 'Signifying Nothing: "culture", "discourse" and the sociality of affect', *Culture Machine*, 6, accessed 17/02/2005, http://culturemachine.tees.ac.uk/frm_f1.htm

Gill, D. and L. Levidow (1987), *Anti-Racist Science Teaching* (London: Free Association Books).

Gillborn, D. (1990), *'Race', Ethnicity, and Education: teaching and learning in multi-ethnic schools* (London: Unwin Hyman).

Gillborn, D. (1995), *Racism and Anti-racism in Real Schools: theory, policy, practice* (Buckingham: Open University Press).

Gillborn, D. (1996), 'Student roles and perspectives in antiracist education: a crisis of white ethnicity?' *British Education Research Journal* 22(2), pp. 165–79.

Gilman, S. (1985), *Difference and Pathology* (Ithaca, NY: Cornell University Press).

Gilroy, P. (1987), *'There Ain't No Black in the Union Jack': the cultural politics of race and nation* (London: Hutchinson).

Gilroy, P. (1989/90), 'Cruciality and the frog's perspective', *Third Text* 5, pp. 33–44.

Gilroy, P. (1993), *The Black Atlantic: modernity and double consciousness* (London: Verso).

Gilroy, P. (2000), *Between Camps: nations, cultures and the allure of race* (London: Penguin).

Giroux, H. (1992), *Border Crossing: cultural workers and the politics of education* (London: Routledge).

Giroux, H. (1993), Reclaiming the social: pedagogy, resistance and politics in celluloid culture, in *Film Theory goes to the Movies* (eds) J. Collins, H. Radner and A. Collins (London: Routledge).

Giroux, H. (1994), *Disturbing Pleasures: learning popular culture* (London: Routledge).

Giroux, H. (1997), 'Re-writing the discourse of racial identity: towards a pedagogy and politics of whiteness', *Harvard Educational Review* 67(2), pp. 285–315.

Giroux, H. (2000), *Impure Acts: the practical politics of cultural studies* (London: Routledge).

Giroux, H. (2004), *The Terror of Neo-Liberalism* (Boulder, CO: Paradigm).

Giroux, H., C. Lankshear, P. McLaren, *et al.* (eds) (1996) *Counternarratives: cultural studies and critical pedagogies in postmodern spaces* (London: Routledge).

Giroux, H. and P. McLaren (eds) (1994) *Between Borders: pedagogy and the politics of cultural studies* (London: Routledge).

Giroux, H. and P. Shannon (1997), *Education and cultural studies: toward a performative practice* (London: Routledge).

Goldberg, D. (2002), *The Racial State* (Oxford: Blackwell Publishers).

Gopinath, G. (2005), *Impossible Desires: queer diasporas and south asian public cultures* (London: Duke University Press).

Gordon, A. and C. Newfield (1996), Introduction, in *Mapping Multiculturalism* (eds) A. Gordon and C. Newfield (London: University of Minnesota Press).

Gore, J. (1993), *The Struggle for Pedagogies: critical and feminist discourses as regimes of truth* (London: Routledge).

Gormley, P. (2005), *The New Brutality Film: Race and Affect in Contemporary Hollywood Cinema* (London: Intellect).

Goulbourne, H. (1993), Aspects of nationalism and Black identities in post-Imperial Britain, in *Racism, the City and the State* (eds) M. Cross and M. Keith (London: Routledge).

Grant, C. and J. Sachs (1995), *Multicultural Education and Postmodernism: movement toward a dialogue*, in Critical Multiculturalism: uncommon voices in common struggle (eds) Kanpol, B. and P. McLaren (Westport, Connecticut: Bergin & Garvey).

Gray, F. (1998), Certain liberties have been taken with Cleopatra: female performance in the *Carry On* films, in *Because I tell a Joke or Two: comedy, politics and social difference* (ed.) S. Wagg (London: Routledge).

Grossberg, L. (1992), *We Gotta Get Out Of This Place: popular conservatism and postmodern culture* (London: Routledge).

Grossberg, L. (1993), Cultural Studies and/in New Worlds, in *Race, Identity and Representation in Education* (eds) C. McCarthy and W. Crichlow (London: Routledge).

Grossberg, L. (1994), Introduction: Bringin' it all back home – pedagogy and cultural studies, in *Between Borders: pedagogy and the politics of cultural studies* (eds) H. Giroux and P. McLaren (London: Routledge).

Grossberg, L. (1996), Identity and Cultural Studies – Is that all there Is?, in *Questions of Cultural Identity* (eds) S. Hall and P. Du Gay (London: Sage).

Hage, G. (2003), *Against Paranoid Nationalism: searching for hope in a shrinking society* (London: Pluto Press).

Hall, S. (1980), Recent developments in theories of language and ideology: a critical note, in *Culture, Media, Language* (eds) S. Hall, D. Dobson, A. Lowe *et al.* (London: Hutchinson).

Hall, S. (1983), Education in Crisis, in *Is there Anyone Here From Education?* (eds) J. Donald and A. M. Wolp (London: Pluto).

Hall, S. (1986), 'Gramsci's Relevance for the Study of Race and Ethnicity', *Journal of Communication Inquiry* 10(2), pp. 5–27.

Hall, S. (1988), New ethnicities, in *Black Film, British Cinema* (ed.) K. Mercer (London: BFI/ICA).

Hall, S. (1989), The meaning of New Times, in *New Times: the changing face of politics in the 1990s* (eds) S. Hall and M. Jacques (London: Lawrence & Wishart).

Hall, S. (1991a), The local and the global, in *Culture, Globalization and the world-system* (ed.) A. King (London: MacMillan).

Hall, S. (1991b), Old and new identities, old and new ethnicities, in *Culture, Globalization and the world-system* (ed.) A. King (London: MacMillan).

Hall, S. (1992a), The question of cultural identity in *Formations of Modernity* (eds) S. Hall and B. Gieben (Cambridge: Polity Press/Open University).

Hall, S. (1992b), What is this 'Black' in Black popular culture?, in *Black Popular Culture* (ed.) G. Dent (Seattle: Bay Press).

Hall, S. (1996), Who needs 'Identity'?, in *Questions of cultural identity* (eds) S. Hall and P. Du Gay (London: Sage).

Hall, S. (1997a), The spectacle of the 'other', in *Representation: cultural representations and signifying practices* (ed.) S. Hall (Milton Keynes: Sage/Open University).

Hall, S. (ed.) (1997b) *Representation: cultural representations and signifying practices* (Milton Keynes: Sage/Open University).

Hallward, P. (2001), *Absolutely Postcolonial: writing between the singular and the specific* (Manchester: Manchester University Press).

Hanssen, B. (2000), Ethics of the Other, in *The Turn To Ethics* (eds) M. Garber, B. Hanssen and R. Walkowitz (London: Routledge).

Hardt, M. and A. Negri (2000), *Empire* (London: Harvard University Press).

Harris, D. (1992), *From Class Struggle to the Politics of Pleasure: the effects of Gramscianism on cultural studies* (London: Routledge).

Hebdige, D. (1987), *Cut 'n Mix: Culture, Identity and Caribbean Music* (London: Comedia).

Henriques, J. (1988), Realism and the new language, in *Black Film, British Cinema* (ed.) K. Mercer (London: BFI/ICA).

Hesse, B. (1999), It's your world: discrepant M/multiculturalisms, in *New Ethnicities, Old Racisms?* (ed.) P. Cohen (London: Zed Books).

Hesse, B. (2004), 'Im/Plausible Deniability: Racism's Conceptual Double Bind', *Social Text* 10(1), pp. 9–29.

Hicks, E. (1988), Deterritorialization and Border Writing, in *Esthetics/Aesthetics: post-modern positions* (ed.) R. Merill (Washington: Maisonneuve Press).

Holland, J., M. Blair and S. Sheldon (1995), *Debates and Issues in Feminist Research and Pedagogy: a reader* (Clevedon: Multilingual Matters/Open University).

hooks, b. (1992), *Black Looks: race and representation* (London: Turnaround).

hooks, b. (1994), *Teaching to Transgress: education as the practice of freedom* (London: Routledge).

hooks, b. (2003), *Teaching Community: a pedagogy of hope* (London Routledge).

Housee, S. and S. Sharma (1999) 'Too Black too Strong'? the making of South Asian political identities in Britain, in *Storming The Millenium* (eds) T. Jordan and A. Lent (London: Lawrence & Wishart).

Huyssens, A. (1986), *After the Great Divide: modernism, mass culture, postmodernism* (London: MacMillan).

Ifekwunigwe, J. (1999), *Scattered Belongings: cultural paradoxes of race, nation and gender* (London: Routledge).

Irwin, W. (ed.) (2003) *The Matrix and Philosophy: Welcome to the Desert of the Real* (Illinois Opencourt Books).

Jamal, M. (1988), Dirty Linen, in *Black Film, British Cinema* (ed.) K. Mercer (London: BFI/ICA).

JanMohammed, A. (1994), Some implications of Paulo Freire's border pedagogy, in *Between Borders: pedagogy and the politics of cultural studies* (eds) H. Giroux and P. McLaren (London: Routledge).

JanMohammed, A. and D. Lloyd (1990), Introduction: toward a theory of minority discourse: what is to be done?, in *The Nature and Context of Minority Discourse* (eds) A. JanMohammed and D. Lloyd (Oxford: Oxford University Press).

Jay, G. (1995), Taking Multiculturalism Personally: ethnos and ethos in the classroom, in *Pedagogy: a question of impersonation* (ed.) J. Gallop (Bloomington and Indianapolis: Indiana University Press).

Jeffcoate, R. (1979), *Positive Image: towards a multiracial curriculum* (London: Writers and Readers Publishing Cooperative in association with Chameleon).

Johnson, B. (2000), Using People: Kant with Winnicot, in *The Turn To Ethics* (eds) M. Garber, B. Hanssen and R. Walkowitz (London: Routledge).

Johnson, D. and S. Michaelson (1997), Border Secrets: an introduction, in *Border Theory: the limits of cultural politics* (eds) D. Johnson and S. Michaelson (London: University of Minnesota Press).

Jones, S. (1988), *Black Culture, White Youth: the reggae tradition from JA to UK* (Basingstoke: Macmillan Education).

Julian, I. and K. Mercer (1988), 'Introduction: de margin and de centre', *Screen* 29(4), pp. 2–10.

Kalra, V. and J. Hutnyk (1998), 'Brimful of agitation, authenticity and appropriation: Madonna's Asian Kool', *Postcolonial Studies* 1(3), pp. 339–56.

Kanpol, B. and P. McLaren (eds) (1995), *Critical Multiculturalism: uncommon voices in common struggle* (Westport, Connecticut: Bergin & Garvey).

Kaplan, E. A. (1997), *Looking for the Other: feminism, film and the imperial gaze* (London: Routledge).

Kawash, S. (1998), Men: moving bodies, or, the cinematic politics of deportation, in *Deleuze and Guattari: new mappings in politics, philosophy, and culture* (eds) E. Kaufman and K. Heller (London: University of Minnesota Press).

Keith, M. (1999), Identity and the Spaces of Authenticity, in *Theories of Race and Racism: A Reader* (eds) L. Back and J. Solomos (London: Routledge).

Kellner, D. (1995), *Media Culture: cultural studies, identity politics between the modern and postmodern* (London: Routledge).

Kelly, U. (1997), *Schooling Desire: literacy, cultural politics, and pedagogy* (London: Routledge).

Kepel, G. (2005), 'Europe's answer to Londonistan', accessed 03/08/2005, http://www.opendemocracy.net/conflict-terrorism/londonistan_2775.jsp

Kincheloe, J. and S. Steinberg (1997), *Changing Multiculturalism: new times, new curriculum* (Buckingham: Open University Press).

Kincheloe, J. and S. Steinberg (1998), *Unauthorized Methods: strategies for critical teaching* (London: Routledge).

Koundoura, M. (1998), Multiculturalism or multinationalism?, in *Multicultural States: rethinking identity and difference* (ed.) D. Bennett (London: Routledge).

Laclau, E. (1994), Why do empty signifiers matter to politics?, in *The Lesser Evil and the Greater Good* (ed.) J. Weeks (London: Rivers Oram Press).

Lather, P. (1991), *Getting Smart: feminist research and pedagogy with/in the postmodern* (London: Routledge).

Lather, P. (1994), Staying dumb?, in *After Postmodernism: reconstructing ideology critique* (eds) H. Simons and M. Billig (London: Sage).

Lawrence, E. (1982), In the abundance of water the fool is thirsty: sociology and the Black pathology, in *The Empire Strikes Back: race and racism in 70s Britain* (ed.) CCCS (London: Hutchinson).

Lawrence, M. (2004), *Like A Splinter In Your Mind: The philosophy behind The Matrix Trilogy* (Oxford: Blackwell).

Levinas, E. (1979), *Totality and Infinity: an essay on exteriority* (Boston: Nijhoff Publishers).

Levinas, E. (1981), *Otherwise than Being, or, Beyond essence* (London: Nijhoff).

Lipsitz, G. (1994), *Dangerous Crossroads: popular music, postmodernism and the poetics of place* (London: Verso).

Lister, M., K. Kelly, J. Dovey *et al.* (2003), *New Media: a critical introduction* (London: Routledge).

Littlewood, J. and M. Pickering (1998), Heard the one about the white middle-class heterosexual father-in-law?, in *Because I tell a Joke or Two: comedy, politics and social difference* (ed.) S. Wagg (London: Routledge).

Lorraine, T. (1999), *Irigaray and Deleuze: experiments in visceral philosophy* (London: Cornell University Press).

Luke, C. (1992), Feminist politics in radical education, in *Feminisms and Critical Pedagogy* (eds) C. Luke and J. Gore (London: Routledge).

Luke, C. and J. Gore (eds) (1992) *Feminisms and Critical Pedagogy* (London: Routledge).

Lusted, D. (1986), 'Why Pedagogy?' *Screen* 27(5), pp. 2–14.

Lusted, D. (1991), *The Media studies book: a guide for teachers* (London: Routledge).

Lynch, J., C. Modgil and S. Modgil (1992), *Cultural diversity and the Schools* (London: Falmer).

Lyotard, J. F. (1984), *The Postmodern Condition: a report on knowledge* (Manchester: Manchester University Press).

Malik, S. (1997), Beyond the cinema of duty? The pleasures of hybridity: Black British film of the 1980s and 1990s, in *Dissolving Views: key writing on British cinema* (ed.) A. Higson (Cambridge: Polity).

Malik, S. (2002), *Representing Black Britain: a history of black and Asian images on British television* (London: Sage).

Marks, J. (1998), *Gilles Deleuze: vitalism and multiplicity* (London: Pluto Press).

Marks, L. (2000), *The Skin of the Film: intercultural cinema, embodiment, and the senses* (London: Duke University Press).

Massood, P. (1993), 'Menace II Society', *Cineaste* 20(2), pp. 44–5.

Massumi, B. (1996), The autonomy of affect, in *Deleuze: A Critical Reader* (ed.) P. Patton (Oxford: Blackwell).

Massumi, B. (2002), *Parables from the Virtual* (London: Duke University Press).

Masterman, L. (1985), *Teaching the Media* (London: Comedia).

May, S. (1994), *Making Multicultural Education Work* (Clevedon: Ontario Institute for Studies in Education).

May, S. (1999a), Critical multiculturalism and cultural difference: avoiding essentialism, in *Critical multiculturalism: rethinking multicultural and antiracist education* (ed.) S. May (London: Falmer).

May, S. (1999b), Introduction: towards a critical multiculturalism, in *Critical multiculturalism: rethinking multicultural and antiracist education* (ed.) S. May (London: Falmer).

May, S. (ed.) (1999c) *Critical multiculturalism: rethinking multicultural and antiracist education* (London: Falmer).

May, T. (2004), *Gilles Deleuze: an introduction* (Cambridge: Cambridge University Press).

Mayberry, M. and E. C. Rose (1999), *Meeting the Challenge: innovative feminist pedagogies in action* (London: Routledge).

McCabe, C. (1988), Black film in 80s Britain, in *Black Film, British Cinema* (ed.) K. Mercer (London: BFI/ICA).

McCarthy, C. (1998), *The Uses of Culture: education and the limits of ethnic affiliation* (London: Routledge).

McClintock, A. (1995), *Imperial Leather: race, gender and sexuality in the colonial contest* (London: Routledge).

McLaren, P. (1995), *Critical Pedagogy and Predatory Culture: oppositional politics in a postmodern era* (London: Routledge).

McLaren, P. (1997), *Revolutionary Multiculturalism: pedagogies of dissent for the new millennium* (Oxford: Westview Press).

McLaren, P. and R. Hammer (1996), Media knowledges, warrior citizenry and postmodern literacies, in *Counternarratives: cultural studies and critical pedagogies in postmodern spaces* (eds) H. Giroux, C. Lankshear, P. McLaren, *et al.* (London: Routledge).

McRobbie, A. (1999), *In the Culture Society* (London: Routledge).

Mercer, K. (ed.) (1988) *Black Film, British Cinema* (London: BFI/ICA).

Mercer, K. (1990), 'Black art and the burden of representation', *Third Text* 10, pp. 61–78.

Mercer, K. (1994), *Welcome to the Jungle: new positions in black cultural studies* (London: Routledge).

Mercer, K. (1999/2000), 'Ethnicity and internationality: new British art and diaspora-based Blackness', *Third Text* 49, pp. 51–62.

Mills, C. (1997), *The Racial Contract* (Ithaca: Cornell University Press).

Mohanty, C. (1994), On Race and Voice: challenges for liberal education in the 1990s, in *Between Borders: pedagogy and the politics of cultural studies* (eds) H. Giroux and P. McLaren (London: Routledge).

Montag, W. (2003), *Louis Althusser* (Basingstoke: Palgrave Macmillan).
Moraes, M. (1996) *Bilingual education: a dialogue with the Bakhtin Circle* (Albany: State University of New York Press).
Morley, D. (1992), *Television Audiences and Cultural Studies* (London: Routledge).
Naficy, H. (1999), Between rocks and hard places: the interstitial mode of production in exilic cinema, in *Home, Exile, Homeland: film, media, and the politics of place* (ed.) H. Naficy (London: Routledge).
Nealon, J. (1998), *Alterity Politics: ethics and performative subjectivity* (London: Duke University Press).
Nicoll, F. (2004), '"Are you calling me a racist?": Teaching critical whiteness theory in indigenous sovereignty', *Borderlands Journal*, 3(2), accessed 10/08/2005, http://www.borderlandsejournal.adelaide.edu.au/vol3no2_2004/nicoll_teaching.htm
Nobil, A. (1999/2000), 'Is East ... East?' *Third Text* 49, pp. 105–7.
NUT (1996), *Anti-Racist Curriculum Guidelines* (London: National Union of Teachers).
O'Shea, A. (1998), 'A Special Relationship? Cultural studies, academia and pedagogy', *Cultural Studies* 12(4), pp. 513–27.
Papastergiadis, N. (1996), *Dialogues in the Diasporas: essays and conversations on cultural identity* (London: Rivers Oram).
Papastergiadis, N. (1997), Tracing Hybridity in Theory, in *Debating Cultural Hybridity* (eds) P. Werbner and T. Modood (London: Zed Books).
Parmar, P. (1982), Gender, Race and Class: Asian Women and Resistance, in *The Empire Strikes Back: race and racism in 70s Britain* (ed.) CCCS (London: Hutchinson).
Parry, B. (1994), 'Signs of our times – discussion of Homi Bhabha's "The Location of Culture"', *Third Text* 28/29, pp. 5–24.
Patton, P. (2000), *Deleuze and the Political* (London: Routledge).
Peters, M. (1996), *Poststructuralism, Politics and Education* (London: Bergin & Garvey).
Pieterse, J. N. (2004), *Globalization and Culture: global melange* (Oxford: Rowman & Littlefield).
Pines, J. (1988), The cultural context of Black British cinema, in *Blackframes: critical perspectives on Black independent cinema* (eds) M. Cham and C. Watkins (Boston: MIT).
Piper, A. (1998), Passing for white, passing for black?, in *The Visual Culture Reader* (ed.) N. Mirzeoff (London: Routledge).
Policar, A. (1990), 'Racism and its Mirror Images', *Telos* 83, pp. 99–108.
Pratt, M. L. (1992), *Imperial Eyes: studies in travel writing and transculturation* (London: Routledge).
Probyn, E. (2004), 'Teaching Bodies: Affects in the Classroom', *Body & Society* 10(4), pp. 21–43.
Puar, J. K. and A. S. Rai (2004), 'The Re-Making of a Model Minority: perverse projectiles under the spectre of (counter) terrorism', *Social Text* 22(3), pp. 75–104.
Puwar, N. (2000), 'Making space for South Asian women: what has changed since Feminist Review 17', *Feminist Review* 66, pp. 131–7.
Puwar, N. (2004), *Space Invaders: race, gender and bodies out of place* (Oxford: Berg).

Puwar, N. (2006), Im/possible Inhabitations, in *Situating Contemporary Politics of Belonging* (ed.) N. Yuval-Davis (London: Sage).

Puwar, N. and K. Powar (2005), 'Khabi Ritz, Khabie Palladium: South Asian Cinema in Coventry 1940–1980', *Wasafiri:* special issue on global cinema.

Rajchman, J. (1995), Introduction: The Question of Identity, in *The Identity in Question* (ed.) J. Rajchman (London: Routledge).

Rattansi, A. (1992), Changing the subject? Racism, culture and education, in *'Race', Culture and Difference* (eds) J. Donald and A. Rattansi (London: Sage/Open University).

Rattansi, A. (1999), Racism, 'postmodernism' and reflexive multiculturalism, in *Critical Multiculturalism: rethinking multicultural and antiracist education* (ed.) S. May (London: Falmer).

Richards, C. (1986), 'Anti-racist initiatives', *Screen* 27(5), pp. 74–85.

Richards, C. (1992), Teaching popular culture, in *English and the National Curriculum: Cox's Revolution?* (ed.) K. Jones (London: Kogan Page/Institute of Education, University of London).

Richards, C. (1998), Beyond Classroom Culture, in *Teaching popular culture: beyond radical pedagogy* (ed.) D. Buckingham (London: UCL Press).

Rodowick, D. (1997), *Gilles Deleuze's Time Machine* (London: Duke University Press).

Roediger, D. (1994), *Towards the abolition of Whiteness* (London: Verso).

Romney, J. (2003), 'Everywhere and Nowhere', *Sight and Sound,* July 2003, pp. 24–7.

Root, D. (1995), *Cannibal Culture: art, appropriation and the commodification of difference* (London: Westview Press).

Rosaldo, R. (1993), *Culture and Truth* (London: Routledge).

Ross, K. (1996), *Black and White Media: Black images in popular film and television* (Cambridge: Polity).

Said, E. (1978), *Orientalism* (London: Penguin).

Saldivar, J. (1997), *Border Matters: remapping American cultural studies* (London: University of California Press).

Sarup, M. (1986), *The Politics of Multicultural Education* (London: RKP).

Scheurich, J. (1997), *Research Method in the Postmodern* (London: Falmer).

Scholle, D. and S. Denski (1994), *Media Education and the (Re)production of Culture* (Westport, CT: Bergin & Garvey).

Schrift, A. (1995), *Nietzsche's French Legacy: a genealogy of poststructuralism* (London: Routledge).

Schroader, E. (2001), 'A Multicultural Conversation: *La Haine, Rai and Menace II Society'*, *Camera Obscura* 46, 16(1), pp. 143–79.

Seay, C. and G. Garett (2003), *Gospel Reloaded: Exploring Spirituality and Faith in The Matrix* (Colorado Springs: Pinion Press).

Sedgwick, E. (1997), Paranoid reading and reparative reading; or, you're so paranoid, you probably think this Introduction is about you, in *Novel Gazing: queer readings in fictions* (ed.) E. Sedgwick (London: Duke University Press).

Seshadri-Crooks, K. (2000), *Desiring Whiteness: A Lacanian Analysis of Race* (London: Routledge).

Sharma, A. (1990), Do they think we're 'uloo'?, in *The Neglected Audience* (eds) J. Willis and T. Wollen (London: British Film Institute).

Sharma, A. (1996), Sounds Oriental: the (im)possibility of theorizing Asian musical cultures, in *Dis-Orienting Rhythms: the politics of the new asian dance music* (eds) S. Sharma, J. Hutnyk and A. Sharma (London: Zed Books).

Sharma, S. (2003), The Sounds of Alterity, in *The Auditory Cultures Reader* (eds) M. Bull and L. Back (Oxford: Berg).

Sharma, S. (2006), Asian Sounds, in *A Postcolonial People: South Asians in Britain* (eds) S. H. Sayyid, N. Ali and V. Kalra (London: C. Hurst & Co.).

Sharma, S., J. Hutnyk and A. Sharma (eds) (1996) *Dis-Orienting Rhythms: the politics of the new Asian dance music* (London: Zed Books).

Sharma, S. and A. Sharma (2000), '"So Far So Good..." La Haine and the Poetics of the Everyday', *Theory, Culture and Society* 17(3), pp. 103–16.

Shaviro, S. (1993), *The Cinematic Body* (London: University of Minnesota Press).

Shohat, E. and R. Stam (eds) (1994) *Unthinking Eurocentrism: multiculturalism and the media* (London: Routledge).

Short, J. (2000), 'Outside of power? or the power of the outside', *j_spot online edition*, 1 (2), accessed 16/03/01, www.yourku.ca/jspot/2/jshort.htm

Simmonds, F. (1997), My body, myself: how does a Black woman do sociology?, in *Black British Feminism: a reader* (ed.) H. Mirza (London: Routledge).

Simon, R. (1992), *Teaching Against the Grain: texts for a pedagogy of possibility* (London: Bergin & Garvey).

Simon, R. (1995), Face to face with alterity: postmodern Jewish identity and the eros of pedagogy, in *Pedagogy: a question of impersonation* (ed.) J. Gallop (Bloomington and Indianapolis: Indiana University Press).

Simons, H. (1994), Teaching the pedagogies: a dialectal approach to an ideological dilemma, in *After Postmodernism: reconstructing ideology critique* (eds) H. Simons and M. Billig (London: Sage).

Sivanandan, A. (1982), *A Different Hunger: writings on black resistance* (London: Pluto Press).

Sivanandan, A. (1990), *Communities of Resistance: writings on black struggles for socialism* (London: Verso).

Sleeter, C. (1996), *Multicultural Education as Social Activism* (Albany: State University of New York Press).

Sleeter, C. and P. McLaren (1995), Introduction: exploring connections to build a critical multiculturalism, in *Multicultural education, critical pedagogy and the politics of difference* (eds) C. Sleeter and P. McLaren (Albany: State University of New York Press).

Spencer, L. (1999), 'Hello Mr Chips', *Sight and Sound* 9(11), pp. 36–7.

Spivak, G. C. (1988a), Can the subaltern speak?, in *Marxism and the Interpretation of Culture* (eds) C. Nelson and L. Grossberg (Urban and Chicago: University of Illinois Press).

Spivak, G. C. (1988b), *In Other Worlds: essays in cultural politics* (London: Routledge).

Spivak, G. C. (1993), *Outside in the Teaching Machine* (London: Routledge).

Stephan, W. and J. Banks (1999), *Reducing Prejudice and Stereotyping in Schools* (New York: Teachers College Press).

Stoler, A. L. (1995), *Race and the Education of Desire: Foucault's 'History of sexuality' and the colonial order of things* (Durham: Duke University Press).

Stuart, A. (1994), 'Blackpool Illumination', *Sight and Sound* 4(2), pp. 26–7.

The Guardian (6/01/2001) Honest truth about lottery films.

The Guardian (20/02/1999) Mirth of a Nation.
The Guardian (23/02/2001) We can't go like this.
The Guardian (31/10/1999) What kind of England do we really stand for?
Timeout (nd), accessed 10/10/2003, www.eastiseast.co.uk
Todd, S. (1997), *Learning Desire: perspectives on pedagogy, culture, and the unsaid* (London: Routledge).
Troyna, B. (1987), *Racial Inequality in Education* (London: Tavistock Publications).
Troyna, B. and B. Carrington (1990), *Education, Racism and Reform* (London: Routledge).
Turney, L., I. Law and D. Phillips (2002), 'Institutional Racism in Higher Education Toolkit Project: Building the Anti-Racist HEI', accessed 02/02/04, http://www.leeds.ac.uk/cers/toolkit/toolkit.htm
Verma, G. (1989), Pluralism: some theoretical and practical considerations, in *Britain: a plural society* (ed.) B. Parekh (London: Commission for Racial Equality).
Walkerdine, V. (1990), *Schoolgirl Fictions* (London: Verso).
Wark, M. (2004), *A Hacker Manifesto* (London: Harvard University Press).
Weiler, K. (ed.) (2001) *Feminist Engagements: reading, resisting, and revisioning male theorists in education and cultural studies* (London: Routledge).
West, C. (1990), The new cultural politics of difference, in *Out There: marginalization and contemporary cultures* (eds) R. Ferguson, M. Gever, T. Min-ha, *et al.* (Cambridge: MIT Press).
Wexler, P. (1987), *Social Analysis of Education: after the new sociology* (London: RKP).
Wexler, P. (1992), *Becoming Somebody: toward a social psychology of school* (London: Falmer).
Whitty, G. (1985), *Sociology and School Knowledge* (London: Methuen).
Willeman, P. (1994), *Looks and Frictions: essays in cultural studies and film theory* (London: BFI).
Williams, C. (2001), *Contemporary French Philosophy: modernity and the persistence of the subject* (London: The Athlone Press).
Williams, P. J. (1997), *Seeing a Color-Blind Future: the paradox of race* (London: Virago Press).
Williamson, J. (1981/2), 'How does girl number twenty understand ideology?' *Screen Education* 40, pp. 80–7.
Williamson, J. (1988), Two kinds of otherness: Black film and the avant-garde, in *Black Film, British Cinema* (ed.) K. Mercer (London: BFI/ICA).
Winant, H. (2004), Behind Blue Eyes: Whiteness and Contemporary U.S. Racial Politics, in *Off White: Readings on Power, Privilege, and Resistance* (2nd Edition) (eds) M. Fine, L. Weis, L. P. Pruit and A. Burns (London: Routledge).
Winant, H. (2004), *The New Politics of Race: globalism, difference and justice* (London: University of Minnesota Press).
Xu, G. (2004), 'Remaking East Asia, Outsourcing Hollywood', accessed 26/03/2005, http://www.sensesofcinema.com/contents/05/34/remaking_east_asia.html
Yeffeth, G. (ed.) (2003) *Taking the Red Pill: Science, Philosophy and Religion in The Matrix* (Dallas: Benbella Books).
Young, L. (1996), *Fear of the Dark: 'race', gender and sexuality in cinema* (London: Routledge).
Young, R. C. (1995), *Colonial Discourse: hybridity in theory, culture and race* (London: Routledge).

Yudice, G. (1988), Marginality and the ethics of survival, in *Universal Abandon? The politics of postmodernism* (ed.) A. Ross (Edinburgh: University of Edinburgh Press).

Zavarzadeh, M. and D. Morton (1994), *Theory as Resistance: politics and culture after (post)structuralism* (London: Guildford Press).

Žižek, S. (1993), *Tarrying with the Negative* (Durham NC: Duke University Press).

Žižek, S. (1997), 'Multiculturalism, or, the Cultural Logic of Multinational Capitalism', *New Left Review* 225, pp. 28–51.

Žižek, S. (1999), 'The Matrix, Or The Two Sides of Perversion', accessed 10/03/2005, http://www.lacan.com/zizek-matrix.htm

Zylinska, J. (2005), *The Ethics of Cultural Studies* (London: Continuum).

Index

affect, 39, 45, 49, 59, 66, 89, 145,
  196n3, 201n15
active/reactive forces, 45, 166, 188
affective investments, xv, 24, 39,
  40–1, 46, 50, 52, 57, 62, 65,
  81–2, 113, 136, 170–1, 187,
  203n19
and emotion, 196n23
and meaning, x–xv, 5, 196n23
agency, x–xviii, 5, 8, 16–17, 23–7,
  31, 33–7, 39–47, 82, 89, 93, 95,
  107, 109, 123, 132, 136, 139–40,
  148, 186, 188, 190, 195n17,
  198n23
Ahmed, Sara, 12
alterity, xii–xviii, 5, 10, 14, 16–25,
  34–7, 42–4, 49–50, 53, 62–5,
  69–70, 80–3, 90, 105–7, 109,
  112–15, 123, 130–40, 144, 147,
  154, 166, 169, 170–2, 174–5,
  187–91, 198n20, 200n6
  see also agency, ethical, other
Althusser, Louis, 93, 99
Alvarado, Manuel, 196n1, 198n19
anti-essentialism, xv, 4, 5, 9, 12, 23–5,
  33, 193n2, 194n4, 195n11
Anzaldúa, Gloria, 29
Aronowitz, Stanley, 28
arranged marriages, 142, 155, 157,
  160, 164–6
assemblage, xvi, 38, 62–3
authenticity, 6, 30, 73, 83–9, 95–6,
  106, 115–16, 124–37, 142, 147,
  156, 162, 182–3, 192, 199n1,
  203n22
  see also ethnicity

Back, Les, xix, 26, 169, 194n3
Badiou, Alain, 194n9
Bakhtin, Mikhal, 24, 119, 123, 194n5,
  195n20
Balibar, Étiene, 93, 99
Banerjea, Koushik, 26, 129

becoming, xii, 42–54, 70, 73–5, 113,
  133, 140, 169, 174, 195n18,
  201n17
becoming-other, xv, 63, 135
becoming-white, 46–7, 52, 135, 187
  see also identity
Belsey, Catherine, 60, 197n13
Bend It Like Beckham, xiv, xvii, 114,
  124, 135–57, 162, 166, 187,
  200n2
Bennett, David, 10–11, 33–4
Bhabha, Homi, 11–15, 24, 29, 30–5,
  43, 123, 194n5, 195n14
Bhangra music, 149
Bhatia, Nandi, 145
Black British Film, xvii, 70, 113–26,
  132–8, 200n3, 201n7
blackness (black body), 80, 88–90
  see also real, the
Bonnett, Alistair, 104
borders, xiv–xvi, 4, 10, 14, 16, 18,
  23–36, 41, 62, 109, 123, 190
  see also pedagogy, third space
Bourne, Jenny, 8
Boyd, Todd, 89
Boyd-Barrett, Oliver, 196n1, 198n19
Brah, Avtar, 145
British-South Asian film, 114, 119,
  122–5, 131–2, 135–41, 188, 190,
  200n3
  see also comedy
British-South Asians, xvii, 29, 114,
  119, 122–90, 194n8, n7, 199n27,
  200n3, n8, n10, n11, 201n13,
  n14, n17, 202n3
Britzman, Deborah, 171, 175–7
Brown, Wendy, 7–10, 17, 23, 36, 39
Buchanan, Ian, 138
Buckingham, David, xiii, 49, 50, 55,
  57, 59–60, 196n1, 197n12, n14,
  n15, 198n18
Butler, Judith, xiii, 42–3, 97, 153, 178,
  195n21

219